D1250610

RUSSIA LOOKS TO THE SEA

David Fairhall

RUSSIA LOOKS TO THE SEA

A Study of the Expansion of Soviet Maritime Power

ANDRE DEUTSCH

First published 1971 by
André Deutsch Limited
105 Great Russell Street
London WC1

Copyright © 1971 by David Fairhall

All rights reserved

Printed in Great Britain
by Ebenezer Baylis & Son Limited
The Trinity Press, Worcester, and London

ISBN 0 233 96224 7

TO MILLICENT FAIRHALL

Contents

List of Plates

9

LIST OF PLATES

List of Figures

Foreword

This is unashamedly a journalist's book. It tries to present the layman with a comprehensive background to the facts of Soviet sea power, explained in non-technical language. It should provide a perspective into which new developments can be set; or – as one of my colleagues on *The Guardian* once defined his job – 'ensure that events never take readers by surprise'. Where I felt my comment or analysis was useful it has been added, but I have deliberately quoted direct from key Russian texts others may not have available or cannot read without translation. On the other hand if a story seemed worth telling for its own sake I have done so.

My thanks go first to my wife Pamela for clearing the decks at home – and with three small children they take some clearing – so that writing has been possible here over the past eighteen months.

As far as the work itself is concerned I am deeply indebted to Bunty Bax, who was responsible for a lot of indispensable research and general organization of the project. Both the US Navy as represented in London by Commander Russell F. Harney, and the Royal Navy in the person of Captain H. Home Cook, have been unfailingly helpful in tracking down source material, putting me in touch with specialists and being ready with advice. I particularly appreciated Commander Harney's offer to read and comment on the manuscript from a technical standpoint. On the merchant naval side the consistent co-operation offered by the Chamber of Shipping through Mr Norman Douglas, and the advice of its expert staff, have been invaluable. Commander Edgar Young kindly loaned me some Russian texts which were not otherwise available in this country.

In dealing with Soviet fisheries and arctic operations I have leaned heavily on the advice and written work of Dr Terence Armstrong of the Scott Polar Research Institute at Cambridge. I am also grateful to John Cashman and his colleagues at Lloyd's Register of Shipping for making their unique statistical records available. Although I cannot mention them all individually, I am particularly grateful to the Russian merchant seamen and officials who offered me their hospitality afloat and ashore, and who did their best to answer my innumerable queries.

Jane's Fighting Ships and the Institute of Strategic Studies's *Military Balance* have been essential books of reference, as the anonymous *Soviet Merchant Ships* has been since its publication last year.

At the last moment, Jean Fairhall helped me out of a difficult situation by kindly agreeing to draw the maps and diagrams.

Chelmsford, November 1970.

CHAPTER I

Alarm and Complacency

The time when Russia could be kept out of the world's oceans has gone forever. The imperialists can no longer have them to themselves. We shall sail all the world's seas – no force on earth can prevent us!

When the Soviet Chief of Staff, Marshal Zakharov, issued his triumphant challenge in 1968 he was not only thinking of the newly formed squadron of Russian warships confronting NATO in the Mediterranean, and the nuclear submarines that were beginning to patrol the United States coast. The rapidly expanding Soviet merchant marine was about to launch its first campaign to break into the Western shipping conferences, declaring that it was 'prepared to go to any lengths to obtain its objective'. Russian trawler fleets organized on almost military lines were sweeping through the grounds traditionally worked by British and American fishermen and ships of the Soviet oceanographic research fleet were turning up in every corner of the world's oceans.

Not since Peter the Great had Russia turned to the sea in this dramatic fashion. If *Punch* cartoonists had still been drawing Russian bears they would have changed the land animal for a polar bear, about to plunge into the Arctic Ocean. But this was no backward eighteenth-century monarchy on the move; it was a centralized Communist bureaucracy, ideologically dedicated to the defeat of capitalism – and one that was capable of integrating the elements of modern sea power so that the whole was equal to far more than the sum of the parts.

The Americans – or rather that minority amongst them which realized what was happening – were already rattled. President Kennedy had said: 'Control of the seas can mean peace. Control of the seas can mean victory. The United States must control the seas if it is to protect our security'; yet the resources available for this great confrontation were an elderly navy still relying heavily on Second World War tonnage, a merchant fleet slowly pricing itself out of existence, a declining fishing industry and a widely fragmented research effort. In contrast, the USSR's equipment had nearly all been purpose-built in the past ten years, unhindered by many of the political and commercial restraints that operate in a Western democracy. The signs were that its use would also be purposive.

'The naval forces now being created by the Soviet Union and the uses of sea power now being made by the USSR are part of the overall Communist design of total victory in the struggle against the United States and other free world nations.' This quotation comes from a report commissioned by the US House of Representatives Armed Services Committee in 1968, which coupled its own alarm with an attack on the alleged complacency of the Administration. The report reminded Americans that the war in Vietnam was being supplied largely by sea and was being fought in conditions of complete naval supremacy – conditions which could not in future be taken for granted. It warned them that the United States was rapidly losing its overseas bases, that the British were pulling out of the Far East and the Persian Gulf and that American naval construction was moving at 'a dangerously slow pace'. The USA was urged to adopt a far more aggressive maritime policy:

To contemplate a loss of US maritime supremacy is to contemplate disaster on an epochal scale. The freedom of the United States and its allies is anchored in the control of the oceans. The construction of ships takes much time, however, as does the establishment of new task forces and fleets. In order to prevent the Soviets from realizing their ambitions at sea, the United States will have to move aggressively in the next few years in a crash build-up of all sea-based strategic forces.

Reactions in Britain were somewhat cooler at first, the Royal Navy having wearily shed most of its world peacekeeping responsibilities since the war. But when the impact of the Russian expansion began to be felt in commercial shipping, where the UK was still the acknowledged leader of the Western world, the alarm signals were run up. In 1968 the President of the Chamber of Shipping, Lord Geddes, spoke of the 'long dark shadow' cast by the growing Russian merchant marine, while his colleagues managed to bring themselves to ask for Government help – which they sometimes affect to scorn. The fishing industry had long ago appealed to the Royal Navy to stop the Communist fleets from trawling the coastal grounds bare, and was uneasily aware that fish conservation policies in the North Atlantic were now dependent on the cooperation of a powerful Russian industry.

The former British Prime Minister Sir Alec Douglas Home summed it up in my own profession's terms when he forcast that the emergence of the Soviet Union as an oceanic power was the subject most likely to occupy journalists' pens over the next twenty-five years.[1]

The first purpose of this study is to put the facts of Soviet maritime expansion into perspective, historically and geographically. The main elements of Russian sea power are then examined in turn to discover what they consist of, how they operate, and the extent to which they are interconnected; comparisons are mainly made with the United States on the naval side, and with Britain where commercial shipping and fishing are concerned. Finally, I have analysed declared Soviet policy in order to assess whether the appropriate reaction should be alarm or complacency: to decide, in other words, whether the Soviet merchant marine is a threat to Western commercial shipping or merely a challenge; whether the scale of Russian deep water fishing and hydrographic research really matters to the West; and whether Soviet naval strategy has shifted from its earlier defensive, land-conscious posture to one that is fundamentally aggressive and world wide.

[1] *Guardian*, May 18, 1968.

CHAPTER 2

Ice and Claustrophobia

If England is a natural sea power, Russia is the opposite. The USSR is a vast land mass bounded to the south and west by frontiers across which armies have often fought, and to the north and east by seas which until the development of the icebreaker seventy years ago might just as well have been land, since they are frozen for most of the year.

It is true that at three points in Europe – on the Barents Sea, the Baltic and the Black Sea – Russians can find their way to the 'ice-free sea' of which the sailors among them dream. In open water to the north they now have the port of Murmansk which, though even nearer to the Pole than its neighbour Arkhangelsk, is normally clear of winter ice; but when faced with the idea of setting sail from this corner of the Arctic in order to carry goods made in Moscow southabout to one's countrymen in Vladivostok, one can see why the Russians should have preferred to build a railway across Siberia instead. And the two narrow routes by which Russian ships can reach warm, open water to the west and south have the great disadvantage that they have always been controlled by foreign powers. Nowadays this means by members of NATO: Turkey straddles the Bosphorus, while Denmark, Norway and West Germany guard the Baltic approaches.

On the Pacific side, only a thin belt of coastal pack ice reaches south to Vladivostok in winter, and the southern entrance to the Sea of Japan is comparatively wide: this was the scene of a spectacular and disastrous Russian effort to exert naval power during the Russo-Japanese War at the beginning of the century. And for obvious political and economic, as well as geographical

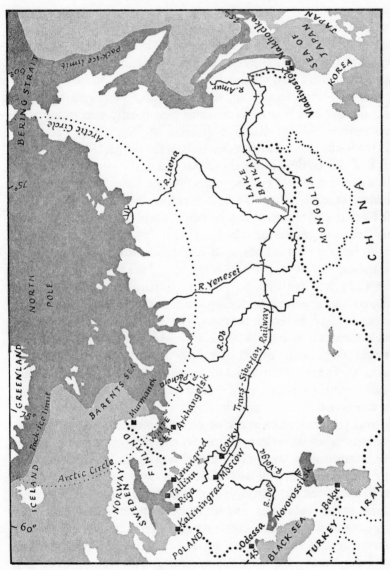

Figure 1   The USSR and its outlets to the open sea. The darker tone marks the area normally covered by winter pack-ice.

reasons, Russians have not felt quite the same maritime claustro-phobia in the Sea of Japan as they have in the Black Sea and the Baltic.

Even in the west, the blockade threat has not been of great strategic significance for Russia's merchant shipping because, at least until recently, she was too self-sufficient. But her naval commanders have always been uneasily aware of how simply their ships could be sealed in with the ice – as indeed they were during the Second World War – and it is hardly surprising that a recurrent theme of Russian foreign policy, from Peter the Great to Stalin, has been the desire to gain political and military control of the outlets from these two seas.

Peter the Great first gained access to the Baltic in 1703, when his forces stormed the Swedish fortress at the mouth of the River Nieva; and just in case anybody should doubt the direction of his imperial ambition, he renamed it St Petersburg and began to build a new capital, spacious and beautiful, out there on the marshes.

The Czar had learned to sail in an English boat on Lake Izmailovo. As a young man frequenting the foreign quarter of Moscow he had listened to men like the Dutch sailor Franz Timmermann. Later he was to visit the shipyards of Holland and the naval dockyards of England to learn something of the seafaring skills at first hand and to recruit men to build and sail his own navy. At the end of his life, after twenty-one years of war at sea as well as on land, he had driven the Swedes from the eastern Baltic and commanded a navy of eight hundred vessels. Russia had become a naval power, if only in the narrowest sense.

Peter's ambitions were not limited to the Baltic however: he fought the Turks as well as the Swedes, and for a time gained access to the Black Sea through Azov. But it was left to Catherine the Great at the end of the century to break permanently through to this southern coastline. She shared Peter's taste for imperial adventure, revitalized the navy he had founded and extended its range. Four years after her spectacular naval victory over the Turks in 1770, at Tchesme in the Aegean, she forced them to sign the Treaty of Kuchuk – Kainardzhy. This gave her ships free navigation in the Black Sea and the right of passage through the Bosphorus and the Dardanelles. A Russian squadron sailed the eastern Mediterranean and the Czarina's advisers began to prepare plans for the partition of Turkey.

Catherine's evident ambition planted seeds of suspicion in English minds which were later to grow into a flourishing 'jingoism'. As the nineteenth century music hall song explained, the idea was to prevent Russia breaking out through the Turkish straits and threatening the route to India:

'We don't want to fight, but by jingo if we do,
We've got the ships, we've got the men, we've got the money too,
We fought the Bear before, and while we're Britons true,
The Russians shall not have Constantinople.'

In fact, the great maritime initiatives of Peter and Catherine were not followed through. The most that can be said is that having acquired a western and southern coastline, the Russians generally mustered a respectable force to defend it. However, they did demonstrate the flair for technical innovation and improvisation by which they are still characterized: in the middle of the last century the Imperial fleet led the world in the development of the mine and gave convincing demonstrations, first of the high explosive shell and then of the torpedo, by sinking Turkish warships with them; in the middle of this one, the Israeli destroyer *Eilat* became the first ship to be sunk by a surface-to-surface cruise missile, launched from a Russian built missile patrol boat supplied to Egypt.

But the flashes of Russian naval inspiration have so often in the past stood out against a background of official indifference and incompetence. Thus, when war broke out with the Japanese in 1904 the Transiberian Railway was just about ready to play a part, but not the volunteer fleet of merchant ships which the Czar was halfheartedly trying to build up in support of his new battleships. During the Second World War, practical necessity – reinforced by inherited military attitudes – limited the Soviet Navy to coastal defence and operations in support of the land forces. Even in the 1960s, the appearance of a Soviet squadron in the Indian Ocean to 'show the flag' – the sort of thing the Royal Navy has been doing for centuries – was so unusual as to attract world wide comment in the press.

In historical perspective, therefore, Russian sea power on a world scale is so sudden a phenomenon that one is bound to wonder how substantial and durable it really is. For the USSR to stand alongside maritime powers like the United States and Great Britain, apparently determined that warships and freighters flying the hammer and sickle shall range every ocean in support of her interests, she must overcome inhibitions deeply rooted in the land. Consider, for example, the by now almost mythical story of the battle of Tsushima.

'We know Russia is not a sea power', said one of the Czar's captains before setting out in 1904. 'There will be no victory, but we shall know how to die and we shall never surrender.' He was right about the dying. More than 10,000 Russians went down with their ships after steaming 18,000 miles to meet the Japanese fleet at 'the island of the donkey's ears'.

But this heroic attempt to send a 'Second Pacific Squadron' round from Leningrad to relieve the First Pacific Squadron, trapped in Port Arthur and Vladivostok by the Japanese Admiral Togo, contained elements of comedy as well as of tragedy. Before Admiral Rozhestvensky could even begin to carry out his orders to 'wipe the infidel from the face of the earth', he had to complete the four battleships that were to lead his fleet, assemble the collection of obsolescent, inadequate craft that was to escort the few good ships he had – the only 'cruiser' to survive Tsushima was in fact a converted yacht – and find enough reservists and conscript peasants to man them.

The admiral calculated that his 42 vessels would burn about 3,000 tons of coal a day. But unlike his opposite number in the Royal Navy, he had no chain of bases at which he could refuel on his way round Africa and through the China Sea. He had to rely on a German firm which promised to send colliers to rendezvous with the Russian warships at sea. This was such a precarious arrangement that when he did manage to load coal at Dakar, it had to be heaped all over his ships – on deck, in the cabins and even in the officers' baths. Any hope of British assistance with coal supplies had been ruled out by what came to be known as the Dogger Bank incident.

Before the fleet sailed wild rumours had reached St Petersburg that the Japanese – presumably in connivance with the British – might try to attack it before it even got clear of the Baltic and the North Sea. As a result, the Russians were in a thoroughly jittery mood as they steamed across the Dogger Bank, in the middle of the North Sea, on the night of October 21, 1904. Suddenly a searchlight picked out the dark shapes of the Hull trawler fleet. The Russians somehow mistook it for a flotilla of torpedo boats; 'Action Stations' was sounded, and the Imperial squadron opened up with its six inch guns, ignoring the trawlermen frantically waving fish in the searchlight beam to identify themselves. One boat was sunk and two fishermen died. A diplomatic crisis seemed imminent, but after a halfhearted apology from the Czar and some lame excuses from Rozhestvensky, the fleet was allowed to continue southward.

After rounding the Cape and steaming 3,000 miles across the Indian Ocean at a ponderous eight knots the Baltic warships arrived off Singapore trailing a rich growth of weed. The Russian consul hurried out in a launch to tell them that reinforcements – a handful of rusty old vessels known as the Third Pacific Squadron – would join them off the coast of what is now Korea. Together the fifty vessels sailed north into the Straits of Tsushima, where the patrolling Japanese cruiser *Shinano Maru* sighted the Russian flagship *Suvorov* approaching through the mist on the morning of May 27, 1905.

By the morning of the following day the battle was over. Only four Russian ships reached Vladivostok. The defeat could not be directly attributed to the fact that the relieving squadron had spent seven months getting there, but it demonstrated with catastrophic vividness a weakness the Russians have been struggling with ever since – that their fleet is divided, as it were, into several watertight compartments.

Even the Romanov administration could hardly fail to take the point. They remembered the ambitious ideas Admiral

Makarov – killed in the war – had been urging on them ten years previously, and built two 1,300 ton icebreakers, the *Taimyr* and the *Vaigach*, for a hydrographic expedition to explore the Arctic sea route. The ships set out in 1913 under Commander Vilkitsky. If he could beat the ice, he would perform a geographical conjuring trick which in one move would help to unify the Imperial navy, give Russia a new coastline and shorten the trading route between Europe and the Far East.

Ice is at least as important in the Russian sailor's environment as mud and sand in the shallow water of the North Sea. And in the Arctic, ice – *liod* in Russian – is not the simple, uniform thing southerners might imagine. Just as British or Dutch seamen distinguish between creeks and channels, swatchways and deeps, so ice may be young or old, layered or rotten; it may be needle ice or pancake ice. Worst of all is the really old ice which has hardened into a rocky mass over a period of three or four years.

The northern shores of the Soviet Union do free themselves for a few weeks in summer, helped by the weight of water flowing down great rivers like the Yenesei and the Liena. But with the thaw comes the fog, which can be as much of a nuisance as the ice is an obstruction. In a bad month – July and August are usually the worst – two out of every three days may be foggy. And the prevailing summer wind is onshore, which does not help matters. In the Baltic, the Pacific and even occasionally in the Black Sea, the Russians have an icebreaking problem as well, but on nothing like the scale presented by the polar ice. The colder, saltier, thicker and older the ice, the harder the icebreaker's job will be.

Attempts to find a North-East Passage from the Atlantic to the Pacific began long before the invention of steam power made the concept of an icebreaking ship feasible. A number of Englishmen tried in the middle of the sixteenth century, closely followed by the Dutch, among them the William Barents who gave his name to the northern sea. None of them got further than the entrance to what is now known as the Kara Sea.

24

The first serious Russian effort was planned by Peter the Great just before he died in 1725. By then the Cossacks had fought their way across Siberia to reach Kamchatka and the Pacific, but they did not know whether the land between the Anadyr and Kolyma rivers stretched on into another continent or was just a remote peninsula. If this was the end of Asia the first thing was to chart the strait dividing it from North America. Next, the Czar wanted to know whether the long coastline of bays and promontories between there and the North Cape of Scandinavia was ever free of ice.

The man chosen for the job was Vitus Bering, a Dane who had made a career in the Imperial Navy. He set out in January 1725 on a Great Northern Expedition which was eventually to last seventeen years. It took him three years to trek eastwards across Siberia, rafting great loads of equipment and two hundred horses across each river as he came to it, and to build his two ships on the shores of the Pacific. After two more years, by which time he seems almost to have lost sight of the expedition's original aim, he returned to St Petersburg to report that he had taken a quick look round what appeared to be – and in fact was – the continent's easternmost cape, and he was inclined to believe the local natives' tales to this effect.

In spite of the hardships Bering and his men had undergone to achieve this inconclusive result, the Czarina Anne was dissatisfied. A much larger expedition was organized, whose tasks were to include charting the whole of the northern coastline.

Meanwhile one of the ships Bering had left behind in the Pacific had reached America but her crew were under the impression they had merely landed on a large island. Bering returned to the east and set sail from Petropavlovsk, named after his new ships, *St Peter* and *St Paul*. He managed at last to cross the strait which now bears his name, but on the way home he was trapped by the approaching winter.

In her study of arctic exploration, *To the North*, Jeannette Mirsky gives a vivid and sympathetic account of the voyage's lonely anticlimax. Bering apparently allowed his scientist only a few hours ashore collecting specimens and would not even wait to fill all the water casks. On the way back, as he feared, the weather overtook them. They were forced to winter on an island so isolated that the blue foxes crowded round as the sailors landed, and were hacked down by the dozen. Bering himself died of scurvy before the spring came.

It was left to Captain Cook, at the end of his third voyage round the world a few years later, to clinch in a few weeks the argument Bering had been trying to resolve for half a lifetime. The Englishman rounded the East Cape and sailed west until the ice stopped him at North Cape. On the way back he had the luck which always deserted Vitus Bering: 'The weather becoming clear, we had the opportunity of seeing, at the same moment, the remarkable peaked hill near Cape Prince of Wales on the coast of America, and the East Cape of Asia.'[1]

Meanwhile the other phases of the Bering plan were steadily proceeding in spite of the enormous difficulties posed by the distances involved, the ice, the fog and the shortness of the arctic summer. The idea was to chart each section of the coastline from a shore base in that area. But the only craft available for most of the work seems to have been a kind of scow, about seventy feet long, called a koch, which sounds like the sort of thing the Vikings used for cargo carrying. In 1740 exploration was halted at Great Bear Cape, east of the Liena, but the expedition had already done enough to demonstrate that if a ship could beat the ice, it could find a North East Passage.

The first ship to do so was the 300 ton *Vega*, sailing from Tromso 138 years later. This Swedish Navy expedition led by the Finn Nordensjold passed Cape Chelyuskin for the first time to seaward on August 19, 1878, but was then icebound within a few miles of open water and did not meet the Pacific swell until the following summer. Two months after Nordensjold's arrival an American boat, the *Jeannette*, set off in the other direction to test the theory that the middle of the Arctic Ocean might be ice free. She drifted across the East Siberian Sea for two years before being crushed by the ice near the Novosibirskie Islands. Some

[1] Quoted by Jeannette Mirsky from *A Voyage to the Pacific Ocean* by Captain James King.

of her crew never reached land again but a piece of the wreckage was washed up on the coast of east Greenland. It was this that prompted Nansen to sail his little wooden vessel, the *Fram*, into the polar ice in the belief – triumphantly vindicated – that she could drift safely across the Arctic Ocean.

CHAPTER 3

Icebreakers and the Arctic Routes

If the Arctic was to become navigable, ships had to be capable not merely of surviving in the polar ice, but when necessary of smashing their way through it. The serious development of what the Russians call the Northern Sea Route – from the White Sea to the Bering Strait – therefore runs parallel to the evolution of the icebreaker.

On a small scale, all kinds of ingenious methods have been used to break ice. The Americans have experimented on the Great Lakes with a sort of floating bulldozer that cracks it from underneath; the Germans produced a boat which wriggles herself along with a set of counter-rotating weights; and the Russians have at least one barge which cuts the ice with rotating saws and lifts it aside on a conveyor belt. Some of the early polar navigation was attempted with strong, but otherwise fairly conventional ships which simply tried to slice their way through. But the most effective method in thick ice is the crudest. All big modern icebreakers have sawn off bows so they can ride up on to the ice and smash it with their own weight, sending long cracks shooting ahead of them.

An icebreaker at work is therefore a decidedly uncomfortable ship. She rears up on the ice, backs off and hurls herself at it again and again until she has forced a way through.

The hull must be immensely strong and may be equipped with three or four propellers to provide the great power required – sometimes two shaft horse power for every ton displaced. Electric drive is normally preferred because it can absorb the shock of a propeller becoming jammed in the ice. Icebreaker captains also like to have a lot of power available for going

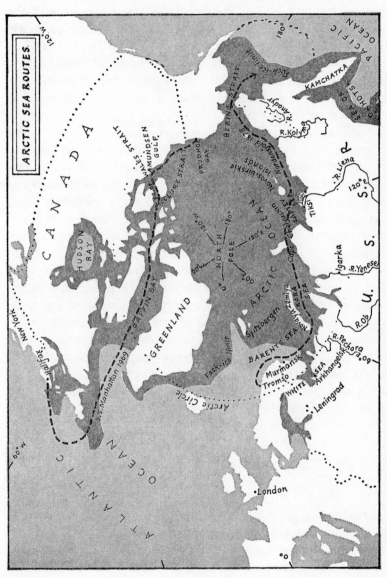

Figure 2 The Arctic sea routes. The darker tone marks the area normally covered by winter pack-ice.

astern and the maximum manœuvrability. Special bow propellers are helpful in soft ice but both the Russians and the Americans have found them too vulnerable for polar work. Even a conventional stern propeller can easily be damaged in heavy ice. To cope with this the Russians have developed a type with separate steel blades bolted together so that if necessary – as happened to the icebreaker *Moskva* in the winter of 1965–66 – it can be repaired at sea.

The ship's log is also easily damaged, whether it be the older kind towed over the stern on a line, or the retractable pressure tube projecting through the bottom of the hull. And in any case measuring speed through the water is not necessarily much use to an icebreaker which is forever turning and backing to work her way through. Russian 'ice captains' have therefore evolved what is known as the 'five minute navigation system'. Every five minutes the course and speed are noted, and later averaged out to give a rough indication of the progress made. When the log has to be retracted in ice, the speed can be judged by timing the passage of some chosen mark along the side of the ship or throwing a chunk of wood overboard to serve the same purpose – an intriguing echo of the technique from which the words log and knot (as a measure of speed) were originally derived. This involved running out a line marked with the ordinary kind of knot, by attaching it to a log of wood which was then pitched over the side of the ship.

The Evolution of the Russian Icebreaker

A continuous experience with icebreakers, dating back to the last ten years of the nineteenth century, when Admiral Makarov forced the experiment of an arctic icebreaker on a reluctant and reactionary Imperial administration, is the only outstanding historical achievement of Russian merchant shipping under both Imperial Russia and the Communist system up to 1945.[1]

[1] John Harbron, *Communist Ships and Shipping.*

The first icebreaker recorded by the Russians was the converted tug *Pailot*, used by the merchant Britniev in 1864 to clear a passage across the frozen River Nieva between St Petersburg and Kronshtat. By the turn of the century there were probably several dozen small craft at work in Russian ports. It was then that Admiral Makarov persuaded his Government to have the 5,000 ton *Yermak* built in Newcastle-upon-Tyne by Armstrong-Whitworth, with steam reciprocating engines giving 10,000 h.p. It was an impressive, ambitious design. But the admiral seems to have oversold his project by painting a vivid picture of his ship carving her way to the North Pole. When she proved not quite up to it, his more practical plans for opening up the Kara Sea were unnecessarily discredited.,

However, as we have seen, the Czar was soon to be reminded of the potential value of a northern sea route by the Russo-Japanese war, and in the First World War icebreakers proved strategically useful in keeping Arkhangelsk open.

By the 1930s the USSR had a substantial fleet of rather elderly icebreakers, most of them British built. The first north-east passage in one season was made in 1932 by the 1,400 ton *Sibiriakov*, built in Glasgow in 1909. But she lost her propeller on the way and only made port under improvised sail. Next summer the leader of that expedition, Professor Shmidt, tried again in the 'ice cutter' *Chelyushkin*, which was hardly more than a strengthened freighter; this time his ship sank under him and the crew had to be lifted off the ice by plane.

In 1934, when the icebreaking fleet was taken over by the Northern Sea Route Administration (*Glavsevmorput* in its characteristic Russian abbreviation) it was immediately decided to lay down the new Josif Stalin class of 11,000 tonners. The first came into service in 1938; the fourth and last, the *Anastas Mikoyan*, reached the arctic by steaming eastabout from the Black Sea while the Soviet Union was at war with Germany. Their design could be traced back to the *Yermak*; and for power they still relied on coal-fired steam reciprocating engines – presumably because coal was available in Spitsbergen, and it was convenient to burn the same fuel as the majority of freighters then in the arctic, so as to be able to supply them if they got stuck in the ice.

Since the war, when the United States started building its seven Wind class 6,000 tonners, the Russians have ordered three new series from Finland. The three Kapitan 5,000 tonners came into service during the 1950s, and five Moskva class vessels, 15,000 tons and 22,000 shaft horse power, in the 1960s. Then in April 1970 it was announced that three even more powerful ships had been ordered from Wartsila in Helsinki for delivery between 1971 and 1975. They would have diesel-electric propulsion giving 36,000 s.h.p. The only Western icebreaker to compare with the Moskva class in both size and power is the Canadian *St Laurent* (13,000 tons and 24,000 s.h.p.), which was completed in 1968. The American *Glacier*, built in 1955, has 22,000 s.h.p. in a 9,000 ton displacement hull – which was simply a development of the Wind class design. The Americans have not built a polar icebreaker since then, although by 1969 plans for a new class were under discussion.

In short, the Soviet icebreaking fleet is by a substantial margin the most powerful in the world. And it contains one unique vessel, the nuclear powered *Lenin*. This 16,000 tonner is not only the world's first nuclear surface ship, just beating the American passenger/cargo liner *Savannah* into service; she is still the only merchant ship with this form of propulsion to do a really useful job as well as being a floating test bed.

It is difficult to credit the Russian claim that the *Lenin* has extended the arctic navigation season by about 50 per cent, particularly since she disappeared, as far as Western observers were concerned, in 1967. But in her first five years, from 1960, she escorted 400 ships and steamed 53,000 miles through the ice. The word 'steamed' is quite legitimate – as well as sounding more natural than 'reacted' – since her atomic reactors are used to heat steam to drive turbines, which in turn are coupled to DC electric motors driving the propellers. Her first supply of fuel lasted three years. She can break ice twelve feet thick and, as the Russians claim with studied nonchalance, 'She could go to the North Pole, but there is no reason to divert her from her duty of convoying ships merely to break one more record.'

The *Lenin* is the prime example of what the Russians call a *linieny liedokol*, which is equivalent to the English expression 'ship of the line'. In this context it means a big polar icebreaker that leads convoys through the ice, that is self-contained with her own workshops and that, in the case of oil-burning ships, carries spare fuel for the freighters she is shepherding: the role of sheepdog, rounding up the stragglers, is given to auxiliary icebreakers. Finally there are the arctic expedition ships which have strengthened, icebreaking bows to get themselves around, and specialized icebreaking freighters.

In 1964 the Russians announced that they would build two more nuclear icebreakers even more powerful than the *Lenin*, the first of which would be commissioned in 1971. The new design was to be simpler, with a lighter and more compact reactor; it would be even more automated, able to go longer without refuelling and manned by a smaller crew. The aim was to make navigation of the arctic possible throughout the year. The few details released since then indicate that the first of the class – to be named the Arktika – would have a displacement of 25,000 tons (compared with the *Lenin*'s 16,000 tons) and carry ten helicopters for ice reconnaissance.

Meanwhile something nasty seemed to happen to the *Lenin*. Early in 1967 the Soviet authorities said it was hoped to have her leading the icebreaking fleet as usual that summer, but she did not turn up; and at the time of writing she has not been reported by Western observers for three years.

The rumours surrounding her disappearance ranged from a vivid picture of her lying abandoned in the polar ice, her reactor running wild, to more prosaic suggestions that a Russian crane driver had dropped a heavy piece of equipment – such as the reactor core container – while she was under repair and had sunk her at the quayside. The first story allegedly reached Scandinavia from Russian sailors coming home suffering from radiation burns, and they sound a little bit like those famous Russian soldiers with snow on their boots. But until the Russians make it clear exactly where the ship is, or the *Lenin* herself hoves

B

into view, Western sceptics are bound to offer their own solutions to the mystery.

Soviet shipping officials either denied the rumours or referred vaguely to operations in the arctic. Yet until 1967 this distinctive vessel was always sighted at some time during the arctic navigation season or mentioned in some circumstantial Russian report. Refuelling, as opposed to major engineering conversion, would take months rather than years.

A reactor can overheat, destroying the core containers and contaminating the primary heat transfer system. But given the elaborate shielding round this or any other reactor compartment, the 'radiation burns' allegedly received by the Russian sailors could have been injuries from high pressure steam – which might nevertheless indicate a serious accident. It is possible that the Soviet engineers ran up against some unexpected problem – metal fatigue or corrosion perhaps – which they did not want to talk about until the *Lenin* could once again take pride of place in their arctic fleet. At a still more pedestrian level, it might have been decided to replace the *Lenin*'s pioneering reactor with a more compact system, possibly as a test bed for the Arktika class. In that case the Soviet authorities have only their own compulsive secrecy to blame for the mystery which has surrounded their great ship.

The Development of the Northern Sea Route

Without a fleet of hefty port icebreakers Russian sea transport would be virtually paralysed for half the year. But the primary task of polar icebreakers like those of the Moskva class is to keep as much as possible of the northern sea route open as long as possible. The original, and still by far the most important motive, was the movement of domestic and foreign trade along limited stretches of the arctic coast, starting with the Kara Sea (when Soviet publications talk about the northern sea route being open for navigation they often mean only part of it). Few Soviet freighters had any occasion to sail from one end to the other, but in 1967 this route was offered to the world's merchant shipping as an international route which would, for example, cut 4,000 miles off the distance southabout from London to Yokohama – and another 4,000 while the Suez Canal remained closed.

Another use for the northern route which is easy to overlook is that it enables swarms of small river craft to reach the waterways of the Siberian interior from shipyards in the west and south of the Soviet Union. There are nearly 200,000 miles of navigable river in Siberia, compared with only 15,000 miles of railway and road, and the Russians make full use of them. Each summer, therefore, a motley convoy of small craft sets out for the Ob, the Yenesei and the Liena escorted by icebreakers. In 1969 it included motor barges, passenger hydrofoils, tugs and floating cranes – enough to try any escort's patience. In twenty-two expeditions of this kind about a thousand vessels have reached their respective rivers along the arctic route.

One of the first cargoes loaded by the English and Russian merchants who spasmodically ventured into the 'ice cellar' of the Kara Sea in the late nineteenth century was timber from the vast Siberian *taiga* forest; and being well suited to sea transport, it is still the characteristic cargo of the northern fleets. In 1968 the Soviet Union exported 13 million cubic metres of round timber and 8 million cubic metres of sawn wood. Much of this will have passed through Igarka, on the Yenesei, which became a boom town in the 1930s, and is quite a familiar port of call for Western tramp skippers. Timber is also carried east from Tiksi, at the mouth of the Liena.

The Yenesei was probably developed further than its neighbour the Ob because it has deeper water on the bar. But the upper reaches of the Ob now carry construction materials for the rapidly expanding oilfields of western Siberia, which will soon be one of the Soviet petroleum industry's main producing areas. Equipment also comes by water to the diamond and gold mines, which seem to have replaced the legendary salt mines. A network of power stations, at least one of which uses atomic power, is being constructed in Siberia as part of an extensive programme of industrialization, and as this sort of development spreads north from the line of the Transiberian Railway new communities will come within reach of the arctic rivers. One of the few occasions on which the nineteenth-century Czarist regimes took an interest in pioneering voyages along the northern route was when the ships carried rails to the Yenesei, for the nearby section of the Transiberian Railway. But in spite of railway development, and later air transport, there is still a long tract of northern Siberia where the economic way to move most freight is by water.

Before arctic navigation could get underway on a regular basis there was a great deal of scientific work to be done. The hydrographers had to prepare reliable charts and pilot books, which were not available for the whole of the northern sea route until the outbreak of the Second World War. The violent magnetic effects, which make compasses so difficult to use near the Pole, and the peculiarities of radio propagation at such high latitudes both needed studying. And the meteorologists had to develop ice forecasts.

This last problem divides itself into two parts: the study of long term ice movements, taking into account the influence of the prevailing winds and ocean currents such as the North Atlantic Drift, which reaches up into the Barents Sea to keep it comparatively ice-free; and the plotting of the immediate situation. For the second requirement the Russians made early use of aerial reconnaissance, starting in 1924. By 1960, according to John Harbron, the Canadian specialist in Communist shipping, the entire northern route was being covered by aerial surveys every ten days, with new ice charts published each month. He considered it a much better service than that provided for Canadian and American navigators at that time. By 1969 the Russians had been experimenting for two years with a helicopter-mounted television camera transmitting clear pictures, it was claimed, up to thirty miles from the parent icebreaker. It was expected to be an easy matter 'to equip all icebreakers with this "Artika" system in the near future', superseding the technique of dropping written ice reports to the ships from aircraft. In

1970 there was talk of feeding information from weather satellites into the forecast system.

In order to standardize their reports, Soviet seamen use what is known as the Zhubov Scale to describe the extent of ice coverage. It is equivalent to the international Beaufort Scale of wind forces and in Russian the same word – *ball*, pronounced with a short 'a' – is used to denote the points on the scale. 'One *ball* ice' covers about 10 per cent of the water visible from a ship's bridge, 'two *ball* ice' about 20 per cent and so on. The scale runs as follows:

1–3 *ball*: sparsely distributed ice; navigable by all vessels without reducing speed.
4–6 *ball*: broken ice; navigable by all vessels at about three-quarters speed.
7–8 *ball*: concentrated ice; vessels require the assistance of icebreakers.
9–10 *ball*: complete coverage; navigation dependent on the type of ice and the effectiveness of the icebreaker escort.

In an effort to speed the break up of ice in the estuaries of the Yenesei and the Liena, the Russians recently tried spraying it with a pattern of coal dust or dye. In a typically enthusiastic account of the experiment, the scientists involved said it enabled 'the spring sun to cut the ice into pieces like a knife going through butter'. The economics were not discussed, but the experiment itself illustrates the methodical way the Russians seem to evaluate any new idea, whether they think of it themselves or pick it up abroad. After widespread public alarm in Britain when several trawlers were lost in the winter of 1967–68 through becoming top heavy with ice, it was noticeable that the Soviet authorities mounted two scientific expeditions to study a problem one would have expected them to know all about. One team of scientists sailed from Murmansk aboard the research ship *Alaid*, while another carried out an identical programme of tests in the Far East. Different parts of the ship's hull were coated with silicon paints in green, black and grey, winches were covered in synthetic materials and a 'magnetic pulse generator' was tried out. Since 1969 the Soviet meteorological service has warned arctic shipping about the onset of icing conditions as well as gales. By 1970, atlases of the Barents and Okhotsk seas had been prepared showing various icing zones and it was announced that similar atlases were being prepared for critical areas of the North Atlantic.

Russian scientists have also been working on the arctic's other big navigational hazard – fog. During a recent experiment in the Kola Gulf, the water was covered with a thin film of emulsion, said to be harmless, which reduces evaporation by 50 to 60 per cent. It was claimed that while the emulsion remained on the surface, a matter of several hours, the fog became 'very thin or disappeared altogether'.

Much of the scientific work in the arctic is done from a chain of research stations along the Siberian coast, some of them ashore, others adrift on the ice. 'Floating Ice Floe Station No I' was established in 1937 under the command of Admiral Papanin, who later became head of *Glavsevmorput*, which is responsible for the northern sea route as a whole. *Glavsevmorput* itself had been founded in 1932. It laid navigational buoys, rigged lights, published charts, established dozens of weather stations and provided reconnaissance aircraft. In short, the first comprehensive attempt was made to open up the polar seas. Dr Armstrong has produced a full analysis of the route's development.[2]

Meanwhile the Soviet Government had vigorously asserted its sovereignty over the islands which lay to the north of the Russian coastline. In the early days the arctic belonged, in a sense, to whoever was man enough to explore it. But as new land appeared on the map and as its potential became clearer, so the lawyers and the politicians took over. Just before the revolution the Imperial regime had declared that any land north of Russia's arctic coastline belonged to her unless specifically conceded to another country. This concept of a sector, drawn from the North Pole to the eastern and western limits of the Russian mainland,

[2] *The Northern Sea Route: Soviet Exploitation of the North East Passage* by Dr Terence Armstrong, of the Scott Polar Institute in Cambridge, England.

was advocated with more determination by the Communist administration of 1926.[3]

It led to disputes, first with the Canadian eskimos who colonized Wrangel Island near the Bering Strait and later with the Norwegian sealers and whalers who used Franz Josef Land. But both these groups were eventually turned out by Russian expeditions and the Soviet flag firmly planted to prevent their returning.

The number of Russian freighters using the northern sea route steadily increased. By the summer of 1936, according to Dr Armstrong, more than one hundred ships moved along some part of it. But the problem of the ice was by no means solved. Next year two dozen vessels were trapped at sea and one of them was crushed and sunk before the old icebreaker *Yermak* could reach her in the following spring.

The simplest answer to such setbacks was more icebreakers. The Josif Stalin class was already under construction. Then during the war three Wind class boats were temporarily acquired from the Americans under Lend Lease. The Finns were forced to hand over half a dozen as 'reparations' afterwards, and between 1954 and 1968 the Russians put nine new polar icebreakers into service, including the *Lenin* (the youngest vessel in the American fleet was completed in 1955). By the late 1960s the shipping authorities were confident enough to offer Russian holidaymakers a three week cruise in the Kara Sea, and as if to emphasize what a tame business arctic navigation had become three Soviet yachtsmen set out in August 1969 to sail from Arkhangelsk to the Yenesei. Since ice conditions turned out to be 'the worst for thirty to forty years' they must have had a rough time.

The important thing was that with more icebreakers working to extend the navigation season at each end, increasing quantities of timber, equipment, construction materials, food and fuel were moving along the northern route, and between 1960 and 1967 the annual total rose by 80 per cent. The 1966 season

[3] The implications of the sector principle are discussed in 'The Soviet Union and the Arctic' by Captain O. P. Araldsen, RNN, *US Naval Institute Proceedings*, June 1967.

lasted for 62 to 133 days, according to which point you choose on the route. The calculation is Dr Armstrong's, and writing in the March, 1968 edition of *Inter Nord*, he gave the following dates for the opening and closing of the season:

Entrance to the Kara Sea: July 3 to November 14 – 133 days.
Igarka: July 17 to October 31 – 106 days.
Mys Chelyuskin: August 7 to October 8 – 62 days.
Pevek: June 29 to October 15 – 109 days.
Bering Straits: June 25 to October 20 – 117 days.

It was a key year, because at the end of that season the Soviet Government decided to offer the northern sea route to the world's merchant shipping as an alternative to the southern oceans. It seemed that the North-East Passage was about to come into its own, four centuries after seamen first started searching for it.

The announcement was made, as we have seen, in March 1967. 'After a careful study of Soviet experience', foreign ship-owners were to be given an opportunity to save thirteen days and about £15,000 in operating costs between London and Yokohama, as compared with the traditional route through the Suez Canal. Icebreakers and polar aircraft would be at their disposal; they could make use of Soviet radio, hydrographic and meteorological services, and take a pilot if necessary; instructions and advice on arctic convoys would be available together with new charts. They might even find themselves escorted by the nuclear powered *Lenin*.

The Russians calculated that the voyage from London to Yokohama via Suez would be shortened from 11,600 miles to 7,300 miles; a saving of 4,300 miles, which they reckoned on average was equivalent to thirteen days. For icebreaking, pilotage and meteorological services they proposed to charge according to a sliding scale, which for ships with a high ice classification varied from about £2 per net registered ton for a 2,000 tonner down to about fifteen shillings per ton for a 7,000 tonner (at 1969 exchange rates). The rate for ships without ice classification or of more than 7,000 tons was to be separately negotiated.

The reaction of British and Norwegian shipowners was distinctly cool. The Danes, Italians, and particularly the Japanese, were reported to be interested. But in fact nothing seems to have come of the Russians' ambitious plans. Their own strengthened freighter *Novovoronezh* loaded an experimental cargo at several European ports in 1967 and apparently reached Yokohama in twenty-eight days, returning at least part of the way before the end of the season. At the time of writing, however, not a single foreign vessel has followed her.

A number of factors may have contributed to this extraordinary anticlimax. One Russian source has since explained that the original cost estimate for providing navigational services was too low; in particular it did not include any allowance for aerial ice reconnaissance. This discovery would make the route less valuable as a source of foreign exchange or less attractive to shipowners, according to how the dues were pitched. Western shipping lines would also have to meet additional insurance charges, which would be further increased by the fact that few, if any, of their existing vessels would be ice strengthened. Russian lines do not normally send their ships along the northern routes unless they are strengthened with a sawn-off icebreaking bow. A conventional ship in heavy ice would, if possible, be lashed hard up against an icebreaker's stern, which is notched and fendered for this purpose, so as to protect her bow. But this is an expensive way of using an icebreaking fleet, and a freighter going northabout would have to save a great deal of money before it became worth paying the economic rate for such a service, even occasionally.

Shipowners who investigated using the route in detail may well have been taken aback by the uncertainty of it all – the danger of a ship being frozen in for the winter could not be completely ruled out – and the short time for which the central sections of the route are actually available. References to its being open for up to 150 days do not tie in with Dr Armstrong's analysis of the 1966 season. It is true the ice was unusually slow to clear in the west that year, but one has the feeling that arctic navigators, like farmers, tend to be grappling with 'the worst season they can remember' every time one talks to them.

A Japanese company which in 1967 was reported to be planning a service for the following season has since complained
about the restrictions placed on its attempts to carry out its own
research of the route. This is consistent with the rumour –
which nevertheless sounds far-fetched even by Soviet political
standards – that after the Middle East war of June 1967, the
Russians decided to stall on the northern sea route in case they
were accused of taking advantage of their Arab friends' difficulties.

The Manhattan Experiment

More recently, since the discovery of oil in Alaska, the international shipping community's attention has turned back to the
great arctic route associated with the names of Franklin, Ross,
Parry and McClure – the North-West Passage. Whereas the
North-East Passage consists of a comparatively straight continental coastline with only a few bays and islands scattered along
it, its counterpart on the west of the Atlantic is almost completely
choked by a barren archipelago stretching from Canada to
Greenland.

But of course those English naval captains who spent the
first half of the nineteenth century trying to find their way
across did not know that. When they started their charts were
blank from Hudson's Bay to the Bering Strait, apart from two
points at which Mackenzie and Hearne claimed to have reached
the sea overland. Discoveries made two centuries earlier by
Davis and Baffin, who could have given them some idea what
they were up against, were either ignored or forgotten. This new
generation of explorers sailed into an icy maze, in which to take
one of the innumerable wrong turnings could mean two or three
long arctic winters trapped in the ice, and sometimes death.

In 1969, the collective route which had been so painfully
charted by wooden, square rigged sailing vessels like the *Hecla*,
the *Fury* and the *Terror*, was retraced in a matter of weeks by the

100,000 ton steam tanker *Manhattan*. Having struck oil in large quantities on the desolate north slope of Alaska, the Humble oil company conceived the idea of a giant icebreaking tanker to bring it to the east coast of the United States. She was to be not merely strengthened, but also fitted with a full icebreaking bow so as to carve an independent channel through the polar pack.

The Russians, for whom the North-West Passage is merely the other side of the ocean which washes their northern coastline, were fascinated by the American scheme but remained sceptical about it – as were a good many other people when they tried to envisage a cumbersome tanker leaping at the pack in the ice-breaker's customary ferocious manner. It was rather as if some-one had suggested that the air force should convert civilian air liners into fighter bombers.

Humble itself described the experiment as a '40 million dollar gamble'. But with potential savings over the cost of a pipeline estimated at forty-five cents for every barrel of oil, it did not intend to accept the conventional wisdom without trying for itself. British Petroleum and Atlantic Richfield, who had also struck oil in Alaska, agreed to put in two million dollars each so as to have access to the results.

In fact the conventional tanker does have one important asset for icebreaking – weight. And the new American bow shape, with a shallow, fifteen-degree angle of attack, is designed to make full use of this; it cracks the ice from above rather than forcing it apart. But most of the icebreaker's other characteristics – the exceptionally high horsepower/tonnage ratio, the large propor-tion of astern power, the outstanding manœuvrability – would be hopelessly uneconomic in the normal oil tanker.

The vessel chosen for the experiment was literally taken to pieces and rebuilt with a long overhanging bow, a protective double skin along the sides, internal stiffening and machinery collision chocks. I happened to have been aboard her some years earlier to inspect the unusual system of flume tank stabilization, and I remember her skipper saying that the twin screws and rudders made her surprisingly manœuvrable for a tanker. This was a help in her new role. But her 43,000 horse power could not be increased, which was obviously going to make it difficult to relate her performance to the much more powerful vessels that would be built if Humble went ahead with its scheme.

The *Manhattan* finally sailed from Halifax in August 1969. With the help of aerial surveys, satellite navigation and two escorting icebreakers she could hardly get into much trouble. But it was still an adventure. After all, it was not until 1903 that Amundsen made the first complete passage from east to west, in an auxiliary cutter, and that had taken three years. The first crossing in a single season had only been achieved in 1954, by the Canadian icebreaker *Labrador*.

For the first few miles of the converted tanker's passage, all went well. The new bow smashed through pack ice up to fourteen feet thick without any trouble. But the ridges formed by floes crushed together were a different matter, particularly in McClure Strait, where the wind had been blowing hard from the north-west for the previous ten days. At one point the *Manhattan* ground to a halt against a twenty-four-foot ridge and the wind-driven ice immediately closed the channel behind her. With insufficient astern power she had to be freed by one of the escorting icebreakers. Conditions continued to deteriorate and the expedition eventually had to retrace its course for about a hundred miles. Heading south into Prince of Wales Strait and Amundsen Gulf she found the going easier and completed her passage at Sachs Harbour, ten days after entering the North West Passage proper.

The site proposed for the loading terminal was further west, at Prudhoe Bay, where the engineers had been trying to provide a berth by spraying two ice 'islands' until they were grounded under the weight of newly formed ice. Unfortunately the islands then broke up, which was one of the problems that remained unresolved as the *Manhattan* retraced her course to Halifax. In the following spring she conducted further trials in Eclipse Sound, to the north of Baffin Island, where she slightly damaged her stern during backing manœuvres.

At the time of writing, Humble has not taken a final decision on whether to build a fleet of icebreaking tankers. But whatever happens in Alaska, the *Manhattan*'s venture may inspire others. The arctic is rich in metals as well as oil – the Mary River iron ore deposits on Baffin Island for example, where the shipping season now lasts for only six weeks. If this could be extended by using icebreaking bulk carriers along the lines of the *Manhattan*, without tackling the inner channels of the North-West Passage, mining might become economic over large areas that have not so far been touched.

Meanwhile General Dynamics, which recently launched its hundredth nuclear submarine for the United States Navy, has come up with the 'simple' solution to the oil transportation problem – a fleet of 170,000 ton submarine nuclear tankers which would dive under the ice at eighteen knots instead of smashing their way laboriously through it. The company clearly takes its own extraordinary proposal seriously, so perhaps it may one day become a reality. For the moment, my own reaction is to feel even sorrier for the crews of such vessels, 'enjoying a steady twenty-eight degree temperature' under the ice, than I do for the men who might be facing the winter's cold above it.

The Strategic Value of the Arctic Routes

There are two main ways in which the Arctic Ocean may be strategically useful to the Soviet Union: as a convoy supply route in wartime, when the entrances to the Baltic, the Black Sea or the Sea of Japan are controlled by the enemy, and as a route by which her warships can move between the Atlantic and the Pacific without leaving Russian coastal waters. Since the development of the Polaris submarine these frozen waters have also posed a potential threat – that a nuclear-tipped ballistic missile might literally be launched against Moscow through a hole in the ice.

For this reason, and because even along such lonely routes convoys are likely to be attacked – as they were by German U-boats in the Second World War – the limitations and advantages of submarine operations in the ice are of special importance.

45

There are few things more awe inspiring, according to those who have experienced it, than to sit in a submarine and listen to the pack ice grinding above you with a dreadful, crushing power; yet the noisy fringes of the ice cap, washed by layers of comparatively fresh water, would probably be a good place for a submariner on the defensive to hide, because of the difficulty of sonar detection.

Venturing far under the ice cap is a different matter, since a diesel powered submarine cannot survive for more than a few days without coming to the surface to charge her engine batteries. To gamble on finding a hole when your time is up obviously takes a good deal of nerve.

Around the North Pole the average thickness of the ice is about eleven feet. Breaks in it can be seen on the submarine's upwards-looking sonar – an echo sounder in reverse. This shows both the change from water to ice and that between the ice and the air above it. To surface, the boat first criss-crosses the hole to plot its shape. She then settles herself beneath it, gently keeping pace with the pack ice, which is almost certainly moving relative to the water – and to hit such a solid mass at even a couple of knots could be dangerous. Finally, having confirmed that there is nothing above her but water or a thin sheet of newly formed ice, she slowly blows her ballast tanks and comes up.

During the Second World War, German U-boats managed to operate with reasonable success in the Arctic, raiding merchant convoys and the few Russian warships they found up there, in spite of the limitations of diesel-electric propulsion. In addition to the famous Allied convoys which tried to break through from the Atlantic, a few freighters carrying American Lend Lease cargoes were sent right along the Northern Sea Route from the Pacific in company with the Russian coastal traffic. The American ships were manned by Soviet sailors, so as to be neutral as far as the Japanese were concerned, but the U-boats were waiting for them in the Kara Sea. According to records cited by Dr Armstrong[4] the Germans succeeded in sinking a dozen merchant

[4] *Geographical Journal*, June 1955.

ships, a destroyer and five escorts at the cost of two submarines and a few bent periscopes.

During their first summer, in 1942, the U-boats were accompanied by the cruiser *Admiral Scheer*, but in the couple of weeks she was in the Kara Sea she found few worthwhile targets. The submarines operated from temporary bases along the shores of Novaya Zemlya. They would rest half submerged in the shallows and then move off to intercept a freighter, lay a few mines or shoot up a Russian shore station. In 1944 they even tried to get through into the Laptev Sea to the east, but the ice blocking the straits was too formidable.

The advent in 1955 of the nuclear submarine, able to remain indefinitely submerged, opened up a whole range of new operational possibilities. Three years later the uss *Nautilus* passed right under the North Pole on passage from the Pacific to the Atlantic. During that same summer another American nuclear submarine, the *Skate*, spent ten days under the ice cap, surfacing on nine occasions. In the spring of 1959 she went under again and this time actually surfaced at the North Pole to scatter the ashes of the arctic explorer Sir Hubert Wilkins. On a third visit, in August 1962, she demonstrated the ability to rendezvous with her sister ship *Seadragon* at the Pole, where they surfaced together.

By then the American submariners felt that their arctic technique – such as their inertial navigation system, which uses devices to sense movement in any direction, so that provided the navigator knows his starting point, he knows where he has got to – was probably as good as anything the Soviet Navy might have developed. But this latest ice spectacular seems to have wounded the Russians' pride in their traditional Polar expertise. On January 27, 1963, *Izvestia* carried pictures of sailors from the submarine *Leninsky Komsomol* planting the Red Flag in the ice at the North Pole, together with a long description of the submarine's 'ice odyssey'. A reproachful caption to the picture explains:

Statements have recently appeared in the American Press wrongly asserting that us nuclear submarines were the first to navigate under the ice of the arctic basin. In fact these boasts have no truth in them.

The honour of opening up the routes beneath the grim ice of the North Polar basin belongs to Soviet sailors. Even in the early 1930s submariners of the Northern Fleet operated bravely and confidently under the ice. And our nuclear submarines were in the high latitudes of the arctic basin considerably earlier than the Americans.

The article explained that the submarine's training mission was to bar the passage of hostile missile submarines which had been penetrating the Barents Sea. The North Pole hardly seems the best place to do this unless the enemy was expected to approach from the Pacific, but the idea of American Polaris boats patrolling the Barents Sea is reasonable, since this is the nearest open water to many of the industrial targets in the central USSR. From the Soviet Navy's point of view, penetration of Hudson Bay might serve a similar purpose in threatening the middle of the United States. But of course the purpose of increasing the range of strategic deterrent missiles like Polaris (since 1960 it has increased from 1,400 miles to 2,900 miles) is to enable the submarines carrying them to back further and further off into the open ocean.

The application of nuclear propulsion to submarines has made it possible for them to use the Arctic Ocean as an underwater short cut from one side of the world to the other and the development of nuclear icebreakers is lengthening the season during which the Soviet Navy can pass warships across the northern sea route on the surface.

But in fact one of the first naval vessels to make this arctic passage in wartime was the German merchant cruiser *Komet*, which in 1940, during the brief period of alliance between Stalin and Hitler, was escorted across to the Pacific by the Russians in a record time of only three weeks. In peacetime the route is apparently used by the Soviet Navy to deliver warships from one ocean to another or to rotate them between the fleets. They proceed in convoys, like the merchant ships, with wooden sheathing to protect sensitive spots on the submarines.

What the traffic amounts to neither Soviet nor NATO sources are inclined to say but it is obviously severely limited by the short length of the arctic navigation season. In the same way, although the ability of nuclear submarines to pass clean under the Polar ice cap has been amply demonstrated, it would be wrong to suppose that they are scuttling back and forth like so many minnows. But here the limitation is one of requirement. Even submariners would not risk the remote, but grim, possibility of breaking down under the ice, unable to communicate or surface, just for the fun of it.

Warming up the Artic

For surface vessels, the problems of the Northern Sea Route remain largely unsolved. For a time it seemed that they might solve themselves, because there was a long term upward trend in arctic temperatures. But according to the British Meteorological Office[5] the improvement petered out during the 1940s and since 1955 the mean winter temperature on Spitsbergen has fallen by nearly six degrees centigrade.

However, the possibility that a fundamental climatic change may be artificially induced is raised by the Russians' recently announced plans to reverse the flow of three great rivers which flow into the arctic – the Pechora, the Ob and the Yenesei. The ostensible purpose of the scheme, which was originally conceived in Stalin's time, is to irrigate the dry lands to the south and raise the steadily sinking water levels of the Caspian and Aral seas. The Caspian has fallen seven feet over the past twenty years and it is feared that the Aral Sea could dry out altogether. The new canals feeding them could be used on their way south to irrigate something like 100 million acres of land and drain an even larger area of swamp. But at the same time, this gargantuan project may have the effect of moving the world's climatic zones further north – only slightly, but enough to produce dramatic results. Anthony Tucker, Science Correspondent of *The Guardian*, has described what is likely to happen[6]:

[5] Citing a paper on *Temperatures in the Arctic during the last Fifty Years*, published in Berlin by Regina Kirchen in 1966.

[6] *Guardian*, February 23, 1970.

49

The reduction in the floating ice area east of Greenland would lead over a number of years to a gradual warming up and a northernward shift of the temperate zone. As Mr H. H. Lamb, a climatic expert at the Meteorological Office at Bracknell said yesterday: 'The real situation is very much more complicated than any of the models used for prediction. Nobody can really say what the effects will be, but the most probable outcome would be a shift of the anti-cyclones to the north.'

This could mean that regions of North Africa, now fertile, would become arid; that the climate of the Caspian Sea area itself could get worse instead of better; and that Britain's climate might warm up to that prevalent for a short time before AD 1300, when vines were common in the south of England and when, in Scotland, the tree line was considerably higher than it is at present.

Whenever this project has been considered during the past twenty years, Russian scientists who predict serious climatic changes have been sufficiently persuasive for the plan to be shelved. But under economic pressure, with a natural climatic change tending the other way, and with the real possibility that a reduction in fresh water in the northern seas will lead simply to thinner ice and to little general change, the Russians may be in earnest this time. The intention, in any case, is to carry out the diversions sequentially so that effects can be monitored over a long period. The danger is that if things look good for Russia, she will take little account of any harmful changes which may take place elsewhere.

If these predictions are realized, the Northern Sea Route may one day become the great commercial waterway the optimistic Russian invitation seemed to envisage in 1967. But the time scale of the river diversion schemes is ten to twenty years. In the meantime, though the new Arktika class icebreakers may make it technically navigable throughout the year, just as the *Manhattan*'s successors may keep the North-West Passage open, its economic use will be severely limited.

CHAPTER 4

Difficult Straits

Since most of Russia's long northern coastline is only available for a few weeks a year, her ships have had to make the best of their limited outlets to the west, south and east. And all of these are unsatisfactory from some point of view.

In the extreme north-west corner of the Soviet Union, Murmansk has acquired strategic and commercial importance because it is kept free of ice by the comparatively warm water moving up from the Atlantic. But it is nonetheless well within the Arctic Circle and not exactly handy for the centres of industry and population to the south, even by Russian standards. Nor of course is the far eastern seaboard, although it is now expanding its own industrial hinterland. In the Baltic, winter ice is a serious handicap and even in the Black Sea some of the Russian ports occasionally have trouble with ice (some small icebreakers were at work there in the winter of 1966/67). From a trading point of view both the Baltic and the Black Sea bite conveniently deep into the land mass, but of course they become a corresponding liability in wartime, when they would have to be heavily defended even if there were plenty of coastline available for naval bases elsewhere.

The Baltic

The Baltic is vitually a tideless sea. Its shallow entrance is choked with islands so that the water is noticeably less salty than in the North Sea outside. Both the Gulf of Bothnia and the Gulf of Finland can be covered with ice — the approaches to Leningrad are frozen for four to five months a year, although icebreakers keep ships moving in and out.

Leningrad is the USSR's most important port. It is the Soviet Navy's main centre for administration, logistics and training (although the Baltic Fleet as such has an ice-free base further west at Kaliningrad). As a commercial port it handles more than ten million tons of general and bulk cargoes a year. One of the two main regional shipping administrations is based there and in particular it is the major terminal of the passenger ship services linking Russia to the West. It is also the biggest shipbuilding centre in the Soviet Union, turning out more than half the country's warships as well as many of the important types of merchant ship. Local industries include electrical engineering, machine tools, armaments, chemicals, timber, textiles and food processing.

The ports of what were formerly the Baltic states – Riga and Ventspils (Latvia), Klaipeda (Lithuania) and Tallinn (Estonia) – have been given their own shipping administrations and developed with the emphasis on handling bulk commodities. For example, Klaipeda (which used to be called Memel) has the largest coal loading installation in the Soviet Union and is a terminal for the Druzhba (Friendship) oil pipeline which runs through eastern Europe. Ventspils is already a big oil exporting terminal and is being provided with a new deep water tanker jetty; special facilities for liquid chemical tankers are under construction. Riga is being developed as a specialized container port and is also a regional headquarters of the Russian fishing industry.

For the Soviet Navy, the Baltic must always have looked like a well designed trap; and so it proved to be during the Second World War. In any future war with the West, warships trying to escape would have to steam hundreds of miles within comfortable range of NATO airfields, through narrow, easily mined channels – which incidentally provide good cover for the fast patrol boats in which all the Baltic navies specialize. The fairly deep basins around the island of Bornholm would probably provide a sanctuary for submarines because there must be plenty of temperature and salinity layers to make things difficult for the sonar operators listening on the surface.[1] But assuming that many of the seventy or so Soviet submarines in the Baltic would wish to reach the Norwegian Sea in the case of war, they face at least one shallow channel in which a big ocean-going boat could hardly remain submerged.

In the circumstances Russian admirals must sometimes despair of their dependence on Leningrad. Certainly it is no wonder they go nagging on about 'settling the problem of the Baltic approaches'. By settling, of course, the Communists mean controlling, and they have tried two lines of attack. They have promoted the idea of a 'neutral sea' from which all but the Baltic powers' warships would be excluded (just as access to the Black Sea is limited by the Montreux Convention). Then during and after the Second World War Stalin made repeated efforts to bargain for a foothold on the Jutland peninsula or in Kiel Bay, to cover the canal linking the Baltic with the North Sea.

What the USSR did gain from the war, of course, was a line of political satellites stretching along the southern shore of the Baltic as far west as the Trave River. The Soviet Fleet now carries out joint exercises, including amphibious operations, with the Polish and East German navies based respectively at Gdynia and Sassnitz. And if one is concerned not with escaping from the Baltic but dominating it, one must take account of the Warsaw Pact's four to one superiority in naval hardware over the NATO countries directly involved there. One of the significant items within this balance is the fleet of missile armed fast patrol boats operated by the Soviet Union, Poland and East Germany. In contrast, the NATO navies in Europe have relied on the availability of air support and virtually ignored the surface to surface missile. It is true that aircraft, if they were available, would make life extremely uncomfortable for any navy in the Baltic. But several members of NATO, including West Germany, are now looking for an equivalent to the Soviet Styx missile. Another basic feature of the physical confrontation in the Baltic is the attention both sides pay to minelaying, matched in the Soviet case by a vast fleet of minesweepers.

[1] See Chapter Nine for a discussion of sonar techniques.

Politically, the Soviet Union is confronting the hesitant northern fringes of NATO. If the forces tending to weaken the alliance persist, as they seem likely to do, Denmark and Norway will probably be among the first to break their links with it. So if the Russians were really looking for trouble, this is one of the places where they might start it.

The Black Sea

Physically, the Black Sea is even more of a backwater than the Baltic. Its only natural outlet is through the long, narrow channels of the Bosphorus and the Dardanelles, which in places are only half a mile wide – and belong to a member of NATO.

The exchange of water between the Black Sea and the Mediterranean produces vicious surface and underwater currents. This makes the straits so awkward that when the Russians were discussing the construction of their first 150,000 ton tanker the ability of such a big vessel to manœuvre through them was questioned in the Soviet technical press. The design eventually emerged with a special bow steering gear.

But whatever the difficulties, this route has carried the bulk of the Soviet Union's seaborne oil exports. The oilfields round Baku date back into the nineteenth century and by the beginning of this century were already connected by pipeline to the Black Sea port of Batumi. The first tanker to pass through the Suez Canal, in 1892, was carrying Russian oil to Singapore and Bangkok. Nowadays the centre of Soviet production is the 'Second Baku', between the Volga and the Ural rivers, from which the oil can be pumped through pipelines to the Baltic and eastern Europe. But the Soviet Union's biggest tanker terminal is still on the Black Sea, near Novorossiisk.

If one adds to this oil trade the large quantities of manufactured goods and other dry cargoes shipped through Odessa (which has a total cargo turnover of fifteen million tons a year) and the new port of Ilyechovsk nearby (six million tons a year), it is not surprising that more than half the Soviet merchant fleet is registered in the Black Sea. According to the Soviet newspaper *Izvestia* at the beginning of 1970, Ilyechovsk was being provided with the biggest ship repair yard in the USSR. Odessa is also a centre for ship repair, as well as for the manufacture of machine tools, agricultural and mining machinery, textiles and chemicals. It has a fishing fleet and is the home port of the Russian antarctic whaling fleet.

The Soviet Navy's Black Sea Fleet, based at Sevastopol, is of particular interest because it provides the squadron which since 1967 has been confronting the US Sixth Fleet in the Mediterranean and having what Admiral Gorshkov describes as a 'sobering effect' on Israel.

Inside the Black Sea, the Russian Navy enjoys some of the advantages it has tried unsuccessfully to obtain in the Baltic. More than half the coastline belongs either to the USSR itself or to other members of the Warsaw Pact, and in the process of reasserting Turkish sovereignty over the straits, the Montreux Convention – which regulates traffic through them – gave certain privileges to the Black Sea powers. But these are no more than minor consolations to a suspicious Russian strategist sitting in Odessa. It is not surprising, therefore, that the Russians should traditionally have had their eyes on Constantinople. In the First World War it began to look as if they might get it, as a result of a secret deal with Britain and her allies; but whatever promises were made, they were repudiated after the Communist revolution.

For some years the straits were demilitarized. Then in 1936 Turkey was allowed to refortify them under the rules established by the Montreux Convention (a shortened text of the convention is given in an appendix). This established freedom of navigation for all merchant vessels not owned by a country at war with Turkey. If Turkey is at war she has complete discretion as to which warships may pass through the straits. In peacetime Black Sea powers may send through capital ships and submarines – on the surface – under certain conditions. Other powers, however, are restricted to 'light surface vessels' (defined as having less than 10,000 tons standard displacement and guns of less than 203 millimetres) which must begin their passage of the straits in daylight and cannot remain in the Black Sea for more than twenty-one days.

The Convention was signed by Bulgaria, France, the United Kingdom, Greece, Japan, Romania, Turkey, the USSR and Yugoslavia. So far the Russians have adhered to it, but they have managed to make some play with it in their long term campaign to erode American naval power in the area and it may one day provide the pretext for a serious conflict. On several occasions since the war, the Soviet Union has suggested to Turkey that she might like to give the Russians a naval base with which to help 'supervise' the Convention. More recently, its terms have been used as diplomatic and propaganda irritants – or, as the Russians would put it, a legal defence – against the passage of United States warships into the Black Sea.

In December 1968, for example, the correspondents of the Soviet newspapers *Pravda* and *Izvestia* caused a considerable stir by protesting at the passage of the US destroyers *Dyess* and *Turner*. It was claimed that the *Dyess* did not meet the Montreux definition of a light surface vessel because she carried the ASROC rocket torpedo, which has a calibre of more than 203 millimetres. Both ships were accused of being engaged in 'provocative' acts intended to heighten tension in the Mediterranean area and diplomatic circles in Ankara were allegedly 'surprised that some experts close their eyes to this violation.'

The Turkish Government replied that it did not regard the passage of the *Dyess* as contravening the Convention. US Navy officials added that by no stretch of the imagination could a 'short range anti-submarine rocket assisted torpedo' be regarded as a gun, therefore its calibre was irrelevant. The weapon simply did not exist in 1936. American ships would continue to carry out 'routine operations in international waters'.

The purpose of the American visit was to assert the freedom of navigation embodied in the Montreux Convention, which the USA accepts but did not sign. American warships had been making similar short forays into the Black Sea at about nine monthly intervals since September 1959.

The genuine point on which the Russians were trying to

capitalize is that in terms of firepower the modern destroyer bears no comparison with the 'light surface vessel' of the 1930s; even if her tonnage is much less than 10,000 and her conventional guns only five-inch, the ASROC, for example, could be used as a nuclear depth charge.

This is the sort of issue that will have to be thrashed out if the convention is renegotiated, but the Russians may be cautious about opening a general argument until they can see the prospect of acquiring some physical control over the straits in the process. In the meantime they must be content with their dominant naval position in the Black Sea itself, bolstered by the modest navies of Bulgaria and, in some circumstances, Romania. Between them, these Warsaw Pact members add two submarines, thirteen escorts, five missile patrol boats, thirty-two minesweepers and eighteen landing craft to the Soviet forces. The main units in the Turkish Navy are ten submarines, ten destroyers, nine coastal escorts, six submarine chasers, seven minelayers and sixteen minesweepers.[2]

The Turks are a tough nation and in the long run the Soviet Union may do a lot better with its recent good neighbour policy than by emphasizing a military threat which is always in the background anyway. In fact Turkey stands at the end of a chain of countries the Russians have cultivated with economic or military aid – Iraq, Iran, Pakistan and India – which helps to secure their southern frontier while they confront China in the east. The more successful this policy is, and the more naval facilities the Soviet Navy acquires in the Mediterranean and the Indian Ocean, the less critical will the Black Sea straits seem.

The Sea of Japan

Vladivostok, terminal of the Transiberian Railway and home of the Soviet Navy's Pacific Fleet, is a magnificent natural harbour at the end of a tongue of Russian territory reaching

[2] These numbers are quoted from the Institute of Strategic Studies publication, *The Military Balance 1970–1971*.

south into the Sea of Japan – but not quite far enough south to be free of coastal pack ice in the winter. The straits leading in and out of these waters are commanded by the Japanese or South Korean coastline except to the north, where the last of the encircling islands, Sakhalin, belongs to the USSR. But the Russian admirals obviously have no intention of letting the sea be Japanese in anything but name and there have been some tense exchanges over naval exercises in the area, as, for example, during the Soviet Navy's elaborate celebration of the Lenin anniversary in April 1970.

Industrially, on the other hand, there is extensive cooperation between the two countries, particularly in oil and shipping. In 1968, for example, they opened a joint cargo liner service to Canada. At the fourth Soviet-Japanese economic conference in Moscow in February 1970 it was agreed that Japan should collaborate in the modernization of the Soviet Pacific ports including a completely new development near Nakhodka. This, it was hoped, would make it possible to increase deliveries of Russian timber and coal to Japan. A part of the substantial Japanese imports of Russian oil have also been supplied direct from the Far East, where there are important oilfields in the island of Sakhalin (until the Second World War the Sakhalin fields were in fact operated by Japanese oil companies under a concession). And some of this oil was used to buy ships from Japanese yards.

The Russian Pacific ports as a whole handle more than thirty million tons of cargo a year. Just as Ilyechovsk was developed near Odessa, so the new port of Nakhodka has been built a few miles to the east of Vladivostok since end of the Second World War. The new port caters particularly for the international trades, handling general cargo, timber, oil, and a range of dry bulk cargoes. It was one of the first in the Soviet Union to be equipped to handle containers, which can be – and to some extent are – brought from Europe across the Transiberian Railway.

The Far Eastern Steamship Company, based at Nakhodka, was naturally given considerable responsibility for Soviet support of the North Vietnamese war effort, but by no means all the supplies have come down the Pacific. Additional cargoes have had to be shipped round from European ports. It was this same shipping administration which in the spring of 1970 applied to the US Federal Maritime Commission for permission to operate an independent cargo service between Japan and the American west coast, in competition with the established 'conference' of lines.

During the 1960s the Russian fishing industry greatly extended the range of its Pacific operations from bases at Vladivostok, Nakhodka, Petropavlovsk and the island of Sakhalin, although the expansion came later than in the Atlantic. Vladivostok is also a whaling centre.

Soviet Ship Canals

In addition to the Transiberian Railway, the Russians have lessened their dependence on external sea routes by digging a great network of ship canals connecting the Black Sea to the Caspian, the Baltic and the White Sea in the far north. Plans are in hand for a second, direct, link between the Black Sea and the Baltic.

The idea of such a network was conceived by Peter the Great but the early canals were too small to be of any use to a modern sea-going vessel. The first of the new deep waterways was completed in 1932, between the Baltic and the White Sea, followed by the Moscow-Volga Canal in 1937, the Volga-Don Canal joining the Caspian and the Black Sea in 1952, and finally the Volga-Baltic Canal in 1964. This last, key section of the north-south link follows the line of the 150-year-old Mariinsky Canal. It runs from Leningrad along the River Nieva, through Lake Ladoga, the River Svir, Lake Onega, the River Kovzha to Lake Byeloe, the River Sheksna and the Rybinsk Reservoir.

By using this canal, vessels can reach the nearest port on the Volga in two and a half days from Leningrad instead of the eighteen days it took previously. In July 1964, one of the first of a new class of specialized river/sea craft of about 2,000 tons deadweight demonstrated the potential of the whole system with a fifteen-day voyage from Murmansk to Baku by way of the Barents Sea, the White Sea, the two north-south canals and the Caspian. It was claimed at the time that her cargo of apatite was carried 30 per cent cheaper than by rail.

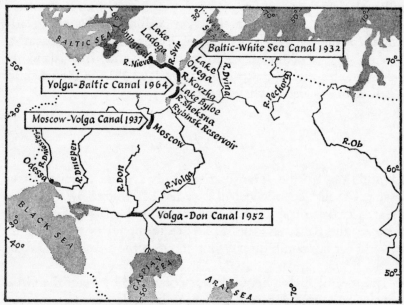

Figure 3 The Soviet canal system.

There are now about seventy of these Baltiisky class mixed navigation ships, and they no longer confine themselves to the Soviet Union's domestic trade. Since 1965, for example, they have run a service from the Iranian port of Pahlevi on the Caspian, through the Volga-Baltic Canal to Dutch and German ports. A call at Krasnovodsk gives transhipment to Afghanistan. More recently the service has been extended to Le Havre and London, giving a transit time from London to Pahlevi of about thirty days – considerably shorter than the southern route into the Persian Gulf.

This particular development can be seen as part of a long term campaign to increase Soviet influence in Iran, which was hopefully described by one early Communist writer as 'the Suez Canal of the revolution'. The Persians have received substantial economic aid from the USSR, including help in the construction of the new port of Ferekhabad on the southern shore of the Caspian.

But British shipping circles are concerned about the new service for more immediate commercial reasons. It is in competition with the 'conference' of lines serving Iran by way of the Gulf, and in 1969 the Russians pitched the freight rates from London slightly below the conference level (which had to be raised after the closure of the Suez Canal). What worries the British owners is not competitive rates as such – they are well used to fighting off outsiders – but the fact that retaliation is limited by the Russians' use of internal waterways and specialized craft.

The Iranian route is by no means an isolated instance. In January 1969 the Soviet news agency Tass announced that a fleet of shallow draught 12,000 ton deadweight tankers which could 'easily transit the Volga-Don Canal' was being built to carry oil from the Caspian to foreign as well as Russian ports. A number of river/sea ships are exporting timber from the Amur River to Japan and bringing back chemicals (a canal project to shorten this awkward and ice-prone route was announced in 1969). Coking coal from Cherepovetsk on the Volga-Baltic Canal is delivered to Denmark and Sweden without tranship-ment. In all, Russian mixed navigation ships tailored to the dimensions of the Soviet canal system called at more than a hundred foreign ports during 1969, and new routes to North Africa and other Mediterranean ports were announced.

From the Soviet merchant marine's point of view all this is natural and practical. It helped to raise the tonnage passed along the Volga-Baltic Canal from 8.0 million tons in 1968 to 9.5 millions in the following year. But it is not a trend that Western shipowners could have been expected to welcome. To take another example of its effect: if the new class of shallow draught

1,200 ton timber carriers the Russians began to build on the upper reaches of the Yenesei in 1969 can be used to load above Igarka – which is the highest point navigable for conventional ships – the already limited scope for British and other foreign owners to pick up tramp cargoes from this river will be further reduced. In general, the Soviet trading agencies have only to specify shipment to or from an inland port in the USSR to exclude Western shipping.

The canals also have some strategic value in allowing light naval craft to move from the Baltic to the Black Sea and the White Sea without venturing into international waters. But this is severely limited by the depth of the canals, in some cases by the length of the locks, and by the fact that most of the waterways are frozen throughout the winter. In war canals are vulnerable anyway, as the Luftwaffe demonstrated in June 1941 by successfully dive bombing the Baltic-White Sea Canal and putting its locks out of action. Even in peacetime navigation can be interrupted, as it was on the Volga-Don Canal in 1969 by reservoir trouble.

Russian references to the capacity of the canals are typically confusing, but it seems that all the new waterways are being dug to a minimum depth of twelve feet.[3] This compares with the Baltiisky class's loaded draught of about ten feet. According to an assessment of the Volga-Baltic Canal's first five years of operation[4] its 'transit depth of four metres' – that is about thirteen feet – makes it navigable by tankers of 5,000 tons deadweight and dry cargo vessels of 2,000–2,700 tons.

[3] V. P. Petrov, 'Soviet Canals', US *Naval Institute Proceedings*, July 1967.
[4] *Novosti*, December 22, 1969.

CHAPTER 5

Economic Pressures and the Merchant Marine

In the mid-1950s the Russians were facing economic pressures which would have made a larger merchant marine seem desirable to any regime, let alone one as politically isolated and suspicious as that of Moscow. With the death of Stalin in 1953, it is true, the Soviet Union became more outward looking and perhaps less concerned about depending on the 'whims of the capitalist freight market'. But a more relaxed foreign policy only served to stimulate the growing volume of overseas trade which had produced that dependence.

Development of the USSR's foreign trade

| | thousand million roubles | | | | | |
	1947	1952	1957	1962	1967	1968
Total	1.4	4.8	7.5	12.1	16.4	18.0
With Socialist Countries	0.8	3.9	5.5	8.5	11.1	12.2
With Industrially Developed Countries	0.5	0.7	1.3	2.2	3.4	3.9
With Developing Countries	0.1	0.2	0.7	1.4	1.9	2.0

Source: Official Soviet trade statistics

By 1968 the Soviet Union's trading partners outside eastern Europe included Cuba (an annual turnover of 810 million roubles), the United Kingdom (580 million roubles), Japan (520), Italy (400), West Germany (390), France (390), Egypt (330), India (330) and North Korea (260).

The immediate result of the increasing demand for sea

transport was that between 1950 and 1955 the proportion of the USSR's foreign trade carried by its own ships fell from about 50 per cent to 30 per cent. Chartering foreign tonnage produced a heavy drain on currency reserves, which might otherwise have been used to finance more trade or to purchase specific elements of Western technology badly needed by Soviet industry. The Russians were bound to react.

In his most recent book, *Soviet Ships on World Sea Routes*, Viktor Bakayev, who retired at the end of 1969 after fifteen years as Minister of the Merchant Marine, explains the motives for expanding his fleet in this way: 'It is not a matter of prestige. It allows our external trade to abandon political and economic dependence on the capitalist fleet and increases the efficiency of that trade. Even pre-revolutionary Russia, having an immeasurably smaller volume of external trade, paid out 150 million roubles a year to foreign shipowners. Now the country is freed from this tribute.'

And, as Bakayev points out elsewhere in the same book, a powerful merchant marine is not merely a means of stopping the drain of foreign currency; it can deliberately be deployed to earn it – and this the Russians certainly do today: 'Every country connected with sea transport tries to have its own fleet, so as to secure economic and political independence for its external trade and, in favourable circumstances, to use the export of shipping services to increase the income side of its balance of payments.'

But in 1958, when the volume of the USSR's seaborne trade with foreign countries had already grown to more than 26 million tons a year, she could muster no more than 250 deep sea freighters with a total tonnage of only 1.4 million. It was a motley fleet composed mainly of pre-war Russian vessels (the first post-war merchant ships built in the USSR were not laid down until about 1951), various craft captured during the war or handed over as German reparations, and a number of American 'Liberties' acquired under Lend Lease.

By comparison with the rest of the world's fleets, it was carrying a heavy weight of vessels more than twenty-five years old. The average size was smaller, nearly half the Russian ships were still powered by steam piston engines (compared with about a third for the rest of the world), and only seven per cent of them had a speed of more than fourteen knots. To keep such a fleet at sea must have required a great deal of time, ingenuity and expense.

Faced with this combination of growing foreign trade, an inadequate fleet and the resulting drain of scarce foreign currency, there is nothing surprising about the Soviet Government's decision to expand its merchant marine. The interesting thing is not the decision in principle but its scale, and the persistent vigour with which it has been followed through.

The fleet planners' job was made a little easier by the fact that, during the 1950s, so much of the trade expansion took place within Eastern Europe. Since then the demand for shipping capacity has continued to be kept somewhat in check by the extension of rail transport and the construction of oil pipelines.

The changing pattern of transport in the USSR's foreign trade

Form of Transport	million tons 1960	1968
Sea	44.7	111.9
Rail	49.5	75.8
River	3.9	8.5
Road	0.3	0.2
Pipeline	1.0	21.5
Total	99.4	217.9

Source: Soviet statistical abstract

The problem of the long route from the USSR's industrial centres in Europe to China was solved by the political rift which developed in the 1960s. Trade between the two countries was strangled as quickly as it had grown.

The USSR's trade with China

million roubles				
1948	*1953*	*1958*	*1963*	*1968*
193	1,055	1,364	540	86

Source: Soviet trade statistics

But in spite of such alleviating factors, the rapid expansion of Soviet foreign trade over a wider geographical range involved a more than proportional increase in its seaborne element.

The demand for sea transport in the USSR's foreign trade

Year	*million tons* 1938	1958	1960	1962	1964	1966	1967
Total exports	10	56	84	117	137	169	185
Exports by sea	9	22	39	60	71	90	98
Total imports	1	13	15	16	21	23	22
Imports by sea	1	4	6	7	12	12	12
% of total carried by sea	94	38	45	50	54	54	53

Source: Soviet trade statistics

The Soviet merchant marine has been expected to cope with the combined requirements of this growing seaborne trade, heavy coastal traffic, and shipments overseas which do not appear in the trade returns (such as war supplies to North Vietnam) while at the same time reducing the country's dependence on capitalist shipping. Not an easy task; but the Russian lines were provided with the means to tackle it.

Output of the Soviet merchant fleet

	1913	1928	1945	1960	1965	1966	1967	1968	1970
Million tons of cargo	15	8	20	76	119	132	141	147	(plan) 187
Thousand million ton miles	11	5	18	71	210	239	285	317	380

Source: Soviet Ministry of the Merchant Marine

At the time of writing statistics on the fleet's performance in 1969 and 1970 have not been issued, but indirect references suggest that the ton/mileage for 1970 will turn out to be 360/370 thousand million – a little below target. The fact remains that by 1960 the Soviet fleet's share of the USSR's seaborne trade had risen again to 40 per cent and by 1967 Russian ships were carrying more than half the total.

Distribution of foreign trade cargoes

	million tons 1960	1967
Carried by Soviet ships	20.1 (40%)	64.3 (52%)
Carried by foreign ships	29.7 (60%)	59.7 (48%)
Total exports plus imports	49.8	124.0

Source: V. Bakayev; *Soviet Ships on World Sea Routes*

Bakayev's figures do not tell us, unfortunately, how many of the 'foreign' ships in fact fly one of the Comecon flags and therefore do not pose a currency problem. Nor does he explain why the totals for 'export-import sea carryings of the USSR' are larger than the figures quoted for seaborne foreign trade in the normal trade returns. It could be that cross trading has been wrongly included.

But such points scarcely blur the sharp contrast between the Soviet Union's substantial degree of independence, and the fact that of the United States seaborne trade in 1967, only 6 per cent was carried by vessels flying the American flag (although in value terms, as opposed to weight, the proportion was 22 per cent). In the same year the United Kingdom handled 48 per cent of its own trade (57 per cent by value).

From a shipping point of view, the significant elements in the growing volume of Russian trade include timber, grain, oil and sugar. As we have seen, the development of the arctic routes was associated from the first with the export of Siberian timber, and total exports have continued to grow steadily throughout the 1950s and early 1960s, although the latest figures available level off.

Soviet timber exports

| | *million cubic metres* | | | | | | | | | | |
	1950	*1955*	*1960*	*1961*	*1962*	*1963*	*1964*	*1965*	*1966*	*1967*	*1968*
Round timber	0.7	1.6	4.4	5.7	7.4	8.0	9.4	11.1	12.4	12.4	12.8
Sawn timber	1.0	2.3	5.0	5.2	6.0	6.5	7.7	8.0	8.0	7.4	7.9

Source: Soviet trade statistics

The Soviet timber export organization has a large fleet of specialized ships at its disposal, but it has been slow to match its competitors in the modern method of handling timber in packages.

The remarkable feature of the USSR's grain trade has been the way the agricultural crisis of 1963 transformed its position from one of substantial export surplus to one involving net imports of several million tons a year. Until the balance was once more reversed in 1967, imports leapt to 6–7 million tons a year while exports were maintained at a lower but still substantial level. The result was a sudden, awkward rise in total movement of this important commodity.

Soviet trade in grain

| | *million tons* | | | | | | | | | | |
	1958	*1959*	*1960*	*1961*	*1962*	*1963*	*1964*	*1965*	*1966*	*1967*	*1968*
Exports	5.1	7.0	6.8	7.5	7.8	6.3	3.5	4.3	3.6	6.2	5.4
Imports	0.8	0.3	0.2	0.7	0.1	3.1	7.3	6.4	7.7	2.2	1.6
Net export	4.3	6.7	6.6	6.8	7.7	3.2	−3.8	−2.1	−4.1	4.0	3.8
Total movement	5.9	7.3	7.0	8.2	7.9	9.4	10.8	10.7	11.3	8.4	7.0

Source: Soviet trade statistics

Whereas most freighters, and even tankers, can if necessary carry grain cargoes, the Russian fleet planners have had to be particularly careful to match the rapidly growing requirements of their oil trade. Oil was probably known in the Caucasus before anywhere in the world – Marco Polo wrote about the 'great fountain of oil which discharges so great a quantity as to furnish loading for many camels.' At any rate both the Czarist regime and the early Communist governments were in the oil exporting business, and it was aggressively resumed in the 1950s.

Soviet oil exports

million metric tons											
1957	1958	1959	1960	1961	1962	1963	1964	1965	1966	1967	1968
14	18	25	33	41	45	51	56	64	74	79	86

Source: Soviet trade statistics

Undercutting prices by up to 40 per cent where necessary the Russian agency *Soyuznieftexport* soon came to rank with the big western oil companies in the scale of its activities. Nationally, the motive was to earn foreign currency, for which purpose oil is the Soviet Union's most important commodity. In a report prepared for the Senate committee on commerce, the American economist Leon M. Herman calculated in 1967 that more than a fifth of the USSR's hard currency sales consisted of oil products.

Throughout the 1960s about one-third of the Soviet Union's oil exports were going to eastern Europe. Bulgaria is supplied by a short tanker route, but Poland and East Germany can make use of the 3,000 mile Druzhba (Friendship) pipeline from the Ural-Volga oilfields. Most of the remaining two-thirds went to western Europe, especially Italy, and to Japan.

During the 1950s the Russians coped with this trade by building a series of standard 12,000 ton tankers, reminiscent of the war-built American T2s, at an average rate of about seven a year. In fact the first deliveries of this type, from Kherson and Leningrad in 1953, were also the first sea-going merchant ships to be built in Soviet yards since the war. These were supplemented by smaller vessels from Finland as well as the home yards.

For a few years after 1962, the Russians not only built rather bigger tankers themselves, but also bought a couple of dozen large vessels from Japan and Italy. These foreign purchases almost certainly represented the Soviet Government's alarmed reaction to the international crisis which accompanied the Communist revolution in Cuba.

When Fidel Castro's regime seized the island's refineries in 1960 it became dependent on supplies of Russian crude oil, which had to be shipped thousands of miles from the Black Sea.

Cuban oil imports from the USSR

million tons								
1959	*1960*	*1961*	*1962*	*1963*	*1964*	*1965*	*1966*	*1967*
—	1.6	3.0	3.6	3.8	3.4	3.5	3.8	3.8

Source: Soviet trade statistics

To carry the oil, the Russians needed chartered tonnage quickly. But the Western oil companies – who themselves own a large part of the world's tanker fleet and are customers to the rest – tried to organize a boycott; and if Castro's move had not coincided with a deep slump in oil freight rates (as a result of overbuilding after the 1957 Suez boom) they might have succeeded. At any rate the message was clear, and as far as one can see the Russians responded to it by a rapid expansion of their own tanker fleet. In the years 1962–65 they doubled its size to a tonnage of about 3 millions deadweight.

The USSR's oil production is already second only to that of the United States and in the past she has declared the aim of surpassing the American level during the 1970s.

World production of petroleum 1969

	million tons
United States	515
USSR	328
Middle East	614
Caribbean	208
Other areas	480
Total	2,145

Source: British Petroleum

But the expansion of domestic Russian production becomes steadily more expensive as the less accessible reserves are exploited. This fact, combined with the Soviet Union's evident desire – particularly since the invasion of Czechoslovakia – to control as high a proportion as possible of the Warsaw Pact countries' supply, has led some observers to predict a levelling off or even a reduction in exports to the West. Since this would mean losing valuable foreign currency sales, the obvious Russian move is to supplement domestic supplies from the Middle East.

This probable chain reaction has caused a good deal of anxiety in Western naval circles, for it is seen against the background of a series of Soviet naval visits to the Persian Gulf ever since Britain announced her intention of withdrawing from the Gulf at the end of 1971. Fortunately the international oil business seems to have a considerable immunity to political pressure, founded on the fact that many of the countries producing oil are entirely dependent on its sale and that crude oil is useless until it has been refined and distributed. This sets out some limit to the extent to which the Soviet Union can use its political infiltration of the Middle East to disrupt commercial relations with the West; a limit which is related to the likely scale of Russian oil imports in the long term.

Addressing the Foreign Press Association in London in February 1969, the chairman of the Shell Transport and Trading Company, Mr David Barran, summed up the situation in this way:

Simply buying Middle East oil on the open market would not be very attractive [to the Russians] either economically or in the sense of security. Other alternatives exist; the most immediately attractive would seem to be if the producing countries could be persuaded to nationalize their oil and call in Russian technologists to help produce it and find more, with payment in the form of oil. Then Russia might at one stroke (so the reasoning might go) be able to supply her own needs, plus those of the satellites, and still have a surplus with which to earn much greater sums in foreign currency in the West, which having been deprived of its own sources would be anxious to replace them, without worrying too much about legitimate ownership.

Unfortunately in this imperfect world there is more to this game than just having crude oil. Nature has thoughtlessly put most of it where it isn't wanted. It is useless unless you take it where it is wanted and then turn it into the products we can use in our cars, houses and factories. The Soviet Government do not have tankers, refineries and distribution systems in western Europe or the world at large. Two-thirds of these facilities are in the hands of the international companies. Unless a marriage could be arranged, which in the circumstances predicted seems improbable, the supply system would suffer almost unbearable strain, if it did not break down completely. Only a trickle of oil would get through.

On the whole, therefore, I think it likely that Russia will shy off this extreme solution and favour some more normal commercial arrangement with the Middle East producing countries. If this is what happens, then she will have the same interest as the rest of us in maintaining political stability, rather than wishing to disrupt everything and create the maximum turbulence and disarray.

The main elements in the Soviet Union's demand for tanker tonnage are therefore an expanded export trade; a growing need for oiler services as the Soviet Navy and fishing fleets range further afield; specific requirements to support first Cuba and then North Vietnam; and, in the future, the possibility of substantial imports from the Middle East. The most important balancing factor has been the construction of land pipelines to carry the large quantities of oil flowing into eastern Europe.

According to the Soviet journal *Vodny Transport*, the net result of the Russians' tanker building programme has been that the amount of oil products carried in their own vessels rose from three million tons in 1955 to twenty-seven million tons in 1965. A report prepared by the maritime administration of the US Department of Commerce in 1967 estimated that about half the Soviet Union's oil exports were being carried in Russian ships.

The requirement to ship oil to Cuba must have been a nuisance to the Soviet fleet planners because of its suddenness, the long haul from the Black Sea, and the reluctance of many Western shipowners to charter vessels for this trade – since they thereby became ineligible for American aid cargoes. John Harbron calculated[1] that it would take about thirty Kazbek class 12,000 ton tankers shuttling back and forth from the Black Sea to keep Cuba's three refineries supplied. This roughly matches the ship count analysed at Southampton University by Captain S. H. Drummond RN. He estimated that there were about twenty-five Soviet tankers in this trade in 1967 – that is numerically about one-seventh of the Russian tanker fleet having a gross tonnage of more than 4,000. Only one non-Soviet tanker discharging in Cuba was identified.

The most important commodity Cuba sends to the Soviet Union in return for its oil supplies in raw sugar, which has in turn become the basis of the Russians' increased exports of refined sugar.

Sugar trade of the USSR

	million tons										
	1958	1959	1960	1961	1962	1963	1964	1965	1966	1967	1968
Raw sugar imports	0.2	0.1	1.5	3.3	2.2	1.0	1.9	2.3	1.8	2.5	1.7
Refined sugar exports	0.2	0.2	0.2	0.4	0.8	0.8	0.3	1.0	0.6	1.0	1.3

Source: Soviet trade statistics

In all, the 'sea bridge' between the USSR and Cuba carried about eleven million tons during 1968: nine million tons of Russian oil, building materials, machinery and food, plus something like two million tons of sugar, minerals and other goods moving in the other direction. In *Soviet Ships on World Sea Routes* Bakayev claims that 'every day Soviet sailors are navigating up to 20–30 large ships across the oceans to Cuba and back.' It is not clear from his statement whether that number of ships is moving in each direction, but this would seem to be the case, since a Moscow Radio broadcast for Cuba in 1969 said that on average, 60–65 vessels are in transit between the two countries all the time.

Allowing for vessels loading and discharging at each end this implies a total of more than one hundred ships involved – that is

[1] *Communist Ships and Shipping.*

more than 10 per cent of those Russian ships that have a tonnage of more than 4,000 gross, or 5 per cent of those over 2,000 tons. This is one of the obvious reasons why the length of the Soviet merchant marine's average voyage should have increased from 900 miles in 1958 to 1,400 miles in 1963.

On an unusually large scale, this trade exemplifies the sort of unpredictable political requirement the Russian fleet has to deal with all the time – the practical implications of what the Communist Party calls 'discharging the Soviet Union's sacred internationalist duty by rendering fraternal disinterested assistance to the Cuban people'. And as Bakayev has himself indicated, the fleet's usefulness in 'breaking down the military, political and economic blockade of Cuba instituted by American imperialism' is considered to be not merely a byproduct of its commercial activity, but a positive responsibility – to which one imagines the Communist leadership would immediately respond when it came to allocating resources.

Yet even allowing for the Russians' desire to maintain their leverage in the Castro regime, it is surprising that they have not handed over some part of the shipping burden produced by their unbalanced trade with Cuba. It is therefore significant that in 1970–71 Soviet yards are delivering three 21,000 ton displacement tankers to the Cuban company Empresa Novegasion Mombisa. They are designed to carry three types of oil product at the same time – as opposed to being simple crude oil carriers – and 'will improve the fuel supply to Cuba's sugar refineries and chemical plants'. These ships are the Cuban fleet's first tankers of any size (in 1969 the tanker fleet consisted of five vessels totalling only 6,000 tons gross).

The same Russian broadcast to Cuba which mentioned the number of ships in transit stated that during 1968 Soviet vessels made a total of 1,600 voyages to the Caribbean island. It is interesting to compare this – though the Russians are extremely careless about defining their statistics – with the count of Soviet vessels calling at North Vietnamese ports published by the US House of Representatives Committee on Armed Services. Its report on the changing naval balance issued in December 1968 stated that the number of Russian merchant ships calling there rose from 47 in 1964 to 79 in 1965, 122 in 1966 and 433 in 1967. It has been disclosed in Moscow that twenty ships of the merchant marine's far-eastern fleet regularly operate between Vladivostok and North Vietnam, but in addition to this, many of the supplies have to come the long way round from the Black Sea. Because of draught limitations in the Vietnamese ports, as in many areas to which the Soviet Union sends aid, the ships need to be fairly small.

The 1969 aid agreement with North Vietnam provided for 'large quantities of food, oil products, transport equipment, complete sets of equipment, ferrous and non-ferrous metals, and chemicals'. But North Vietnam also uses large quantities of Soviet arms, for the carriage of which the Russians would wish to use their own vessels even if tramp shipowners flying other flags were prepared, in principle, to enter this trade.

Another 'sea bridge' carrying armaments as well as a range of non-military cargoes is that connecting the USSR and Egypt, the main terminals being Alexandria and the new Black Sea port of Ilyechovsk. A significant proportion of the ships on this route are Egyptian but in spite of this Russian vessels were arriving in Egypt at a rate of more than one a day in 1966. By then the Aswan Dam project alone had absorbed 300,000 tons of equipment and materials shipped from the Soviet Union. Egypt's engineering, shipbuilding, oil and chemical industries were also being equipped by the Russians, with cargoes of cotton and rice moving in the opposite direction.

The USSR's offer to help finance the dam in October 1955, accompanied by an arms deal, marks the beginning of Russian involvement with the cause of Arab nationalism in the Middle East. It also marks the start of a systematic programme of economic aid to 'progressive' non-Communist countries. Before Stalin's death in 1953 this method of buying influence outside the Soviet bloc was ruled out because of the political compromise it implied, but the Russians have made extensive use of it since. In the case of the Aswan Dam the Soviet offer was followed by an American and British decision to withdraw their support for the project; this led to Nasser's nationalizing the Suez Canal and the disastrous Anglo-French invasion of 1956.

Considering that was the first time the Russians had played this game, they must have been delighted with their performance. In general, the financing of such a scheme is based on the understanding that the money will be spent in the Soviet Union and the equipment it buys will be installed by Russian engineers. It guarantees some degree of technical infiltration, and if the project involves advanced technology, or is dependent on a steady flow of spares, it may give some degree of permanent control. (About 5,000 Russian technicians worked on the Aswan project.)

Such schemes also involve training local personnel in Russian methods, where they might otherwise have sought their education in Britain or the United States. A recent Moscow broadcast, for example, stated that as a result of the various aid agreements which had by then been concluded with twenty-five African countries – most of them involving industrial development – 6,000 Africans were studying in the Soviet Union. The Congolese government alone had sent 300 students to the USSR and sixty Russian teachers were working in the Congo itself. Translated into shipping terms, this scale of involvement meant a doubling of the calls by Russian freighters at African ports between 1960 and 1965 – from about 500 to 1,100. By then, ten West African countries were regularly served.

Cargoes moving between the Black Sea and India – Russian equipment and materials for just the first stage of the Bhilai steel works project, for example, apparently accounted for half a million tons: the equivalent of perhaps sixty voyages – are carried by a joint Indo-Soviet shipping service. This was established by an agreement signed in 1956, by which each country provided six vessels. The agreement has since been revised, but the new terms have not been published.

That such a politically sensitive trade should be shared out on a fifty-fifty basis by the two governments may seem natural enough, however much it irritates Western shipowners. But it noticeably did not stop the Soviet shipping minister complaining about the United States Government's practice of reserving 50 per cent of its aid cargoes for American flag ships on the grounds that this 'violated generally recognized international principles'.

The total of Soviet credits extended to developing countries now stands at more than 4,000 million roubles, according to a Moscow broadcast in May 1969: it must represent a significant element in the demand for Soviet shipping capacity.

Some indication of the pattern of this aid programme can be devised from the exports of 'equipment and materials for complete undertakings,' under the broad heading of machinery and equipment.

Soviet exports of complete installations

| | millions of roubles | | | |
	1965	1966	1967	1968
Algeria	5.3	1.5	2.6	12.4
Afghanistan	27.0	40.5	25.7	16.3
Ghana	7.3	0.6	0.0	0.0
Guinea	1.7	3.1	1.0	1.9
India	90.8	57.9	81.4	101.8
Indonesia	11.9	3.4	0.3	0.0
Iraq	4.8	3.9	4.1	4.2
Iran	0.0	4.3	20.2	33.0
Yemen	1.4	4.9	5.5	1.9
Mali	2.3	3.4	4.7	3.3
Mongolia	32.7	51.5	64.9	73.3
Egypt	77.5	76.9	72.7	60.2
Pakistan	3.0	4.7	3.8	7.7
Syria	3.9	5.3	18.9	15.1
Somalia	5.1	2.1	2.0	0.8
Tunisia	2.0	2.6	0.9	0.6
Turkey	0.0	0.1	0.0	3.2
Ceylon	0.0	0.8	1.0	0.4
Ethiopia	5.5	2.6	0.3	0.5

Note the sudden changes in the case of Ghana, Indonesia, Iran, Syria, Algeria and Turkey.

Source: Soviet trade statistics

The net effect of all these factors – the effort to reduce the Soviet Union's dependence on foreign shipping, the changing alignment of her trade, rising oil and timber exports, the uncertainties of the wheat harvest, sugar imports and the demands of the various aid programmes – was to double the tonnage of cargo carried by the Russian merchant fleet between 1960 and 1968, and to double the average distance each ton was carried. At the same time the demand for oil transport became more important relative to dry cargoes.

The expanding operations of the Soviet merchant fleet

	1960	1968
Liquid cargoes (M. tons)	32.5	70.1
Dry cargoes (M. tons)	42.3	76.1
of which Coal	7.1	9.0
Ores	7.5	11.7
Timber	3.3	9.3
Metals	2.8	5.8
Machines and equipment	0.9	2.3
Other dry cargoes	20.7	38.0
All cargoes (M. tons)	74.8	146.2
Average length of voyage (miles)	935	2161
Ton/mileage (Thousand M. ton/miles)	71	317

Note: the timber totals do not include the rafted timber normally included in the Soviet ministry's statistics.

Source: Soviet Ministry of Merchant Marine

CHAPTER 6

The Merchant Fleet in Perspective

The pressures which led to a rapid expansion of the Soviet commercial fleet began to appear in the late 1950s. The expansion itself – from about four million tons deadweight in 1959 to thirteen millions in 1969 – gathered its full momentum in the early 1960s. Throughout this period the fleet was under the control of Viktor Bakayev, who became Minister of the Merchant Marine in 1954. The structure on which he had to build was little more than a collection of remnants held together – except in the special case of the arctic – by only a loose thread of experience and tradition.

Under the Czars the shipping lobby had been no match for the railway enthusiasts in the competition for patronage. At the outbreak of the First World War the Russians possessed just over a million tons deadweight of merchant ships. By the end of it, even this modest fleet had virtually disintegrated under the the impact of revolution. Vessels were sunk, captured or commandeered; many were left to rot or rust. Those that remained were nationalized by decree of the Congress of Soviet People's Commissars on January 23, 1918. But by the time the fleet was counted, in 1922, it was found that only about a fifth of the steamers and a tenth of the sailing vessels had survived in Soviet control. The Far East authorities could apparently muster no more than ten ships of any size.

In 1924 the job of piecing a fleet together again and centralizing its control was given to an organization whose name abbreviates, in the Soviet manner, to *Sovtorgflot*. A year later official records show that 133 vessels had been assembled under the hammer and sickle.

RUSSIA LOOKS TO THE SEA

To begin with, the job was one of repair and improvisation. Two light cruiser hulls, for example, were converted into steam tankers of 5,000 tons; the *Aznieft* and the *Groznieft*. But by 1925 the Leningrad shipyards had begun to turn out new ships in standard classes – the form of production which has since characterized Communist shipbuilding. Among the first were the Worker class of 3,000 ton timber carriers and the Co-operation class of refrigerated 2,000 tonners for cargo/passenger service between London and Leningrad.[1]

But the Soviet shipbuilding industry was limited both in capacity and experience (a fact which was later to hinder Stalin's plans for building battleships and aircraft carriers), and the bulk of the freighters acquired between the wars were bought second-hand off the buoys, where Western shipowners had laid their ships up during the world-wide slump of the 1930s. That the Russians were not exactly choosy can be seen from their purchase in 1928 of what must have been their oldest sea-going ship, the *Sotchi*. As the brig *Olga*, she had been built in Sunderland in 1870. A pioneer tanker built at Newcastle upon Tyne in 1886, the *Loutsch*, was also still on their register.

But however curious the mixture may have been, the net effect was to increase the merchant tonnage by 1.7 million tons deadweight between 1928 and 1940, when the total stood at 2.1 millions. The 1913 figure for cargo turnover had been regained in about 1930 and the Russians claim to have been reasonably satisfied with the scale of shipping operations achieved by the outbreak of the Second World War – although even they admit that the large proportion of coal burners gave the fleet a dismally low average speed.

During the war, major shipyards at Leningrad, Odessa, Nikolayev and Sevastopol were destroyed, as were the Polish and East German yards which were later to supply large numbers of ships to the Soviet Union. The Russians did not start turning out merchant ships again until the early 1950s, when the first of their standard 12,000 ton tankers were laid down at Leningrad and Kherson. But they nevertheless ended the war with a bigger

[1] *Development of the USSR's Merchant Fleet.*

fleet – 2.4 million tons deadweight in 1946 – than they had at the beginning.

One reason for this is that under the Lend Lease agreement, the Americans handed over about fifty obsolete freighters, plus about forty war-built 'Liberty ships', which were never returned. At the end of the war the Soviet Union's share of German reparations included about 180 ships, out of which she agreed to provide for Poland as well. Most of these were small dry cargo freighters, among them a number of smart little Hansa class 3,000 tonners recently built by the Germans to carry supplies round occupied Europe; but they also included fifteen liners which were to form the backbone of the Soviet passenger fleet. Finally came those ships – about sixty of them – which were acquired after the defeat of Finland and the annexation of the Baltic states of Estonia, Latvia and Lithuania (it is possible that the figures of 2.1 million tons quoted above for 1940 includes this tonnage, since it comes from a Soviet Government source).

Even when her own yards had been rebuilt, the Soviet Union under Stalin devoted much of their capacity in the late 1940s and early 1950s to building Sverdlov class cruisers and the world's biggest fleet of submarines. She therefore turned to Poland for the supply of merchant tonnage, and the second sea-going ship to be launched from a Polish yard after the war, a collier, was renamed and handed over to the Russians in 1950.

Deliveries from East Germany did not begin until a few years later; since then she has become a major supplier, particularly of passenger liners and other complex types. Hungary, and to a much lesser extent Bulgaria, have also built ships for the Russians.

Outside the Communist bloc, Finland was an important source of new tonnage in the early post-war years, specializing, among other things, in icebreakers. And at various times – in the early 1960s, for example, when the Russians badly needed some big tankers – the Soviet purchasing agency *Sudoimport* had signed contracts with all the major shipbuilding countries in the capitalist world: Japan, Britain, West Germany, Sweden, Denmark, Holland, France and Italy. The United States is, of course, a major exception, but her shipbuilding industry is not internationally competitive in any case.

If one adds domestic production to her purchases abroad, the Soviet Union was acquiring new sea-going ships at a rate of something like fifty a year throughout most of the 1950s, and this was stepped up to about one hundred a year in the 1960s. The intention was that under the 1966–70 plan, 40 per cent of the tonnage should be home built, 50 per cent should come from other Communist countries and the remaining 10 per cent from capitalist shipyards.

The records collected in *Soviet Merchant Ships* – a catalogue of Russian ships assembled by an anonymous Royal Naval Reserve Commander who, for all his reticence, has performed an extremely valuable service for any student of Communist shipping – indicate that in the five years 1958–62 the Russians were able to supply nearly 40 per cent of their new tonnage from their own yards, but that in the following five years the proportion fell to less than 30 per cent. Over the ten years a substantially smaller proportion of dry cargo tonnage than of tankers and fishing vessels was home built. (Fishing vessels are here considered as part of the merchant fleet, although their operation and development are discussed separately in Chapter 9.)

If one examines the sources of the Soviet post-war merchant fleet by type of ship, the pattern looks like this:

General cargo vessels: many were home built, using diesel, diesel-electric and even gas turbine propulsion, but large numbers have also been bought from Poland, other members of the Soviet bloc and several countries outside it.

Colliers: appropriately enough, the Russians have relied on Poland for this type; for example, dozens of the B 31 class 5,000 tonners, handsomely traditional with their three-island layout and tall straight funnels.

Timber carriers: some of them were built in Russian yards but most came from East Germany, Poland and Finland.

Refrigerated dry cargo vessels: as an example of the way in which the Russians turned to western sources when they saw an urgent need which could not be fitted into long-term Communist plans to build standard ships, *Sudoimport* suddenly bought fifteen secondhand fruit carriers from West Germany and Sweden in the space of a few months in 1963–64.

Tankers: the Russians have built quite a large proportion of their own tonnage and take particular pride in their 50,000 ton Sofia class ships. But they have also bought a number of large vessels – large by Soviet standards, that is – from non-Communist countries. In 1960–61, for example, tankers already under construction for Western owners in Japan, Holland and Italy were taken over by *Sudoimport*. This was presumably to meet the sudden requirement to supply Cuba, although the world surplus of tankers at that time would also have made it a good moment to buy. At the same time the Russians ordered eighteen big vessels from Japan for delivery between 1962 and 1965.

Fishing vessels: Russian, Polish and East German yards have all supplied large numbers, including herring fleet mother ships, fish factories and trawlers from Poland, and an important class of factory trawlers from East Germany. Among the few vessels of this kind built in non-Communist yards were two whale factory ships from West Germany, and some fish factories from Japan.

Polar vessels: the Soviet fleet has relied on Finland for all its big modern icebreakers except for the *Lenin*. It also had six Polar supply vessels built in Holland. But the Amguena class of diesel-electric arctic freighters is home built.

Passenger liners: this is another type for which the Russians have relied almost entirely on foreign sources; in this case East Germany, which has turned out both the 5,000 ton Mikhail Kalinin class and the 20,000 ton Ivan Franko class.

The Soviet Union's dependence on foreign built tonnage, albeit mainly from her political satellites, is balanced only to a small extent by the sale of Russian built ships. But this form of export could become important in the future.

Soviet trade in ship and maritime equipment

million roubles										
	1950	*1955*	*1960*	*1961*	*1962*	*1963*	*1964*	*1965*	*1966*	*1967*	*1968*
Import	25.8	237.5	340.4	203.1	332.9	366.1	483.9	489.7	493.7	445.9	503.2
Export	1.1	3.0	10.6	16.9	25.3	17.3	31.8	29.4	32.2	45.4	54.6

Source: Soviet trade statistics

The Russian types which have so far attracted foreign customers include trawlers, freighters and passenger-carrying hydrofoils. If it can overcome political resistance and customers' anxiety about the supply of spare parts, by agreeing to install western equipment for example, the Soviet industry has one important economic advantage: it builds ships in long standard series, something European shipyards always strive for but rarely achieve. But of course this is a meaningless benefit unless the standard happens to be roughly what the customer wants.

To illustrate the sort of problems that arise when the Russians try selling in the West, one might examine the recent campaign to introduce the *Komieta* hydrofoil launch into Britain. The Russians found themselves an enthusiastic agent, who went out to see the craft demonstrated on the Black Sea and helped to ferry it back by way of the canals, the Baltic and the North Sea. Its arrival was given a lot of publicity, and one of the first people to step aboard in Dover harbour was a representative of British Rail, which was considering running a hydrofoil alongside its hovercraft ferries.

The chances of one or two sales seemed quite good, especially as the price being asked was low. But first the *Komieta* had to obtain a British passenger service licence. I happened to be on board when the two Board of Trade inspectors took their first wary ride. They were a suspicious pair, but I gather they were prepared to grant at least a limited licence provided they could carry out a routine inspection of the production facilities, including the factory which made the diesel engines. This was perfectly standard procedure, but the Russians suddenly took fright. They refused to allow anyone near their engine works where, it transpired later, they also make naval equipment. The

British sales agent tried vainly to persuade them that the solemn looking men carrying briefcases really were from the Board of Trade and not the secret service, as the Russians seemed almost to suspect. The Soviet authorities protested; they even put the word about that the chances of concluding a deal to buy British ships from the Clyde might be improved by waiving the engine inspection rule. But in fact neither side would budge and later that summer the *Komieta* began her long voyage back to the Black Sea.

The centrally planned expansion I have outlined has raised the status of the Soviet merchant marine in ten years from that of a maritime nonentity to sixth place in the world's shipping league table.

The world's principle merchant fleets in 1969.

million tons gross *(inclusive of fishing vessels which are also shown separately in brackets)* *Flag*	*Tonnage*	*% of world total*
Liberia	29.2 —	14
Japan	24.0 (0.9)	11
Great Britain	23.8 (0.2)	11
Norway	19.7 (0.2)	9
United States (including reserve fleet)	19.6 (0.1)	9
USSR	13.7 (3.4)	6
Greece	8.6 —	4
Italy	7.0 (0.1)	3
West Germany	7.0 (0.2)	3
France	6.0 (0.2)	3
Panama	5.4 —	3
Netherlands	5.3 (0.1)	3

Source: Lloyd's Register of Shipping

If one regards the fleets operated by Comecon as a single unit – and there is an arguable case for doing so – the total is not far short of the American tonnage even including the reserve fleet. Poland now has about 1.5 million gross tons of ships, East

Germany 0.9 million, Bulgaria 0.6 million and Romania 0.3 million; so the combined Comecon tonnage is around 17 million tons (including 3.7 million tons of fishing tonnage).

Excluding the United States Government's reserve fleet of 6½ million tons of 'mothballed' ships, and including the USSR's exceptionally large tonnage of fishing vessels, the Soviet fleet apparently surpasses the American. But in a strategic context, which is how the Americans tend to view the Soviet merchant marine these days, the reserve is an asset to be counted even though it is commercially obsolete.

In purely commercial terms there is in any case a much more important qualification to these figures – the fact that Liberia, Panama and to a small extent Honduras, provide 'flags of convenience' to enable foreign shipowners to escape the costs of operating under their own flags. British owners do not use these flags but their American counterparts, facing extremely high wage costs and well organized unions at home, have turned to them in a big way. Most of the ships involved are tankers, plus a fair number of bulk carriers. At the beginning of 1969 more than nine million gross tons of shipping that flew these flags of convenience was considered by the American Navy Department to be 'under effective US control', even though in a minority of cases the ships belonged to companies where less than half the stock was owned by American citizens. The important assumption is that, in time of war, this tonnage would be at the disposal of the United States.

Ships registered in Liberia and Panama but under effective US control as at December 31, 1968 – million tons deadweight (gross tonnage)

Flag	Tankers	Dry Cargo	All Types
Liberia	8.4 (4.9)	3.3 (1.8)	11.7 (6.7)
Panama	3.5 (2.1)	0.2 (0.2)	3.7 (2.3)
Total	11.9 (7.0)	3.5 (2.0)	15.4 (9.0)

Source: US Department of Commerce

If one adds this tonnage to the United States fleet quoted in the international table (as at July 1969) the total under American control is something like 29 million tons – more than twice the Soviet figure and by a substantial margin the biggest national fleet in the world. Excluding the reserve fleet for purposes of commercial comparison the United States still deploys some 22 million tons, that is five million tons more than the combined Comecon fleets.

The ownership of the Liberian and Panamanian fleets, which the United States shares with Greece and a number of other countries, is too often ignored by chauvinistic American admirals lecturing on the 'threat of Soviet sea power'. In the same way the impressive growth of the Russian fleet is sometimes contrasted with the slow decline of US flag tonnage without the even greater increase in Liberian and Japanese tonnage being noted – or the comparatively powerful position of a small nation like Norway.

Growth of the world's principal fleets.

| | million tons gross | | | | | |
	USSR	UK	USA	Liberia	Japan	Norway
1950	2.1	18.2	27.5	0.2	1.9	5.5
1955	2.5	19.4	26.4	4.0	3.7	7.2
1960	3.4	21.1	24.8	11.3	6.9	11.2
1965	8.2	21.5	21.5	17.5	12.0	15.6
1970	14.8	25.8	18.5	33.3	27.0	19.3
Growth since 1960:	11.4	4.7	−6.3	22.0	20.1	8.1
Growth as % of 1960:	335	22	−25	195	291	72

These figures somewhat exaggerate the Soviet fleet's growth because records of fishing vessels, included in the Lloyds definition of the merchant fleet, were inadequate in the earlier years.
Source: Lloyd's Register of Shipping

Looking at these figures with the important connection between Liberia and the USA in mind, the nation that has most reason to be dissatisfied with its comparative performance is Great Britain. But even if the amount of American controlled tonnage is considered sufficient from the us Government's strategic point of view – as a guarantee that the usa has the shipping capacity to support a major overseas war effort, and cannot be subject to economic blackmail in a 'cold' war – the decline of the us flag as such is hardly a satisfactory state of affairs.

The strategic requirement for a national merchant marine, and the shipyards to expand it in hurry, was brought home to the United States during the First World War. Most of the foreign ships which at that time carried nearly 90 per cent of the country's overseas trade, were suddenly withdrawn. Exports piled up on the quays, imports had to be cancelled and astronomical freight rates were paid on those goods that were carried. When the usa entered the war matters became even worse, in the sense that it was dependent on its allies even to transport its army and military supplies. A crash programme of shipbuilding was started, but too late. The Government was merely left with hundreds of ships, of which only a small proportion was really suitable for commercial operation.

It was to prevent the same thing happening again that the Merchant Marine Act of 1936 was passed. This laid down the policy of maintaining a fleet which would be:

(1) Sufficient to carry the domestic waterborne commerce and a substantial portion of the foreign commerce of the country;

(2) Capable of serving as a naval auxiliary in time of war;

(3) Owned by, and operated under, the United States flag by citizens of the usa;

(4) Composed of the best equipped, safest and most suitable types of vessels;

(5) Manned by trained and efficient citizens of the United States.

One wonders what the legislators would have made of today's widespread use of flags of convenience. To persuade shipowners to buy vessels from American yards and operate them under the us flag it has proved necessary to offer a whole range of subsidies to cover, for example, wage costs two to five times higher than abroad. These include operating and construction subsidies, trade-in allowances and the insurance of loans and mortgages. In addition the American Government pays for specific 'defence features' which make ships readily convertible to a wartime role of naval auxiliary.

In the post-war years it was paying out an annual average of nearly 80 million us dollars in subsidies. By 1960 more than half the 500 or so us flag vessels in foreign trades were subsidised. Yet the tonnage registered under the American flag (including the reserve fleet) continued to decline at a rate of about half a million tons a year throughout the 1960s. Towards the end of 1969, therefore, President Nixon announced a new support policy intended to 'replace the drift and neglect of former years and restore this country to a proud position in the shipping lanes of the world.'

The objective of the new policy is to subsidize the construction of thirty ships a year in American yards over the next decade compared with the previous average of about ten a year. The Government will commit itself to building a certain number of ships over a period of years to enable yards to streamline production and economize in materials and overheads. The subsidies will also be paid direct to the shipbuilders instead of through the owners. But at the same time the proportion of total building costs that may be covered by subsidy is limited to 45 per cent in 1971 and this is to be progressively reduced to 35 per cent. The principle of the construction subsidy, which is now to be extended for the first time to tankers and bulk carriers, is that it should cover the difference between world shipbuilding prices and the American ones.

The President proposed that operational subsidies be continued only to cover the American shipping lines' higher wage and insurance costs, eliminating payments for maintenance and repair. But instead of comparing foreign seamen's wages with those paid on American ships – which meant that operators lost in subsidies what they saved in costs – the comparison will now be with an index representing a comparable average level within the United States.

Finally, it was announced that there would be more research to develop the advanced cargo handling systems, such as container ships, in which American lines might hope to become internationally competitive without subsidy. In fact the research appropriations requested from Congress in February 1970 were almost doubled, to 20 million US dollars.

If a merchant vessel is built with government aid the Secretary of the Navy can and does request the inclusion of national defence features to ensure, under the 1936 Act, that it shall be 'capable of serving as a naval auxiliary'. American commentators on Soviet sea power are fond of pointing out ways in which new Russian merchant ships could be adapted for military use in wartime – for example the Vostok fisheries mother ship, carrying a fleet of small catchers on deck, could be converted for amphibious operations – without reminding readers of the explicit nature of their own Government's provisions in this respect.

For example, the liner *United States* was easily able to capture the Blue Riband of the Atlantic for the fastest crossing because she was equipped with extra boilers to provide the speed to outrun submarines if she were ever required as a troop ship. During the Second World War, the Cunard liners *Queen Mary* and *Queen Elizabeth* relied on their speed of around thirty knots in the same way. Even when the *Queen Mary* sliced the British cruiser *Curaçao* in half approaching the Irish coast in 1942, she dare not stop for the survivors and risk being torpedoed with 10,000 American troops aboard. The *United States* (withdrawn from service at the end of 1969) took the Blue Riband at speeds of about thirty-five knots and was said to be capable of even more. She could quickly be converted to carry a complete division, of perhaps 14,000 men, but at the time of writing her future is still unclear.

Other examples of defence features are heavy lift gear, roll-on and roll-off facilities to load military vehicles, extra evaporator capacity to provide extra water for troops, and duplicated controls which would be less vulnerable to damage. If the Federal Maritime Board judges that such equipment is not commercially necessary it is paid for by the Government. For example a freighter costing about 13 million US dollars might include 90,000 dollars' worth of defence features.

But although the American merchant marine is dependent on government support, it is not a creation of government, like its Russian counterpart. The growth rate of the Soviet fleet is determined not by the profits to be made under flags of convenience, or even the attractions of a given form of state subsidy, but by the central political decision to allocate resources to this type of development in preference to any other. The machinery for this allocation is of course the five-year plan.

While long-term national planning does not by any means guarantee efficiency, it does allow the Soviet effort to be co-ordinated and directed; and it allows political and economic objectives – such as the support of Cuba or a high level of foreign currency earnings – to be injected straight into the programme. At the same time, however, the plan signals these objectives to the rest of the world.

One reason why Soviet shipping activity has received so much anxious attention by comparison with, say, the explosive growth of the Japanese fleet, is that a crude graph of the Russians' progress is so easily drawn and projected – which is not to underestimate the many reasons why it should receive attention. Speech writers and Press commentators have been able to point to declared growth rate of a million tons a year during the 1960s, reaching a specific total for 'transport' tonnage of 13,136,000 tons deadweight at the end of the 1966–70 five-year plan, and a long-range target of more than twenty million tons by 1980. It would have been nowhere near as easy to produce comparable predictions for Japan, based on an analysis of commercial trends: so the Japanese comparison simply did not appear.

Although the USSR's plan for 1971–75 has not been published at the time of writing, the shipping minister forecast in 1969 that by the end of that five-year period his country's fleet would have grown to 17–18 million tons (the context indicated that these were deadweight tons). The best way of putting this continued growth rate of about a million tons a year in the context of other maritime nations' intentions is to compare the tonnages already on order.

Dry cargo vessels on order – October 1969
(totals for container ships and bulk carriers are given in brackets)

Flag	Tonnage on order 000 tons deadweight	Number of ships excluding container ships and bulk carriers	Average size tons deadweight
USSR	1,411 (393)	256	5,500
West Germany	820 (1,143)	141	5,800
Greece	716 (700)	75	9,600
Japan	661 (1,100)	100	6,600
Liberia	531 (3,072)	43	12,400
UK	375 (3,231)	56	6,700
Norway	311 (1,889)	42	7,400
France	302 (301)	26	11,600
Holland	92 (118)	13	7,100
Panama	51 (207)	7	7,300
Italy	51 (336)	4	12,700
United States	13 (1,048)	4	3,300

Source: *Fairplay International Shipping Journal*

The conservative but highly flexible nature of Russian shipping operations is quite clearly reflected in this table, prepared from Fairplay's quarterly supplement *World Ships on Order*. While other countries, and especially the United Kingdom, build new fleets of container ships and big, specialized bulk carriers, the Soviet Union is still concentrating on conventional freighters plus its own specialities, like the timber carrier.

The other striking feature of the Russian construction programme shown up by these figures is the small size of the new ships. The only country whose orders for conventional freighters have a lower average tonnage is the United States, and since only thirteen ships are involved it is hardly significant.

The rest of the dry cargo tonnage ordered by the Americans (shown in brackets) is almost all designed to carry containers. By contrast, the USSR does not appear at all in the list of container ship orders, although she has since announced plans to build one vessel of this type for the Australian trade. The Russians have a modest 393,000 tons of bulk carriers on order, but there is no sign of the 50,000 and 100,000 tonners one finds sprinkled through the British and Japanese lists.

Bulk carriers on order – October, 1969

Flag	Tonnage on order 000 tons deadweight	Number of ships	Average size tons deadweight
Liberia	2,946	93	31,700
UK	2,402	53	45,300
Norway	1,822	53	34,400
Japan	1,010	30	33,700
West Germany	847	11	77,000
Greece	598	18	33,200
USSR	393	12	32,800
Italy	336	5	67,300
France	216	5	43,200
Panama	207	7	29,600
USA	143	3	47,600
Holland	74	3	24,500

Source: *Fairplay International Shipping Journal*

Warnings that the Soviet merchant fleet is 'doubling in ten years' seem less alarming when one realizes that its full weight will not be felt in the new container and bulk carrier markets currently attracting the attention of Western shipowners. And a similar situation is reflected in the Russian tanker programme. While Britain and Norway have literally dozens of specialized 200,000 tonners on order, prompted in part by the possibility of the Suez Canal remaining closed, few of the Soviet vessels even exceed 20,000 tons deadweight.

The largest tankers so far operating under the Soviet flag are the Sofia class 50,000 tonners, whereas the Western oil companies

Tankers on order – October, 1969

Flag	Tonnage on order 000 tons deadweight	Number of ships	Average size 000 tons deadweight
Liberia	16,107	88	183
UK	9,354	92	102
Norway	8,338	73	114
France	4,362	28	156
Japan	2,723	21	130
USA	2,195	30	73
Panama	2,194	15	146
Italy	1,698	23	74
Greece	1,057	21	50
USSR	1,030	77	14
West Germany	432	35	12
Holland	5	3	2

Source: *Fairplay International Shipping Journal*

already have many of their 200,000 tonners at sea plus a few 300,000 tonners. The reason for building bigger and bigger ships is simply the economy of scale. The cost of carrying a ton of oil in a 200,000 ton tanker might be only one-third of the cost in a 20,000 tonner. This puts the Soviet merchant marine at a severe disadvantage if it has ambitions to compete in the open market for the carriage of oil; a reassuring thought for independent Western tanker owners. International oil companies like Shell charter the occasional Russian ship, but apparently only as a gesture of commercial goodwill.

The trouble with the giant tankers is that they require deep water terminals specially built and dredged for them. This is economic when they provide a link in the permanent chain of supply from the oilfields of the Persian Gulf to the factories and filling stations of north-west Europe. But the pattern of the Soviet oil industry in the 1960s was entirely different. It supplied a big domestic demand, piped large quantities to Communist neighbours in eastern Europe and then exported the surplus on an opportunist basis wherever hard currency was to be earned. One of the few routes which resembles a typical west European operation is that between the Black Sea and Cuba. This may well be the trade, therefore, for which the Russians decided to build their first real 'supertanker' – a 150,000 tonner named *Mir* (Peace) which is considered the biggest they can use.

The ship design department of the Ministry of Merchant Marine had for a long time been itching to tackle the construction of a really big vessel. But for at least a year before the order for the *Mir* was announced, towards the end of 1969, the ship operators resisted the idea. There was at the same time quite a lively discussion in the Russian technical press. The limited port facilities available to such vessels were mentioned. It was also argued that if a tanker of more than 80,000 tons was to navigate the twisting narrows of the Dardanelles and the Bosphorus she should have her superstructure amidships. And if the supertanker experiment was to be tried, some were apparently in favour of building abroad to take advantage of western experience and prices.

At all events the design was eventually entrusted to a team in Leningrad. The ship was to have a 30,000 horsepower steam turbine installation giving a speed of 16½ knots. The propeller was to be 'regulated' and the hull fitted with some sort of bow steering device to 'make her more manœuvrable in narrow straits or canals and when entering ports'. The crew would number 34–36, about a third less than in the Sofia class, and a series of pumps shifting 5,000 tons an hour should enable her to unload in ten or twelve hours.

There are general factors governing the size of Russian merchant ships which apply to dry cargo vessels and tankers alike. Many of the Soviet Union's harbours and estuaries, for example in the arctic, can handle ships of only limited draught. The same is true of ports in the developing countries with whom she has deliberately cultivated trading contacts or supplied with aid cargoes. The Russians also have a large requirement for vessels which can penetrate their great rivers and use their network of ship canals – for example the Baltiisky class of 2,000 tonners – in both coastal and foreign trades. Finally, although shipping operations are managed on a regional basis and many ships –

such as the ice-strengthened ones – show a regional speciality, it is reasonable that the central planning of shipbuilding and design should take account of the wide range of commercial and military trades a Russian freighter may be asked to serve.

Through a mixture of deliberate design and physical necessity, therefore, the Soviet fleet is an extremely flexible one. The typical ship is smaller than the world average, and since a ship's economic speed is partially a function of size, it is not surprising that the Russian merchantman should also be comparatively slow – in contrast to the exceptionally high speed of many Soviet warships.

Comparative size and speed of Soviet cargo ships

	Freighters				Tankers			
	Average Deadweight		Average Speed		Average Deadweight		Average Speed	
	World	USSR	World	USSR	World	USSR	World	USSR
1956	7,600	4,700	11.7	10.3	15,500	7,300	13.0	11.2
1965	7,800	5,900	13.1	12.6	25,100	14,900	14.3	13.3

Source: US Department of Commerce

Taking the Soviet merchant fleet as it stands now, another major characteristic – in addition to conservative design and small average size – is simply its newness. In this respect Russian tonnage contrasts sharply with the elderly vessels registered under the United States flag – half of them more than twenty-five years old.

The Soviet merchant fleet in a world perspective, 1969

	All Types of Merchant Ships				Tankers only			
	M. gross tons	% of World Fleet	Av. Size	% less than 10 yrs. old	M. gross tons	% of World Fleet	Av. Size	% less than 10 yrs. old
USSR	13.7	6.5	2,400	70	3.2	4.1	8,200	77
World	211.7	—	4,200	56	77.4	—	13,200	62
UK	23.8	11.2	6,200	58	10.2	13.2	16,900	70
USA	19.6	9.3	6,200	15	4.6	5.9	12,200	22

Source: Lloyd's Register of Shipping

While the proportion of British tonnage less than ten years old is slightly larger than the figure for the world as a whole, and the Soviet proportion substantially so, only 15 per cent of the American fleet was built during the 1960s.

The changing age structure of the Soviet fleet in percentages

	Less than 10 years	10–20 years	20–30 years	More than 30 years
1939	24	26	23	27
1959	47	18	14	21
1969	70	20	4	6

Sources: *Development of the USSR's Transport, 1917–62* and Lloyd's Register of Shipping

Among the individual cargo ship types of which the Russians themselves seem most proud are the 49,000 ton Sofia class tanker, freighters of the 16,000 ton Leninsky Komsomol and 13,000 ton Poltava classes, and the Amguema type of icebreaking freighter.

The *Poltava* herself, with her comparatively high speed of seventeen knots and unusually long No 4 hatch, became internationally famous in 1962 when she was used to carry missiles to Cuba. Ever since then American commentators have invested this sort of hatch design in Soviet ships with sinister implications, while the Russians themselves insist that it simply follows the modern trend in cargo handling. The Leninsky Komsomol series, the first of which appeared in 1960, reflects the Soviet planners' concern to inject a bit more speed into the fleet: steam turbines give them a speed of 18–19 knots. In the past few years the Russians have also experimented with freighters powered by gas turbines, a form of propulsion which in the West is associated with fast small warships.

The Amguema class ships which appeared in the mid-1960s embody a concept the Russians were already exploring in the 1930s – freighters which do their own icebreaking. They have a deadweight of 8,000 tons and are apparently used to convoy conventional ships as well as operating independently. As one would expect for this sort of work the propulsion is diesel-electric (which absorbs propeller shocks more easily), giving a speed of fifteen knots. Appropriately, they were built in Siberia, on the Amur River.

The Sophia class tankers, nineteen of which were delivered between 1963 and 1967, are the largest vessels so far built in the Soviet Union (although a pair of whale factories built in 1959–61 are almost as big). When they appeared the Russians claimed that in some respects – for example their speed of seventeen knots and their economic use of steel – they surpassed world standards. It was also pointed out that they were equipped with insulated lifeboats which could be lowered by remote control and if necessary motor safely through burning oil. At all events the design team in Leningrad was nominated for a Lenin Prize.

Until 1963 the Leningrad yards had been turning out the Pekin class (an unfortunate name as it turned out) of 30,000 tonners. But the real workhorses of the Soviet tanker fleet have been the sixty or so Kazbek class 12,000 tonners, built over a period of eight years from 1953. The basic hull resembles the American standard war-built T2 tanker, but a series of this length gave plenty of scope for progressive refinement of the design as well as production economies.

A number of new designs have already been mentioned by Soviet officials as being scheduled for construction during the 1971–75 five-year plan, in addition to the 150,000 ton tanker discussed earlier. They include bulk carriers of 40–50,000 tons, a wine tanker, a 12,000 ton timber carrier, a specialized vehicle and machinery carrier (Western military intelligence will no doubt prick up its ears at this one) and a vessel which carries 40–50 barges. This last design seems intended to serve coastal areas which have no deep water ports rather than being an alternative form of container ship intended to secure a fast cargo turnround. But it sounds similar to the LASH ships now plying between New Orleans and Rotterdam – Japanese-built 40,000 tonners each carrying 73 barges which are distributed and collected by pusher tugs.

The Russians have also announced tentative plans for a deep-sea container ship. Early discussion of the design mentioned speeds of up to 23/24 knots and a capacity for 500–600 containers. But since at the time of writing the Soviet vessel is intended to represent Baltic Steamship in the trade between Europe and Australia, using a terminal in Hamburg, one would expect her to be a lot bigger and closely matched to the British Continental tonnage on this route.

The Passenger Fleet

The sixty or so deep-sea vessels in the Soviet passenger fleet reflect the overall pattern in that many of them were built in the past ten years, but averages of age or speed are weighted by the important element of really old ships that remains. After the Second World War the Russians assiduously salvaged, refurbished and in many cases re-engined a total of fifteen German passenger liners. They include the 21,000 ton *Sovietsky Sojus* (Soviet Union), built as the *Hansa* in Hamburg in 1923, which re-emerged from an East German yard in 1955. She is used on the regular run between Vladivostok and Petropavlovsk, carrying up to 1,500 passengers at a time, and is still the biggest passenger ship flying the Hammer and Sickle.

North German Lloyd, Hamburg – America, German East Africa; most of the great names in German shipping between the wars contributed to the reconstructed Communist fleet. Especially ironic was the transfer of the *Marienburg*, third of the Nazi workers' cruise liners. Launched in Stettin at the outbreak of war, she survived to become the *Abkhazia*. The deserving workers who were building the Third Reich have been replaced by worthy Communists who have over-fulfilled their production norm.

The newly built element of the passenger fleet is based on three main types: 3,000 tonners of the Kirgizstan class, the Mikhail Kalinin 5,000 tonners, and most recently the 19,000 ton Ivan Franko class.

The nine Kirgizstan ships were home built in Leningrad between 1959 and 1963 for cruising and the short Black Sea and

Baltic routes. They carry 240 passengers. Russian diesels give a speed of sixteen knots and their shallow draught of only twelve feet opens up a wide range of small ports.

For the two bigger classes, which were to carry the Soviet flag into the Mediterranean, the Pacific and the North Atlantic, the Russians turned to the East German yard of Mathias Thesen at Wismar. The *Mikhail Kalinin* herself was completed in 1958, and by 1964, when the Wismar yard switched to the Ivan Franko series, nineteen ships had been built to this rather elegant design, with its long rakish bow. There is accommodation for about 300 passengers and diesels built by the German firm of M.A.N. give a cruising speed of eighteen knots. This is the type used on the Soviet merchant marine's longest passenger route, between Leningrad and Havana.

However, the spearhead of the Russians' effort in the international cruise market and on the North Atlantic route to Canada is provided by the four Ivan Franko class ships. These carry 700 passengers in fully air-conditioned accommodation. Sulzer diesels give twenty knots. After the *Aleksandr Pushkin's* first season on the North Atlantic without stabilizers a set was bought and fitted.

A senior shipping ministry official has indicated that a new class of liner carrying about 500 passengers may be built for foreign routes. If so, the primary justification will no doubt be the potential foreign currency earnings. It is extremely doubtful whether some of the foreign operations in which the big Russian liners are engaged, for example the North Atlantic run between Britain and Canada, could be justified in conventional commercial terms. But when foreign exchange revenue is weighted by whatever factor the Soviet shipping ministry uses in its internal accounts, the result looks rather different.

In addition to the network of scheduled passenger services radiating from Leningrad, Odessa and Nakhodka, the Russian agencies have used their 20,000 tonners for cruises from the Mediterranean, Britain, Canada and Australia, in between two-way charter voyages from the UK. Starting in 1971, the brochures also offer trips from British ports to the Caribbean, a rich and expanding cruise market for which several European shipping lines are building specialized new ships.

For the future, the Russians probably see the Caribbean operation as a source of US dollars, but American passengers will be hard to attract. There is political antagonism to be overcome; the competition is vigorous and more experienced. The Russian liners I have been aboard give an impression of bright, clean efficiency, but like Russian air liners they could do with a lot less proletarian plastic in primary colours. No one could call them sophisticated. Still, the direct Soviet style may well suit American tastes more than it does European, and there are some cruise managers who would give a great deal to be able to dress their product with the unique trimmings available to the Russians – caviar, vodka, Siberian salmon, Georgian wines and the music of the balalaika.

The Soviet passenger fleet carries more than three times as many people each year as it did before the war, and there has been a substantial expansion of traffic during the 1960s, in parallel with the growth in cargo shipments. The short distance travelled by the average passenger reflects the heavy weight of coastal ferry services.

Passenger transport by sea

	1940	1960	1965	1966	1967	1968
Millions of passengers carried	9.6	22.7	31.3	32.3	34.0	34.0
Million passenger/miles	479	715	789	879	889	945
Average passenger voyage, in miles	50	32	25	27	26	28

Source: Soviet statistical abstract

Hydrofoils

A form of passenger shipping in which the Russians have shown a unique interest is the hydrofoil – a vessel which rides clear of the water on slender legs fitted with submerged 'wings'. In most parts of the world this type of craft is still a slightly exotic rarity, rather like the hovercraft; but it is as natural to see one sweeping down the Nieva in Leningrad at forty knots as it is to see a sedate Thames launch sliding under Westminster bridge. There are now well over a thousand hydrofoils in operation in the Soviet Union, making use of the country's great network of rivers, lakes and canals. On the Volga alone there are eighty services. By 1969, eleven years after the first route was opened, more than three million passengers a year were using this form of transport. This is still quite a small number compared with the total of 150 millions carried annually on Russian inland waterways, but the Soviet authorities forecast that hydrofoils will eventually replace almost all the conventional vessels.

By rising on its legs, a hydrofoil offers much less resistance to the water, and if there is enough power available it can reach speeds that would be completely beyond a displacement craft of similar size. For example the *Buryeviestnik* (Stormy Petrel), the Russians' first gas turbine powered passenger hydrofoil, has a maximum speed of sixty knots. Although its water jet propulsion leaves a great cloud of spray astern, the wake is comparatively smooth – an extremely important asset on rivers and canals. And once it is riding on its foils, the 140 foot hull, seating 130 passengers, draws only sixteen inches of water. Even floating as a conventional boat its draught is no more than 6 feet 7 inches.

The problem with foilborne craft is to make the lifting system stable. Most of the Soviet designs have so far made use of a shallow, fully submerged foil system. It is stabilized in a downward direction by small surface planing foils and relies on the main foils' loss of lift as they come near the surface to prevent the vessel leaping out of the water. The same basic system can be adapted for fairly rough water, but Soviet designers have also developed a range of specifically sea-going craft of the Striela (Arrow) type which have V-shaped surface piercing main foils. They are similar in concept to the Supramar designs, the main Western hydrofoils to be seen in service in the Mediterranean and Scandinavia.

The *Striela* is also important because from it the Soviet

Navy has developed its Pchela (Bee) class of fast inshore patrol boats. Two dozen of these boats have been delivered, armed with twin mounted heavy machine guns.

It is on the potential naval applications of the hydrofoil, as a gunboat or a submarine chaser, that the Americans have so far concentrated. For this purpose they have developed a range of experimental designs using fully submerged movable foils automatically controlled by an autopilot. Boeing's seventy foot gunboat *Tucumcari* rides high out of the water on three re-tractable foils, driven at more than forty knots by water jets. Grumman's *Plainview*, the world's largest hydrofoil, is a rakish 200-footer built to investigate the possibility of an ocean-going anti-submarine craft, and is designed to reach eventually speeds of more than seventy knots.

Passenger derivatives of these sophisticated craft are beginning to appear. For example a Grumman Dolphin with automatic retractable foils operates in the Bahamas. But the Americans have not followed the Russians in the widespread application of simple, rugged hydrofoils. As for Britain, she has virtually ignored the whole concept, preferring instead to put her effort into a British invention, the hovercraft. However, there are signs that this attitude may be changing; the United Kingdom's first hydrofoil ferry service opened on the Solent in 1969, using a Seaflight H 57, and but for Russian sensitivity about the Board of Trade's licensing requirements, as I described earlier, it might have been preceded by a Soviet Komieta. One of the few commercial operators in the United States with really ambitious plans, International Hydrolines Incorporated, operates two Soviet craft – a Rakieta and a Komieta – through its subsidiary Trinidad and Tobago Hydrolines, and has more on order.

Meanwhile Russian designers have no doubt been keeping a close watch on the long-legged, automatic us Navy craft. In December 1969 they launched the 100-seat sea-going ferry *Typhoon*, described as the first Soviet design with automatically controlled foils. These are said to copy the principle of aircraft control surfaces. Gas turbines will give a speed of about forty knots, which should be maintained in Force 5 seas.

The Russian hull designs are characterized by an old-fashioned, somewhat superfluous streamlining reminiscent of that generation of American automobiles which sprouted huge fins. They generally provide aircraft style seating, a bar and sometimes a promenade deck.

There are four basic types (details of performance and capacity are quoted from *Jane's Surface Skimmer Systems*):

Rakieta: the prototype for this class of 33-knot 50-seaters was launched in 1957. Hundreds are now in service and a number have been exported. This was the type which really proved the Alexieyev foil system. From 1971 it will be replaced by a family of Voskhod 65-seat designs, one of them with an especially shallow draught and another powered by gas turbines.

Meteor: this 120–150-seater entered service in 1960. The cabins are air-conditioned; there is a bar and a small promenade deck. Diesel engines give a maximum speed of 35 knots. The sea-going version of this design is known as the Komieta.

Sputnik: a 100-ton 260-seater introduced in 1961. It cruises at 41 knots. A sea-going version, the Vikhr, is designed to operate up to fifty miles offshore.

Striela: A specifically sea-going design to carry 92 passengers at 40 knots in up to Force 4 weather. Built in Leningrad, as opposed to the main hydrofoil shipyard of Krasnoye Sormovo in Gorky, it entered service in 1961. It operates on the Baltic and, together with Vikhrs and Komietas, provides Black Sea services throughout the year.

CHAPTER 7

A Planned Industry

The Soviet shipping industry is organized into fifteen regional agencies responsible to the Ministry of the Merchant Marine. In addition, there are a number of functional agencies, the most important of which is *Sovfrakht*. This long established organization controls all cargo ship chartering. There is an equivalent central organization for international passenger operations, but it seems to leave the regional agencies – or companies, as they are usually styled in translation – much more to their own devices. *Sovinflot* provides agency services for all vessels using Russian ports.

The shipping Minister remained unchanged from 1954 until 1969, when Viktor Bakayev retired at the age of 67 and handed over to his deputy, Timofei Guzhenko. Bakayev once recalled that he had invited three Italian ministers to the Soviet Union but none of them survived long enough in office to take up the offer. His own career covers the successive phases of reconstruction and expansion since the death of Stalin, and as a member of the powerful Council of Ministers he probably deserves a great deal of credit for the priority shipping has received within the successive five-year plans. He must also have had considerable personal responsibility for rationalizing the political objectives of Soviet shipping policy; for example the encouragement of governmental regulation through the United Nations Conference on Trade and Development (UNCTAD) while at the same time pushing ahead with commercial infiltration of the Western shipping 'conference' system. The question, therefore, is whether the change of minister will significantly change the policy.

Bakayev trained as an engineer, specializing in port operations and construction, and held a number of academic posts before being appointed a deputy minister in 1945. His 51-year-old successor is a graduate of the Odessa Institute of Water Transport. He was at one time director of the port of Murmansk and ran a combined shipping and port administration in Sakhalin. For the past four years he has been First Deputy Minister of the Merchant Marine.

This last fact suggests a continuity of policy that seems to be confirmed by Guzhenko's first public statements as Minister. But he is a comparatively young man, and in the past has concerned himself with future planning and development rather than finance and administration. One would therefore expect some new initiatives now he is in full control. The word 'creative' has been used of him; we must wait and see whether for Western shipowners this should be translated as 'aggressive' or 'co-operative'.

In addition to the operation of all sea-going merchant ships, including icebreakers, the ministry is also responsible for port operations and ship repair. The same co-ordinated structure is reflected in the regional agencies. This is in striking contrast to the Western pattern, where only the most specialized shipping companies – some of the big tanker operators, for example – organize their own terminals, let alone repair facilities.

The director of the Baltic agency in Leningrad, for example, presides over a management board of departmental heads running not only the ships based there, but also the various port undertakings, repair yards and other associated facilities in the area. The pyramid structure of centralized planning in the Soviet Union means that each agency receives an annual plan, and hopefully has the necessary resources allocated by the relevant department of the shipping ministry. How far local managers can feed back requirements not already perceived in principle by the central planners is difficult to discover, but one of the declared aims of the economic reforms introduced in this industry in 1968 was to give individual undertakings more commercial independence.

More than half the Soviet merchant fleet is registered in Black

Sea ports. This group of agencies has also shown the highest average growth rate during the 1960s – in 1966 a new ship was being delivered every ten days. One reason is that Black Sea ships handle a large proportion of Russian oil exports, which have grown rapidly, through newly built tanker ports like that at Novorossiisk, for example. In particular 'sea bridges' to Cuba and Egypt have been maintained from the Black Sea. In the latter case the Russian end of the bridge is Ilyechovsk, near Odessa; in 1957 it was nothing but a shallow lagoon, but it is now one of the biggest Soviet ports on that coast. The individual agencies in this area, with their associated ports, are:

Black Sea Steamship Company (Odessa, Ilyechovsk, Kherson): this operates the largest dry cargo fleet in Soviet Union, mostly new tonnage, and a lot of coasters; is responsible for joint services to Egypt, India and dozens of other international routes including those to Latin America and Australia; and also has an important passenger section, with routes throughout the Mediterranean.

Azov Steamship Company (Zhdanov, Berdiansk): apart from coastal operations, it specializes in bulk carriers.

Novorossiisk Steamship Company (Novorossiisk, Tuapse): the Soviet Union's principal tanker operator.

Georgian Steamship Company (Batumi, Poti): coastal operator in Mediterranean and Red Sea.

Soviet Danube Steamship Company (Izmail, Reni, Kilia): operates river cargo and passenger services.

Although less tonnage operates from the Baltic than from the Black Sea, the Baltic group of agencies is in some ways more important. The Leningrad company operates the Russians' major international passenger services; it represents Soviet shipping in a number of Western 'conferences' and takes part in joint cargo liner operations with the East European fleets – a significant trend for the future. Until the 1960s there was virtually no Russian tanker fleet in the Baltic, but by 1966 it had grown to more than 200,000 tons. Since the beginning of 1969, when the Lithuanian Steamship Company was formed, four individual agencies have operated from this sea:

Baltic Steamship Company (Leningrad, Vyborg): responsible for passenger services to London, Havana and Montreal; it has a large fleet of general cargo vessels and timber carriers, the former serving many long routes including Australia and South America.

Estonian Steamship Company (Tallinn): specializes in West African cargo liner trades; also coastal traffic and local passenger services.

Latvian Steamship Company (Riga): tanker specialist handling all liquid cargoes in the Baltic.

Lithuanian Steamship Company (Klaipeda): subdivided from Baltic Steamship to concentrate on bulk coal and timber exports; originally allotted nineteen ships, the port and a repair yard.

In the arctic, timber, ore and coal are among the important cargoes, and the ships are designed accordingly. They are strengthened for ice and used to working with icebreakers. There are two individual agencies:

Murmansk Steamship Company (Murmansk): Murmansk marks the western end of the Northern Sea Route, and the main fleet of ice-breakers for that route is based there.

Northern Steamship Company (Arkhangelsk, Oniega, Mezen, Naryan-Mar): operates a large fleet of timber carriers and ice-strengthened ships of various kinds; also provides passenger ships on the Northern Sea Route.

The USSR's inland sea has its own agency, the Caspian Steamship Company. Based at Baku, it is more in evidence than it used to be because of the ship canals giving an outlet to the Black Sea and the Baltic. Ships operated by this agency – which has a mixed fleet of freighters, tankers, passenger liners and ferries – range as far as the North Sea.

In some respects the Pacific fleets seem to have been the cinderellas of Soviet shipping: for example, nearly half the

Kamchatka agency's ships were still coal burners until 1958, although few of them are left now. But their basic job of contributing to the industrial development of the Soviet Far East has been extended to include the establishment of closer trade links with Japan, involving passenger as well as cargo services, and the support of North Vietnam. Soviet-Japanese cooperation in the exploitation of Siberian timber and oil has specifically included the extension and modernization of the Russian ports. A joint commission was established for this purpose in 1967.

Three individual agencies operate from this part of the Soviet Union:

Far Eastern Steamship Company (Nakhodka): operates a mixed fleet of freighters, tankers, passenger ships and icebreakers, and has played an important part in opening up the Northern Sea Route. Nakhodka was one of the first Russian ports to be equipped for handling containers, but the typical cargo is timber.

Sakhalin Steamship Company (Kholmsk): mainly responsible for domestic support of Sakhalin Island from the mainland.

Kamchatka Steamship Company (Petropavlovsk): as with Sakhalin, this is responsible for some deep sea timber trade but is mainly concerned with general cargo and local passenger services.

The overall pattern of the fifteen companies' operations can be seen from the number of calls they make at foreign ports in different parts of the world.

The pattern of Soviet merchant shipping – 1967

	Number of calls	Percentage
North-West Europe	7,270	38
Mediterranean, Black and Red Seas	4,960	26
North, Central and South America	2,330	12
West Pacific, including Japan	1,890	10
Indian Ocean, including East Africa	1,290	7
South-East Asia, Oceania and Australia	760	4
West Africa	480	3

Source: V. Bakayev: *Soviet Ships on World Sea Routes*

It is noticeable that some of the new routes about which the Russians make a lot of noise for political reasons, such as to the developing countries of West Africa, still play only a small part in the fleets' activities. By comparison with the industrialized nations of the West, the scope of the Soviet Union's trading along the deep sea routes is still quite limited, focusing on specific requirements – support for Cuba, or grain imports to cover a bad harvest at home – of the kind discussed in Chapter Five.

The co-ordination and specialization found among the fifteen Soviet agencies extends to the other Comecon fleets to a significant extent. In some respects – their joint shipbuilding programmes, and the emphasis on earning hard currency for example – it is reasonable to discuss them all as a single entity.

'Comecon' is the usual abbreviation for the Council for Mutual Economic Assistance; in maritime affairs, as in other industries, mutual is a misleading way to describe its early development under Stalin. A Polish shipyard's job, for example, was to provide cheap colliers for the reconstruction of the Soviet fleet, just as the Silesian pits were expected to supply cheap coal. By the end of her first six-year plan, in 1955, Poland was still sending about 90 per cent of her ships to the Soviet Union.

Under Khrushchev, however, genuine economic integration began to replace coercion as the means of ensuring Russian control. Credits were distributed, the notorious 'gift' prices were replaced by ones that gave the East Europeans the chance to make a profit, and the maritime nations among them were able to start rebuilding their own fleets. By 1959 the Soviet Union even launched a couple of tankers for East Germany.

A basic framework for maritime cooperation is provided by Comecon's permanent council. Annual conferences are also held in each of the shipping 'basins' to discuss 'the allocation of free tonnage, the state of the freight market, joint chartering and tariff policy, relations with Western conferences and the organization of joint services'. Such activities are than co-ordinated through a joint 'chartering bureau'. The Russian agencies in the Baltic rely heavily on Polish ship repair facilities. Comecon fleets already share a number of standard ship designs and there is said to be a plan to reduce the number of different types from about fifty to less than twenty. Inland water transport, for example along the Danube, has been rationalized. In June 1970 the Comecon countries formed an International Shipowners Association, based in Gdynia, which is apparently intended to be equivalent to the Western shipowners' International Chamber of Shipping and represent the Communist fleets in legal and technical matters.

In Communist economic theory, the advantages of such 'fraternal internationalist' cooperation between Socialist countries are matched domestically by national co-ordination of the various forms of transport:

The Socialist economic system in the USSR makes possible the most rational development of different forms of transport, as component parts of a national transport system. The Complex Transport Problems Institute operating under the State Planning Committee of the USSR, supreme planning organ of the Soviet Union, draws up scientifically corroborated recommendations for developing individual branches of the transport services. This permits us to ensure dependable transport communications at least possible cost.[1]

To a Western shipowner, this process of centralized planning is probably the most striking feature of the Soviet merchant marine's operation. But the term requires cautious definition – with the emphasis on the word 'centralized'.

For although by comparison with an airline or a motor manufacturer the average British shipping company may use rough and ready management methods, many of its decisions are likely to be more 'rational' – in the sense that more factors are introduced into the economic equation – than those of its Russian counterpart. The difference is that in the Soviet Union some factors are declared to be more rational than others.

Equally, no one could doubt that the most elaborate 'planning' goes into the passenger operations of the P & O group or that the tanker requirements of Shell and BP are 'scientifically

[1] *The Soviet Merchant Marine Today and Tomorrow.*

corroborated'. OCL and ACT combine road, rail and sea transport in a door-to-door container service half-way round the world, demonstrating a degree of integration which I understand the Soviet authorities have found difficult even within their own borders. A shipping line in the United States may not operate its own computer, as some of the bigger Russian agencies now do, but it will have plenty of computer services available and the American executive might well be more aware of their potential than his Russian opposite number.

Nor does the Russians' passion for statistics – which they share with the Americans – in itself indicate a concern for efficiency. The figures as published are often selective, incomplete or inconsistent. They may well be irrelevant. A Russian journalist writing about a new tanker would throw in a few percentage increases in productivity as habitually as an American public relations man feels obliged to mention that it carries enough fuel to take the average family car half-way to the moon.

But Soviet statistics have a reality of their own. In a state-owned, centrally controlled industry, whose funds are allocated from above, it is even more important to quantify success than in a capitalist economy. Existence is only possible as an entry under the five-year plan. The Central Merchant Marine Research Institute, which develops new standard ship designs and improves the efficiency of existing ones, justifies its work by pointing to the five million roubles it has saved the economy; and the individual seaman knows that his earnings are directly related to the percentage 'above plan profit' achieved by his ship.

It is not planning as such that characterizes the Soviet shipping industry, but the centralized structure and the nature of the planning criteria that are applied. Political objectives, such as the development of 'peace routes' to newly independent African states, can be directly introduced into the system, as can military requirements or differential subsidies designed, for example, to stimulate foreign currency earnings.

The system's biggest drawback is the familiar danger of bureaucracy. The Russians have become increasingly worried by this, and by their own lack of economic sophistication, as they have begun to match themselves against Western standards of commercial efficiency. Hence the progressive refinement of the cost accounting system they use – *khoxraschiot* – in the absence of the capitalist balance of profit and loss.

In the late 1950s freight earnings replaced cargo tonnage and ton/mileage as the main indicator of the merchant fleet's performance. Then in 1968 a whole range of reforms – 'new conditions of planning and economic stimulation' – were introduced. The two principal aims were to give the shipping companies more independence from central control and to apply economic methods of management more widely, with a new emphasis on the profitability of the individual ship.

The next step, according to Bakayev, is the progressive transfer on to a system of 'automatic management' using computers: 'The theoretical work is going well. In the near future the computer will be a real aid to the sailor. It provides the answer to the main problem – increasing productive work while reducing the administrative apparatus.'

The Russian industry may well go through a phase of disillusionment with the computer, as many American firms have done. For the moment, it seems to have reached the stage at which every self-respecting shipping company has to have a computer, even though many of the problems of putting them to work have yet to be solved. Bakayev himself implies as much. But in the long run he may have hit on the one thing that can transform a rambling bureaucracy into a smoothly functioning economic machine. And judging from the way in which every aspect of Soviet shipping operations is expressed statistically, right down to its effect on the average seaman's productivity in ton/miles, there is plenty of routine arithmetic for the computers to tackle in the meantime. It may be difficult to get a simple series of figures showing how the merchant fleet's tonnage has grown since the war, but it is easy to discover that the Russian seaman's annual production is four million ton/miles, or that the average ship's annual utilization has increased from 278 days to 330 days in the past ten years. In absolute terms such statistics are almost meaningless but the changes over time, as with annual utilization, may be interesting. In this case the Soviet authorities claim that most of the improvement is due to a new system of repairs and servicing at sea, using either the ship's crew or special repair teams, intended to guarantee at least two years between dockyard overhauls. By 1966 about 400 vessels were operating the system.

As I suggested earlier, a proliferation of statistics is natural to a centrally planned economy relying on the principle of payment by results: 'Tapping their internal reserves, the crew of the MS *Mednogorsk* of the Black Sea Steamship Company have saved 179 tons of fuel and lubricants in the past four years and brought the country 146,000 roubles of extra profit. The vessel was awarded the Order of the Red Banner of Labour. Eleven members of the crew were given government awards. [2]

One of the paradoxes of the Russian method is that the terms profit and profitability tend to crop up more often in conversation with a Soviet shipping executive than with a capitalist shipowner – although in another context the Russian might feel obliged to remind you that there is no such thing as 'profit' under the Communist system. The Ministry of the Merchant Marine itself has to show a rate of return by which its performance can be compared to that of other industries. In 1967 it was 13.2 per cent, 'after covering all the expenses of a rapidly expanding merchant fleet, including capital investment'. Before the percentage is calculated, the industry's earnings are weighted by 'centralized additional payments', the main function of which seems to be to allow for the fact that foreign currencies are relatively more valuable, because of their scarcity, than the official rouble exchange rates indicate.

On this basis shipping's performance was better than average for the Soviet economy. But exactly how such a profit compares with the much lower rates declared by many British shipping lines is extremely difficult, if not impossible, to say without access to the Russian accounts, and I certainly do not have the information to attempt such a comparison here. The fleet's earnings from the carriage of Soviet cargoes (domestic traffic, cif exports and

[2] *The Soviet Merchant Marine Today and Tomorrow.*

fob imports) are determined by the tariff of notional freight rates it charges customers in other ministries and agencies. The tariff was calculated in 1965, based apparently on average world freight rates, and came into effect in January 1966. Since then I understand there have been few changes, although it is open to the shipping companies to appeal for an adjustment through the Ministry's tariff department if they believe a particular rate is inadequate.

However the profit is calculated, it is of immediate importance to everyone aboard a Russian freighter, because the elaborate system of incentive bonus payments is based on it. The professionally ambitious and the Communist Party members no doubt feel pride and satisfaction at winning the title of 'Communist Labour Personnel' or being awarded the Order of the Red Banner of Labour. It secures a mention in despatches to the trade union conference and the attention of the shore management. But the whole crew benefits from the increased productivity the award is supposed to acknowledge:

Famous for their labour accomplishments on the Black Sea are the crew of the tanker *Vladimir*. They make thrifty use of every kopeck of fuel, lubricants and technical supplies, organize flawless mooring and cargo handling operations, seek ways to transport above-plan cargoes and to increase the ship's speed. As a result of all this, the crew have yielded a saving of 186 tons of fuel and 11 tons of lubricants during the past few years, increased the service life of the ship and carried large amounts of above-plan freight. The tanker has been awarded the Order of Lenin, the highest award of the Soviet Union, for her labour successes.[3]

A detailed comparison of the ship's planned targets and her actual performance is posted in the crew's quarters. The above-plan profit may be achieved either by economizing, for example in fuel, or by increasing the revenue. The captain of, say, a timber carrier, might be able to load more than his nominal cargo tonnage by loading only the absolute minimum of oil and water.

[3] *The Soviet Merchant Marine Today and Tomorrow.*

The bonus paid to an individual is not simply related to his ship's performance but also to his contribution. For example, as part of a foreign exchange economy drive Soviet captains have been encouraged to dispense with pilots in foreign ports wherever possible, unless pilotage is compulsory. I gather that 10 per cent of the money saved (this figure, quoted to me in the port of London, may be different elsewhere) is distributed to the crew, but only to those members – the captain, who gets half, the chief engineer and one or two others – who have additional work or responsibility. Similarly, seamen who make proposals for increased efficiency are rewarded in proportion to the extra profit the idea yields.

Ironically, the comparison which came to mind when I first saw the production charts, the slogans and the pictures of the 'top workers' aboard a Russian freighter, was with the Boeing Company's aircraft factory in Seattle, where these same three techniques for instilling a corporate spirit are much in evidence. The two organizations also have in common a well-disciplined paternalism which many people would associate more readily with life in the armed services. But there can be no real comparison, the Boeing man will protest, between paternalism exercised by a private company, however large, and that of a political dictatorship.

To Western eyes, the sinister feature of the Soviet organization is of course the presence of Communist Party members on board each ship, ensuring some degree of political activity and taking care, I should imagine, that shore contacts are in the main either professional or 'cultural'. Certainly the journal *Vodny Transport* periodically reminds Russian sailors that their first duty is to support the Communist system in its ideological struggle with capitalism. Soviet writers warn them about subversion by foreign intelligence services and complain about their being subjected to 'religious propaganda'. The proportion of party members varies, but Russian sources indicate that a ship's crew of thirty-five would probably include about five of them.

The state-sponsored seamen's trade union plays a separate

and, it is claimed, decisive role in establishing living and working conditions. On a modern vessel this means single and double berth air-conditioned cabins, a 41-hour week (with emergency work paid as overtime) and 24 days paid leave, plus days off earned at sea. Ashore, the union provides subsidized holiday accommodation.

Crew sizes are 'scientifically determined'. Figures quoted in 1966 indicated the following standards – (in each case the numbers look rather high by current British standards):

Tanker of 25,000 tons gross – 48
Tanker of 8,000 tons gross – 40
Dry cargo freighter of 9,000 tons gross – 40

Soviet seamen appear to be comparatively well paid, although the Soviet statistical abstract is confusing on this point because it lumps together 'water' (*vodny*) transport without specifying which categories are included or whether any are excluded.

Average monthly wages

| | *roubles* | |
	1960	*1968*
Whole Economy	80.6	112.6
Industry	91.6	121.9
Agriculture	53.8	92.1
Transport	87.0	126.0
Rail	82.9	116.0
Water	106.9	154.4
Road and Urban	88.0	128.8
Communications	62.7	88.0
Construction	92.4	131.2
State Administration	86.4	118.0

Source: Soviet Statistical abstract

In general, there are many similarities between service life as we know it in the West and the life of a Russian merchant seaman: the specially allotted housing and recreational facilities, the organized sports with clothing and equipment provided, the regular broadcasts 'for those at sea', the special shore visits, and the libraries stocked with scarcely touched classics – including Dickens – and well-thumbed paperbacks. No doubt it suits some people.

CHAPTER 8

Russian Shipping Policy

The maritime policy of the USSR stems from the task of extensive participation by the cargo fleet in the economic competition between the socialist and capitalist systems, of fully satisfying the demands of the economy and its external trade, of fulfilling the country's own transport needs at home and abroad, and increasing the Soviet fleet's share of international sea transport. (V. Bakayev, *Soviet Ships on World Sea Routes*.)

In other words the growth of the Soviet merchant fleet is admittedly a challenge to the established maritime powers, even if the Russians deny that it constitutes a threat. By 1965, according to Bakayev, the Soviet Union had 'freed herself from the whims of the world freight market'. The next stage, he wrote in the magazine *Za Rubezhom*, was to enter into 'free competition with the capitalist fleet'. In the process the Russian ships would 'restrain the expanionist intentions of certain agressive states and render real assistance to the newly developing countries in the growth of their economy and foreign trade.'[1] These last two objectives – which in practice involve complaining about the United States protective discrimination in shipping, and encouraging the developing countries' suspicions that they have been exploited by conferences of European shipowners – are neatly combined in the USSR's policy towards UNCTAD. In *Soviet Ships on World Sea Routes*, published in Moscow just before he handed over to Guzhenko, Bakayev presents a sort of 'Bakayev Plan' for the eventual supervision of world shipping through the United Nations.

He starts with the contention that for various different

[1] *Za Rubezhom*, March 27, 1965.

reasons, governments are playing an increasing part in international shipping, among capitalist nations and in the developing countries as well as in the communist ones. He has no objection in principle – naturally enough – provided there is some degree of international control. 'Trade and shipping are becoming more and more international. The regulation of shipping, bearing in mind its global character, cannot exist on a basis only of national laws within each country.' The Soviet Union recognizes this, for example in her active membership of IMCO (the Intergovernmental Maritime Consultative Organization, which drafts international safety conventions). But in his view UNCTAD has a special importance.

Since the developing nations have vitually no fleets of their own, they are forced to make use of the services of the capitalist shipping conferences, 'which arbitrarily establish unnecessarily high freight rates, restraining the economic development of the developing nations'. Hence the need 'to establish international control, with the help of the United Nations, over the activities of the conferences and over freight rates'.

The conferences Bakayev refers to are groups of private shipping companies who combine to provide scheduled cargo services on certain routes, sometimes pooling revenue as well as tonnage. In return for offering a consistent service, they fix a common tariff of freight rates. And to keep other shipowners out of the trade while at the same time keeping their regular customers happy, they often give 'loyalty rebates' to firms which ship with them for more than a stipulated period. Many of the important conferences are dominated by big British groups like P & O, Ocean Steamship or Furness Withy. Their ships are cargo liners as opposed to tramps.

To say that the conferences would oppose the principle of governmental control, even on an international basis, is an understatement. As maritime common carriers they have tried to resist the trend towards 'flag discrimination'; that is government action to direct certain cargoes, or a fixed proportion of them, into ships of its own national fleet. And during the 1960s British and European shipowners in particular have been fighting a running battle with the US Federal Maritime Commission, and in UNCTAD, to prevent other forms of interference with their commercial activity.

The FMC argued that to carry out its statutory responsibility to defend the interests of US commerce it must be given full details of the dual-rate agreements between the Atlantic freight conferences and their shippers, and reserved the right to declare agreements illegal under the Bonner Act of 1961. The conferences refused to open their books, let alone abandon their dual-rate system to suit the Commission. But to the extent that they traded into US ports and operated in partnership with American firms, they had to accept American jurisdiction. Hundreds of thousands of dollars have been spent on the legal actions which resulted.

In a sense the dispute was a conflict between the USA's anti-trust tradition – without which embarrassed American business-men would not have tolerated some of the FMC's more extreme antics – and the obsessive secrecy of the traditional British conference. One healthy result was a more open, formal relation-ship between conferences and their customers, the shippers. This improvement also made the shipowners less open to suspicion when they resisted proposals for economic analysis by UNCTAD, which were really designed to check whether countries like India and Pakistan were being exploited by the established maritime nations.

Bakayev is in no doubt about the answer. He goes on to argue that although many Western countries proclaim the principle of non-interference with commercial shipping, in fact they do interfere – 'for them the term "freedom of the seas" means the right of unlimited activity for private enterprise shipping companies.'

It is true that European governments supported their ship-owners' opposition to the FMC's campaign. In the early 1960s the British Government even went so far as to forbid companies to hand over commercial information where it claimed the business concerned was outside American jurisdiction. But I can vouch for the initial reluctance with which the United Kingdom

Chamber of Shipping turned to the Ministry of Transport for help. The old guard of British shipping were still instinctively suspicious of Whitehall, but they did not feel able to take on the American administration by themselves.

Nowadays the industry would concede the Soviet Minister's point that governments are bound to play a larger role. It recognizes, for example, the desire of developing countries to create national fleets, and would much prefer to see them as respectable members of the conference system than fighting it from outside. But this does not mean approving of government participation for its own sake.

In the Bakayev doctrine, extensive participation is taken for granted – even if the particular policy of the US Government is not – because of the alleged inadequacy of traditional commercial methods:

The further development of international shipping demands that its problems be reviewed on a broad representative basis. The basis for that consideration exists in UNCTAD.

In spite of the difficulty of resolving questions such as the level and structure of freight rates, of conference practice and the relation of a shipping system to essential demands, it is essential to find a solution. In this context an international agreement or convention might be useful on the basic problems of shipping. Such an agreement would undoubtedly discharge the tension in international shipping in connection with the growing demand for the regulation of tariffs and freight rates and the political discrimination practised by some countries.[2]

So much for the gospel according to Bakayev. But until the day when private enterprise shipping organizations 'gradually die off or merge with intergovernmental bodies', as he forecast on another occasion, the Ministry of the Merchant Marine is busy infiltrating the existing commercial structure. Russian participation in the various intergovernmental organizations that do exist seems just as much designed to create an image of competent respectability among Western shipowners and traders as it is to further the principle of international regulation.

[2] V. Bakayev, *Soviet Ships on World Sea Routes.*

The USSR has been a member of IMCO since 1958. The Organization deals with a whole range of technical matters on which cooperation is essential, such as rules of navigation, and the Russians play an active role. When a system of one-way routes for the Baltic was being discussed – to lessen the collision risk, particularly for tankers – the interested countries were invited to Leningrad, and the Novosti news agency duly noted that 'a Soviet draft was the basis for the decisions adopted.' The Russians also claimed that their Sofia class tankers were the first vessels to meet all the requirements of the 1960 Convention on the Safety of Life at Sea.

Other international organizations concerned with shipping of which the Soviet Union is a member include the International Labour Organization and the Permanent International Association of Navigation Congresses. These have been supplemented, as far as the Russians are concerned, by a series of bilateral shipping agreements with individual states. The first was signed with France in April 1967. An Anglo-Soviet agreement followed a year later, and in May 1969 one was signed with the Dutch. Since then talks have been held with Spain to establish the right of entry of Soviet cruise liners and freighters into Spanish ports, and a shipping office has been set up in Madrid – a nice political irony.

The Russians claimed that the Anglo-Soviet treaty 'put the seal on the desire of the Soviet Union and Britain to support in every way freedom of merchant shipping and develop two-way business contacts'. A joint commission would be set up to discuss various unsolved problems. In acknowledging this principle of freedom, the Soviet press felt obliged to comment, we should remember the notorious way it was violated by the Americans.

The main provisions of the treaty covered the conditions under which the two countries' ships carried goods between their ports and from those ports to third countries, the treatment of ships in port, and arrangements for consultation. Specific articles dealt with the entry of seamen without visas, the jurisdiction of the signatories' courts aboard ships, the treatment of shipwrecked vessels, and the exemption from certain shipping taxation of 'enterprises which have their central management and control in the territory of the other Contracting Party and do not carry on business through a branch or agency'.

In the long term, this agreement must do something to improve the climate for cooperation with British shipowners, but at the time it cut no ice with them. They and their continental colleagues looked at matters much more directly. With growing apprehension they had been watching the rapid expansion of Russian shipping capacity. They were alarmed by instances of Soviet competitive rate-cutting – in 1968, for example, the president of the UK Chamber of Shipping pointed to rates 40–70 per cent below the conference level in the South American trades – and above all they wondered just where it would stop.

Would the Communists use their powerful state trading monopolies to direct nearly all their seaborne trade into ships flying the hammer and sickle, regardless of previous protests against American flag discrimination? Or worse, would they perhaps use their growing cross trade capacity (between non-Soviet ports that is) deliberately to topple the delicate structure of the shipping conferences, which was already undermined by the nationalism of the developing countries?

By the autumn of 1968 the UK Chamber was so worried that it sent a delegation to the Board of Trade to enlist the Government's aid in meeting the Soviet 'threat', just as it had done when the US Federal Maritime Commission started throwing its weight about. And the International Chamber of Shipping, representing 65 per cent of the world's tonnage, warned that 'the general approach of Communist shipping operators to the problems of economic rate fixing is so fundamentally divergent from that of normal commercial practise that the possibility of understanding between the two interests is remote.'[3]

Against this background of distrust, Bakayev and his senior colleagues have devoted a good deal of effort over the past few years to calming shipowners' fear wherever possible. Critical articles in the British and American Press have been replied to in Soviet magazines and pamphlets; allegations by leaders of the

[3] *The Times*, October 17, 1968.

shipping industry have been challenged. In particular, the Minister has refuted the 'absurd idea' that the Soviet Union is trying to monopolize its own foreign transport – that is carry 100 per cent of its seaborne trade in its own ships.

As Bakayev himself admits, the argument is something of a red herring in this simplified form. But it is one that is often raised, and his reply is worth quoting at length. Writing in *Za Rubezhom* in March 1965, he had this to say:

Anyone who is familiar with the practical side of international trade knows that no country can hope to ship all the goods it buys or sells in its own ships. In making deals, the trade partners take into account and defend the interests of their national shipping lines. That is why the volume of shipments of Soviet goods on foreign ships is growing year by year. Inasmuch as it is envisaged, according to the most conservative estimates, to increase the volume of Soviet foreign trade fourfold by 1980 as a result of the USSR's tempestuous progress, Soviet cargo shipments on foreign vessels will grow too.

What then is the Soviet merchant marine 'striving' for? It is striving to have its own ships transport the greater part of the goods bought and sold on terms stipulating the use of its own means of transport. I think that hardly anyone with commonsense would deny that this is quite a legitimate aim and in no way affects the norms of mutual relations between the states that have been established in the world.

It is merely inexpedient to raise the question of ensuring 100 per cent transport on Soviet ships. Every trader knows that even with a big fleet of one's own available, very often it is more convenient to charter vessels for the transport of particular consignments of goods. Often it is advantageous to charter a vessel on the spot where the goods have been bought, rather than to send one's own vessel there in ballast.

We declare that the basic task of the Soviet merchant marine during the next years is to ensure shipments of its own goods bought and sold on condition that they are transported by our own means of conveyance. This is the main task. Naturally, the volume of shipments of goods of foreign shipowners bound in the same direction will likewise grow. Here we shall enter, using the terminology of our Western colleagues, into free competition with the capitalist fleet. And, as is known, in the West competition has never been described as an expansion.

Accepting Bakayev's point that a 100 per cent monopoly of one's own seaborne trade is an impracticable objective, one is left with the two real questions for the Western shipowner: how far can, and will, the Soviet Union use the power of its state trading monopolies to increase the proportion of its seaborne trade 'bought and sold on condition that it is transported by our own means of conveyance'; and how far is it prepared to subsidize drastic rate-cutting or use political pressure to break into cross trades for which it must have a growing capacity?

What purports to be an answer to the first question is given in the introduction to *The Development of the Soviet Merchant Marine*, published in Moscow in 1967 to mark the fiftieth anniversary of the revolution: 'The important result of the development of the Soviet cargo fleet is the achievement of independence from the world freight market for the USSR's external trade. However, this certainly does not mean that all goods will be carried only by the home fleet. The Soviet Union buys and sells about 50 per cent of goods on condition they are carried by foreign buyers or sellers.'

This is reassuring, except that it appears to exclude third parties from the international shipping business. But it is difficult to believe that when they have suitable shipping capacity, the Russians will not take advantage of their centralized trading system to save as much foreign currency as possible; and the chances of their having the capacity increase year by year. In the trade between the United Kingdom and the USSR, for example, it is instructive to compare the situation in the two important bulk trades, timber and ore.

The Russians have a large, modern fleet of timber carriers and their state agency *Exportliess* has a monopoly of sales; with the result – if that is the right word – that in 1968 UK flag ships carried only 1 per cent of British timber imports from the Soviet Union. But in the ore trade the position is reversed. While the Soviet merchant marine is noticeably short of bulk carriers (other than for timber) there are plenty sailing under the UK flag; and in this case Britain has its own state trading agency BISC (Ore), which has a virtual monopoly of iron ore imports, with the result that in 1968 91 per cent of UK iron ore imports from the USSR were carried in British ships. Such specialization is not necessarily 'unfair', but it does remind me of something Bakayev wrote about the importance of having a powerful merchant fleet: 'It is well known that the leading capitalist countries, basing on a widely popular formula – "He who owns the ships dictates prices, determines buying conditions and freight rates" – pressed hundreds of millions of dollars out of trade with Russia in the form of freight tributes.'[4]

The shipping balance

| | *million tons* | | | | | | | |
	1960	*1961*	*1962*	*1963*	*1964*	*1965*	*1966*	*1967*
Tonnage carried by Soviet ships for foreign charterers	—	—	2	—	—	9	—	16
Soviet seaborne trade carried by foreign ships	30	—	—	—	51	50	54	60
Total seaborne trade of USSR	45	59	67	76	84	92	103	109
Percentage carried by foreign ships	67	—	—	—	61	54	52	55

Source: Various official Soviet statistics

It rather looks as if other people will be paying tributes in the future. At any rate, by 1969 Bakayev was able to claim that the Soviet Union was 'freed' from this form of economic subservience to capitalism. By this he presumably means that the cost of chartering foreign vessels to carry goods for the shipment of which Soviet trading agencies are contractually responsible – that is cif exports and fob imports – is comfortably covered by the earnings of Soviet ships chartered to foreigners. Even by 1966 90 per cent of such goods were carried in Russian vessels[5] and, according to Bakayev, hard currency expenditure

[4] *Za Rubezhom*, March 27, 1965.
[5] Philip Hanson, of Birmingham University, cited E. M. Kramarov's *External Trade in Maritime Transport* to this effect at an LSE conference in 1969.

127

on chartering foreign tonnage was reduced by 75 per cent between 1962 and 1965.

It is in fact a stated aim of the 1966–70 plan that the chartering out of Soviet ships on the international freight market should be increased by two to two and a half times, and what figures there are certainly indicate a rapid growth. Bakayev insistently points out that the rapidly expanding capacity which makes this possible has not prevented the total tonnage of Russian trade carried by foreigners from growing as well. But it has naturally tended to reduce the proportion, as opposed to the absolute amount, available to Western shipowners.

As for the trade between Britain and the USSR, in 1968 ships flying the UK flag carried 36 per cent by weight, the same as in the previous year. The Soviet flag's share increased to 43 per cent, apparently at the expense of other non-British shipowners. But according to the Russians' fifty-fifty rule (which the British shipping industry would never accept as a general principle because it would exclude it from so many cross trades) the UK percentage should rise parallel with the Soviet one.

The sharing of UK – USSR seaborne trade

	1967	1968
United Kingdom imports from USSR (tons)	*3,357,000*	*3,862,000*
% carried by UK ships	37	37
% carried by Soviet ships	37	43
% carried under other flags	26	20
United Kingdom exports to USSR (tons)	*186,000*	*219,000*
% carried by UK ships	15	15
% carried by Soviet ships	67	48
% carried under other flags	18	37
Weighted average share in total seaborne trade (%)		
UK ships	36	36
Soviet ships	39	43
Others	25	21

Source: UK Chamber of Shipping

The atomic icebreaker *Lenin*, the world's first nuclear powered merchant ship and pride of the Soviet merchant marine – at least until her 'disappearance' in 1967. (APN *photograph*)

The *Manhattan* ploughing steadily through the pack-ice in Melville Sound on her way back through the North West Passage. (*Humble Oil Company photograph*)

The 100,000 ton icebreaking tanker *Manhattan* temporarily fast in the fourteen feet thick ice-pack of the McClure Strait during the summer of 1969. She eventually broke clear by repeatedly ramming the ice with her slanting bow and completed the North West Passage to Alaska. (BP *photographs*)

Baltiisky 57 loading in London's Surrey docks. She is one of a large fleet of 'mixed navigation' ships whose shallow hulls enable them to pass through the Soviet Union's canal system from the Baltic to the Black Sea. Vessels of this type can and do carry cargo from West European seaports to the canalside wharves of Moscow. (*Bunty Bax photograph*)

The 50,000 ton *Sophia*, built in Leningrad and registered in Odessa. This is the vessel which gives her name to the largest class of tanker so far constructed in Soviet yards. (APN *photograph*)

A Komieta passenger hydrofoil of the type which came all the way from the Black Sea – by way of the Baltic – to make a sales demonstration tour of British ports. She is typical of the rugged hydrofoil designs which now carry more than three million passengers a year on Russian lakes, rivers and canals. (APN *photograph*)

The *Aleksander Pushkin*, the 20,000 ton liner which carries the Soviet flag in the North Atlantic passenger trade, thereby earning badly needed foreign currency. She and her three sister ships were built in the East German yard of Mathias Thesen between 1964 and 1968.

The spectacular Soviet research vessel *Cosmonaut Vladimir Komarov* preparing to sail from Odessa. The great white domes protect her sensitive tracking equipment. (APN *photograph*)

The *Sovietskaya Ukraina* is one of a fleet of Russian whale factory ships. She was built at Nikolayev in 1959.

The launch of the *Vostok*, pride of the Russian fishing fleet. She acts as 'mother' to a fleet of fourteen sixty ton catchers which she carries from one fishing ground to the next on her deck. (APN *photograph*)

Admiral of the Fleet S. G. Gorshkov, commander-in-chief of the Soviet Navy. At the age of 31 he became the youngest admiral in Russian naval history. Since his appointment by Khrushchev as head of the Navy he has not only protected his service from the more bizarre enthusiasms of his political masters, but transformed it from a coastal navy – 'faithful helper of the Red Army' – into an independent, ocean going force. (APN *photograph*)

A Sverdlov class cruiser in the Mediterranean. Stalin is said to have had a 'curious passion' for heavy cruisers but Khrushchev thought they were fit only for the scrapyard, and, but for Admiral Gorshkov, might have sent most of the Sverdlovs there. It was one of these vessels which visited Portsmouth in 1953. (*Ministry of Defence photograph*)

A Russian freighter bound for Cuba in October 1962, with a deck cargo which may have contained some of Khrushchev's missiles. The crisis which followed probably did as much as anything to convince the Soviet leadership that it should develop an ocean going navy to match the US Navy. The pictures were taken by an American reconnaissance aircraft. (UPI *photographs*)

The 18,000 ton helicopter carrier *Moskva* (Moscow) which created such a stir in Western naval circles when she appeared in 1967. She is equipped with large anti-submarine helicopters and anti-aircraft missiles, but she could also be used to land 'naval infantry'. (*Ministry of Defence photograph*)

The Hawker Siddeley Harrier, the world's first operational vertical take-off aircraft with fixed wings, landing on the helicopter deck of the Royal Navy's cruiser HMS *Blake* in the Channel. (*Hawker Siddeley photograph*)

The prototype of an equivalent Soviet aircraft, a crude looking design by Yakovlev, being demonstrated at the Domodedovo air show in 1967. (APN *photograph*)

The USS *Pueblo*, captured by the North Koreans while collecting electronic intelligence. (*US Navy photograph*) She is the American equivalent of the *Bakan*, one of a fleet of Soviet 'spy trawlers' which doggedly follow NATO Exercises in the Atlantic and the Mediterranean. (*Ministry of Defence photograph*)

Mutual deterrence: The nuclear powered fleet ballistic missile submarine USS *George Washington Carver* under way in the Atlantic. The first of the United States 41 Polaris boats went on patrol in November 1960. (*US Navy photograph*)

The equivalent Soviet Y class probably became operational in 1968. The missile shown breaking the surface may have been fired from one of these boats. This photograph of it was released in 1967. The submarine on the surface observing the test is a conventional diesel boat converted to carry cruise missiles on deck. (*Express photograph*)

The American aircraft carrier *John F Kennedy*, escorted by the cruiser *Little Rock*, is shadowed by a Soviet Kynda class light cruiser. The Russian vessel's surface-to-surface cruise missiles can be seen on deck fore and aft, housed in a row of big cylindrical tanks. (*US Navy photograph*)

A Soviet Z class diesel submarine; a large ocean going type capable of laying mines as well as firing torpedoes. (*Ministry of Defence photograph*)

The Soviet helicopter carrier *Moskva* refuelling at sea, watched by the British frigate HMS *Undaunted*. (*Ministry of Defence photograph*)

A Kotlin class destroyer passing close under the stern of HMS *Ark Royal* as she shadows the British aircraft carrier in the eastern Mediterranean. A few hours later the Russian vessel cut it too fine and two of her sailors were flung overboard and drowned as the ships collided. (*Ministry of Defence photograph*)

A Soviet Kotlin class guided missile destroyer taking on fuel at sea from one of the fleet of auxiliaries which now enable Russian warships to cruise throughout the world, independent of foreign bases. Note that the ships are steaming in line astern rather than side by side, as is the practice in the more experienced US and Royal navies. (*Ministry of Defence photograph*)

A Riga class light destroyer, of which about fifty were built, some of them later being transferred to other navies. (*US Navy Photograph*)

In any case the picture is much less satisfactory from a British point of view if one excludes bulk cargoes of timber, ores and oil, and considers only the more lucrative general cargoes consisting mainly of manufactured goods. Here the UK share between 1965 and 1967 came to no more than 9 per cent – and it fell away even further in 1968, to 5 per cent. This type of cargo is typically shipped in small consignments by scheduled cargo liner services, for example between London and Leningrad. A British stake in the Baltic liner trade is nominally secured by a fifty-fifty tonnage pooling agreement with the Russians, but it is noticeable that when extra ships have to be put on the berth they always seem to carry the sign of the hammer and sickle.

Another statistical comparison worth making is between the rate of growth of the USSR's seaborne trade and that of its merchant fleet, in deadweight tons.

| | Soviet seaborne trade | | Soviet merchant fleet | |
	million tons	index	million tons dwt.	index
1961	59	100	5.3	100
1963	76	129	7.0	133
1965	92	156	9.6 (8.6)	181 (162)
1967	109	185	10.4 (10.0)	196 (189)

Source: Soviet trade statistics, the US Maritime Administration and – for the figures in brackets – V. Bakayev's *Soviet Ships on World Sea Routes*. The American series, shown for all four years, includes cargo/passenger tonnage but this could not completely account for the divergence from Bakayev's figures, which are defined as the 'transport' fleet in a context that implies cargo transport.

These indices would appear to show that Soviet shipping capacity kept only slightly ahead of trade growth even during its period of most rapid expansion, although a more accurate ton/mileage comparison might show a rather different picture. However, the most important aspect of the Soviet fleet's growth from a British shipowner's point of view is likely to be its impact on what for the Russians are cross trades – from the Far East to UK and continental ports, for example, or from West Africa to Europe.

To take a specific instance referred to earlier, a Soviet vessel carrying arms or supplies to North Vietnam from the Black Sea might prefer to pick up the occasional homeward cargo at well below liner conference rates rather than return in ballast.

The point about Soviet seaborne trade as a whole is that it shows a permanent and heavy bias towards exports. And as Philip Hanson has shown[6] the same bias exists in each of the Soviet Union's main shipping 'basins' – the Baltic, Black Sea, Far East and so on.

The imbalance of Soviet seaborne trade

	million tons Total seaborne trade	Exports	Imports	Exports minus Imports
1960	44.7	38.8	5.9	32.9
1961	58.5	51.2	7.3	43.9
1962	66.9	60.0	6.9	53.1
1963	75.6	66.7	8.9	57.8
1964	83.7	71.5	12.2	59.3
1965	91.8	79.1	12.7	66.4
1966	102.7	90.3	12.4	77.9
1967	108.8	98.5	10.3	88.2

Source: Soviet trade statistics

Every deep sea shipowner tries to move his vessels round the world so as to have as few ballast voyages as possible, but the Russian fleet planners have a peculiarly difficult task in this respect. Looked at from a British shipowner's viewpoint – and even more so from that of a Norwegian or Greek owner – Soviet fleet expansion to meet the requirements of a lopsided and wider ranging trade has an ominous built-in tendency to create cross trading capacity.

Another peculiarity of Russian shipping – the fact that many of its own ports are icebound in winter – makes additional tonnage available for part of the year. *Sovfrakht* is particularly

[6] In a paper presented to the LSE conference on Soviet Trade and Technology.

proud of the increasing employment it has found for its ice-strengthened freighters on the winter run between Europe and the St Lawrence. The first Soviet vessels appeared on the route five years ago and by 1970 they were calling at Montreal more than once a week during the coldest part of the year. On three occasions a Russian captain has won the trophy presented to the first ship to reach the Canadian port in the New Year.

A basic policy decision to move out into the cross trades, as illustrated by the Canadian service, seems to have been taken in 1964. The Soviet lines' efforts since then are reflected in the tonnages of foreign chaters quoted in the table earlier. The trades now include ore from the Indian Ocean to the Adriatic, steel from Japan to Europe, copra from Indonesia to Europe and grain from Mexico, Brazil and Argentina to Europe.

In the early days the Russians were handicapped by Western businessmen's fear that Communists simply could not be trusted to fulfil a contract, particularly if it involved some additional verbal understanding. These doubts have largely been dispelled, although they have left a good deal of resentment on the Soviet side. European shippers and shipowners generally seem to accept that Communist lines have commercial objectives of their own, albeit different from those of their private enterprise competitors: but this does not prevent shipowners from using every weapon they can lay hands on to combat Russian infiltration of their organizations and markets.

The first big issue of this kind was Soviet membership of London's Baltic Exchange, on which much of the world's shipping is chartered. When the Russians' first approaches were rebuffed they went off feeling angry and humiliated, determined to bypass the Exchange wherever possible. At least this was the Soviet shipping Minister's own reaction, according to a graphic account of the affair he gave at a press conference in London later: 'I told this Government official "If that is the way they treat me, I can do the same to them. Cancel all business with the Baltic Exchange. If they don't want to take any more of those millions of pounds of sterling, I will find another market. So let them suffer for it!" – and that is exactly what happened.'

Whether or not this histrionic outburst occurred quite as Bakayev described it, his tactics eventually persuaded the Baltic to elect a Russian representative. On the same occasion, in September 1965, he argued that the West had only itself to blame if it was worried by the expansion of Soviet shipping. The USSR was the victim of blockades and blacklists (an obvious reference to the United States, although she was not named), and was no longer prepared to beg for tonnage from other nations to carry her growing external trade.

'I can assure you', he went on, 'that if there were no discrimination against us we would give it another thought before embarking on this build-up of the merchant navy.' It would be cheaper and simpler to hire British ships. He had thought of inviting the instigators of the blacklist policy to a party, to thank them for helping him make out a case for a large Soviet fleet.

The policy to which he refers prohibits vessels which have traded to Cuba, North Vietnam or China from bunkering in United States ports for a specified period. Those trading to Cuba and North Vietnam also cease to be eligible to carry American Government aid cargoes, 50 per cent of which are in any case reserved for US ships.

Finally Bakayev discussed an issue of crucial importance to such nations as Norway, Greece and Britain, which hire out a lot of shipping to the rest of the world to balance their national trading accounts with 'invisible' earnings; namely whether the USSR's fifty-fifty agreements with its trading partners would exclude the freelance shipowner from a third nation. The answer seemed quite clear. The Russian Minister accepted that a maritime nation like Britain could not accept such discrimination and promised that the Soviet Union would support participation by third countries whenever it made shipping arrangements.

Again, the words are reassuring, but British shipowners are not yet convinced. They continue to fear that when she has the opportunity, the USSR will simply carve up the trade between her own fleet and that of the country with whom she is bargaining. As evidence of this tendency they cite the Soviet-Indian agreement of 1956 which established a cargo liner service be-

tween Bombay/Calcutta and Odessa/Novorossiisk: each government nominated six ships, and rates for a wide range of general
cargoes were agreed.

I have no doubt that British fears will be justified to some
extent. It is inconceivable that the Russians should take no
advantage of their increasingly powerful position; and in a sense
their attitude parallels that of the European conferences, which
accept in principle that the new national fleets of the developing
nations should have a stake in their own trade – but not too big
a stake. The most that the freelance shipowner can expect from
either the Soviet or the us Government is that they will exercise
reasonable restraint in disrupting an economically sound system
of international freight services for political ends.

For the moment at any rate, formal tonnage pooling agreements between Soviet and foreign lines account for only a small
amount of cargo. Eleven 'joint lines' are currently in operation,
including the Egyptian, British and Indian services to which I
have already referred. According to Soviet statistics, the total
cargo handled in 1967 was about 1.2 million tons.

Joint cargo liner services – 1967

Participants	Thousand tons carried
USSR – India ⎫ USSR – Ceylon ⎭	450
USSR – Bulgaria	276
USSR – Japan	156
USSR – Egypt	77
USSR – UK	75
USSR – West Germany	63
USSR – East Germany	47
USSR – Belgium	40
USSR – Holland	35
USSR – France	29

Source: V. Bakayev, *Soviet Ships on World Sea Routes*

By far the most important Soviet initiative as far as the world
shipping establishment is concerned has been the Russians'

deliberate infiltration of the Western rate-fixing conferences. It has produced the first big public clash between capitalist and Communist lines, and has shown the Russians at their most aggressive. Yet at the same time it has left European shipowners wondering whether their original fears – as exemplified in the statement by the International Chamber of Shipping quoted earlier – were entirely justified. For although the Communists have pilloried the conferences in UNCTAD for their alleged exploitation of the developing countries, in the Canadian and Australian trades they have been eager to join the capitalist club. And having become members, they seem quite prepared so far to stick to the rules and get on with maximizing their profits like everyone else.

The bewildered editor of the Australian Communist newspaper *Tribune* reproached senior officials of the Soviet shipping ministry in Moscow for reaching a compromise with the conferences, only to be told that such working agreements were inevitable within the policy of peaceful coexistence. The Russians explained, he reported in the issue of November 19, 1969, that irrespective of capitalist profit motivation the two conferences involved were 'the most highly sophisticated shipping complex in the world'. They enjoyed the official protection of the Australian Government, and to continue the Soviet challenge would have been to collide headlong with the Government. If one built a big merchant fleet, it had to be used without incurring avoidable losses. Agreement meant 'a total saving of work in world society', and would incidentally enable the Soviet Union to buy more Australian goods.

The first conferences to accept a Russian member – the Baltic Steamship Company – were those controlling the east- and westbound passenger services on the North Atlantic, with headquarters respectively in New York and Folkestone, England. It took place in September 1965, at a time when Cunard still operated a big passenger fleet, including the *Queen Elizabeth* and *Queen Mary*, in competition with United States Lines and Canadian Pacific. The conferences' primary function is to fix fares for various classes of accommodation, and Baltic Steamship's application was in preparation for the opening in the following year of its Leningrad–London–Montreal service with the newly built 19,000 ton *Aleksandr Pushkin*.

In November 1965 Baltic Steamship was accepted as a member of BIMCO (Baltic and International Maritime Conference), four years after it first applied. BIMCO, which has its headquarters in Copenhagen and represents something like one-third of the world's merchant tonnage, is not a conference in the usual sense. It is a trade association for the exchange of technical and commercial information which also arbitrates in disputes involving charter parties, bills of lading and other agreements.

Then in 1969, after months of commercial skirmishing, the Russians achieved three of their objectives in rapid succession. In January, the Baltic Steamship Company was accepted as a member of the outward and homeward bound freight conferences between Europe and Australia; in March, the Black Sea Steamship Company became a member of the east- and west-bound freight conferences serving routes between Canada and Mediterranean; and in October, the Baltic Steamship Company joined the New Zealand to Europe conference.

On top of all this, the Russians had, by December, opened negotiations with the Europe–South America conferences.

In the Australian trade the skirmishing nearly developed into a full-scale rate-cutting battle. The way in which a compromise was eventually reached is worth considering in some detail both as a case study in Soviet commercial tactics and because this is likely to be only the first of many similar clashes.

For some years before the Russians approached the conference with their request for 'cooperation' in the summer of 1968, they had used the Western shipowners' service to carry part of their wool imports from Australia. Soviet vessels were only used if they happened to be suitably placed, which often meant dropping down from Haiphong after delivering a cargo of military supplies to the North Vietnamese. To avoid embarrassing the Australian Government, whose troops were fighting in Vietnam, the Russians shrewdly diverted ships from the Cuba-Japan sugar trade instead once they began negotiating with the conferences. But there was nothing pussy-footed about their opening proposal. This was for twenty-four Russian sailings in each direction, far more than they needed for their wool imports, which were not balanced by Soviet exports to Australia. According to the London chairman of the conference lines, Mr W. R. Russell, it was backed by an open threat that the Russians 'had unlimited funds and would be prepared to go to any lengths to obtain their objective'.

When a Soviet delegation arrived in London several weeks later they adopted an even tougher line, saying that they now intended to operate thirty-six sailings in each direction. 'The conference lines were therefore being asked to "cooperate" by handing over more than 25 per cent of the outward trade from Europe to Australia – despite the fact that exports of Russian goods to Australia were virtually nil.'[7] Again they were told that their proposals were unacceptable, but a conference delegation agreed to continue negotiations in Moscow.

At this point the shipowners claim they encountered unexpected difficulties obtaining visas. The Russians seem to think they were just stalling, but in the event it made no difference either way because the invasion of Czechoslovakia intervened. Negotiations were resumed some months later, but in the meantime the Soviet side showed that it meant business by signing up five major wool importers – the English firms Sir James Hill and Sons, and Woolcombers, and the continental firms Kreglingers, Prouvost Lefèbvre and Vanlaine – at rates reported to be $7\frac{1}{2}$–15 per cent below the conference level.

Australian shippers, however, remained loyal to the conferences, in spite of their continual grumbling about freight rates. So when the first Russian ship, the *Karachayevo Cherkessia*, started loading in Brisbane, the Australian Government came under pressure to do something about the Communist threat, or at least about those ships which continued to ballast down from North Vietnam. But the Minister of Shipping and Transport, Mr Sinclair, argued that Australia was a signatory to a 1923 treaty calling for the free use of ports by international merchant

[7] Mr W. R. Russell's statement to the Press, November 6, 1968.

shipping – even though the USSR was not – and as such she could not ban the Russians. In any case, he added, only one in six Soviet ships was coming from Haiphong.

Some union leaders tried to organize a boycott in protest against the Czechoslovakian invasion. But this also fizzled out and the shipowners were left to sort the problem out for themselves – which they proved quite capable of doing.

Under the agreement reached in January 1969, the Russian share of the trade was approximately related to the amount of Soviet wool imports, as the conferences had always maintained it should be. But of course the Russians ships now had the benefit of outward bound cargo from Europe they would otherwise have had to fight for as outsiders. It was arranged that Baltic Steamship should have the right to twelve sailings from Australia, four of which would serve Soviet ports only. From Europe, the Russian line would have nine sailings, but three of these would lift cargo from the Baltic only.

The Russians put on some of their smartest new tonnage and did their best to create a good impression. At first they seem to have suspected that they were being discriminated against within the conference organization, but a reasonable working relationship appears to have been established, the fundamental point of which is that they combine with the other members to charge and defend an agreed tariff of freight rates.

The British shipping industry, represented in this trade by great names like P & O, Blue Funnel and Port Line, greeted the settlement with a general sigh of relief. The president of the Chamber of Shipping, Lord Geddes, who had previously talked gloomily of the 'long, dark shadow' cast by the Soviet fleet, admitted that he was most encouraged. It showed, he said, that Russian and Western shipping could after all exist side by side in harmony.

On March 15, 1969, *Izvestia* produced its own summing up of the confrontation: 'Discrimination against the Soviet Union is a hopeless enterprise these days. It is good that the Australian conferences have understood this at last. Still better, it is also understood by other representatives of Western shipping organizations. Our planet is a large one and on its seas and oceans there will be found work for the peaceful fleets of all countries.'

Just over a year later came the first moves in what promised to be an even more fascinating confrontation, in the trans-Pacific trade. The Far Eastern Steamship Company of Vladivostok announced plans for the first regular Soviet shipping service to the United States in twenty years. But this time the Russians had to deal not only with an established conference of American and other Western lines, but also with a governmental regulatory authority, the us Federal Maritime Commission. In principle, they could not object, although they had in the past attacked the Commissions' policy under the Bonner Act for helping to bring the USA 'notorious fame as supporters of discriminatory measures in shipping'.[8]

In April the Soviet line applied to operate three cargo liners between Japanese and American North Pacific ports. A few weeks later Mrs Helen Bentley, the Commission's chairman, told the Senate committee on commerce that the proposed tariff had been thoroughly investigated and the Russian rates were found to be 13–47 per cent below the conference level. However, she had to admit that 'they do not seem to be lower than other independent operators on the route'.[9]

In other words it was going to be difficult to claim, in the words of the Bonner Act, that the Russian rates were 'so unreasonably high or low as to be detrimental to the commerce of the United States'. It might have been suggested that since there were already 28 other independent operators there was no room for another competitor, but this was not an argument the Commission could respectably use since it is supposed to uphold the principle of free access to the us trades. The application was rejected, but apparently on purely technical grounds.

Mrs Bentley's staff pointed out that the Far Eastern Steamship Company proposed to settle claims in the USSR, which would be contrary to us law. The bill of lading liability was only $110 instead of the $500 minimum required by the us Carriage of

[8] V. Bakayev, *Za Rubezhom*, October 24, 1964.
[9] *Liverpool Journal of Commerce*, May 30, 1970.

Goods by Sea Act. A full record of the Soviet line's organization and operation had not been provided. Neither the service nor the rates were fully defined. An approved inland carrier had not been identified in connection with overland rates and, finally, abbreviations used by the Russians were not explained.

At the time of writing it remains to be seen how long these irregularities in the application – the first of which is potentially of great importance but the last no more than a bureaucratic quibble – will delay the start of a Soviet service. Yet even a temporary delay is significant. As the *Journal of Commerce* commented in the editorial accompanying one of its reports: 'The Americans have been as concerned as the British, perhaps more so, over the growth of Russian maritime activities. But as we have noted on a previous occasion, the American maritime laws which are anathema to so many European shipping men are the same laws which can be used by the Americans to prevent disruption of their trade should the Russians ever decide to use their ships as political weapons.'

In fact British shipowners had already taken the point, except that they were more concerned about flag discrimination against themselves – particularly by some of the South American governments – than about keeping the Russians out. By the time they came to give evidence to the Rochdale Committee of Inquiry – which published its report as a Government White Paper in May 1970 – the Chamber of Shipping reluctantly suggested that the British Government should take reserve powers to retaliate against countries which discriminated in favour of their own flag on a large scale.

The Rochdale Committee made no clear recommendation to this effect, but its report did produce an intriguing echo of Bakayev's thinking on the regulation of the conference system in recommending the establishment of a code of conduct, which might eventually be embodied in an international treaty:

From our consideration of the international problems now surrounding the operation of shipping services . . . we have reached the conclusion that a multilateral inter-governmental agreement on shipping will increasingly be seen as desirable by all concerned with the future efficiency and prosperity of shipping. The type of agreement we have in mind would be one which established an agreed code of principles within which governments should develop their national shipping policies and which provided for regular consultation on the practical operation of the code. We consider such an agreement should embody the most favoured nation principle, a general prohibition of flag discrimination in international trading and provisions designed to curtail operations under flags of convenience.

Another trade in which it began to look as if the Australian pattern would be repeated – competitive rate-cutting followed by an attempt to break into the conference – was the Malayan rubber trade to Europe. This followed a dispute between the Far Eastern Freight Conference (including British, Continental, Scandinavian and Japanese lines) and the rubber shippers in Malaysia and Singapore. Many of the shippers refused to sign a new contract with the conference and at the height of the argument, early in 1969, the Soviet shipping agency in Singapore intervened with an offer to lift other people's cargoes of rubber as well as its own.

During February and April three Soviet vessels loaded in Singapore at rates reported to be about 25 per cent below the conference level – about the same as two other communist 'outsiders' already operating on the European route, the East Germans and the Bulgarians. But a fourth ship advertised by the Soviet agency never turned up (one rumour had it she was already full of manioc loaded in Bangkok) and when the two sides in the 'rubber row' managed to settle at least their public differences, the Russians called off the challenge. From the start, their long-term objective had probably been membership of the conference, but they apparently decided that in this case discreet negotiation was more likely to get results than loud-mouthed bullying.

In a way it is surprising the Soviet lines have not made more use of ships ballasting back from North Vietnam, many of which evidently bunker in Singapore. Perhaps they felt it would be politically embarrassing (as it certainly was in the Australian trade) or that generally they find it convenient to keep war supply operations separate from normal commercial traffic. None of the three vessels which intervened in the rubber trade arrived in Singapore from Haiphong.

The next obvious source of tension in the Australian trade is the conversion from conventional tonnage to container ships. By 1972 the Western lines should have fourteen 30,000 tonners on the UK/Continent–Australia route, each carrying about 1,300 containers at 22 knots. The Russians decided that their first deep sea container vessel should also operate in this service, probably using Hamburg as its European terminal. And understandably, since they wanted their representative to be fully competitive, her speed and size were to be closely matched to the rest of the fleet.

The trouble, as the conference pointed out, is that one big, fast container ship can do the work of a fleet of conventional cargo liners: if the Baltic Steamship Company simply operates a single vessel throughout the year, and withdraws its conventional tonnage, it nevertheless increases its share of total conference capacity by a substantial amount. And the Soviet line's fellow members claim the trade cannot stand a fifteenth container ship anyway.

The Russians were obviously not going to be deterred by the prospect of getting a bigger slice of the conference cake. But at the time of writing they are considering a proposal from their Western colleagues that they might do better both for themselves and the other lines by building a roll-on, roll-off, ship which could take vehicles as well as the standard containers.

Whatever the result of this particular argument, the Soviet planners clearly regard the use of containers and pallets as a major line of development. Bakayev forecast in 1969 that by the mid-1970s four to five times as much cargo would be carried by these methods. However, since in the previous year the Black Sea fleet moved only 12,500 tons of cargo in containers this may not mean much.

One reason for the slow start is said to be the difficulty of establishing an integrated service that involves interdepartmental cooperation between sea, road and rail transport – an ironic illustration of the conservative, bureaucratic nature of the centralized Soviet system. One of the Russians' major objectives is evidently to establish the Transiberian Railway as a link in the large-scale movement of container traffic between the UK, Europe and the Far East – in competition with Western shipping services. Some containers are already moving along this 'land bridge', and at the end of 1969 plans were announced for providing a sea shuttle service between the port of Nakhodka, at the eastern end of the railway, and Japan. The new port complex being built with Japanese assistance near Nakhodka is reported to be designed to handle 120,000–140,000 containers a year. At the western end there is an awkward change of railway gauge, and one wonders how much guaranteed spare capacity there can be on the Transiberian Railway itself.

For the moment, anyway, the Poles and the East Germans seem to be setting the pace in container development among the Communist fleets. The East German line Deutsche Seerederei (DSR), with a terminal at Rostock, is building a fleet of twenty ice-strengthened coastal container ships, each carrying 34 containers or 100 cars, and has already opened a full container service to London's Tilbury docks. In a discussion of deep sea container development, the East German weekly *Seewirtschaft* suggested that routes from Europe to South America and East Asia would be suitable for this type of ship by the late 1970s. The article said that DSR's 'partners in cooperation', presumably meaning the Poles and the Russians, would also be interested.

Polish shipping circles have certainly argued that the best way to reduce the risks and spread the investment would be to form container consortia with other Comecon countries on particular routes – while not neglecting to put in a plug for the use of their own ports as terminals. The construction of Poland's first container ship was reported in the spring of 1969. She was said to be a 12,000 tonner which at 23 knots would be the fastest ship ever built in a Polish yard. However, the five identical vessels included in Fairplay's *World Ships on Order* in February 1970 were 13,000 tonners, carrying 700 containers at 22 knots.

As for the Russians, they welcome any development which

helps to cement Comecon into a more solid economic and political bloc, and where conventional shipping is concerned, cooperation has already reached the point at which for some purposes the combined Comecon fleets must be considered as a unit.

Between them they operate about a dozen joint cargo liner services. Among the most important is the Baltic–Cuba line provided by a mixture of Soviet, Polish and East German ships. Another is the 'Baltafrica' service operated jointly by DSR and Polish Ocean Lines. This partnership caused a tremendous stir in British shipping circles in 1969 by capturing nearly the whole of the United Kingdom's coffee imports from East Africa for the coming year. They were reported to have offered cuts of 20–25 per cent on the British conference lines' rate. The major importers, Nestlés, Lyons and Maxwell House, jumped at the chance to reduce their costs, and there was a cordial exchange of liquor and speeches when the MV *Wilhelm Florin* docked at Tilbury with the first cargo. The senior DSR representative, Mr H. J. Lassen, denied that the rates quoted by the Communist lines amounted to undercutting: 'Baltafrica do not undercut freight rates. In fact, we have restricted ourselves to the internationally accepted outsider rebate and worked for stability of freight charges. Baltafrica has contributed to this in that a continuous rise in the East African freight charges has been prevented and we have, in our opinion, thus supported the economic policy of the East African countries as well as the interests of the shippers.'

By the beginning of 1969, the combined deadweight tonnage of the East European fleets was more than four millions – and growing fast.

Combining these figures with the planned growth in the Russian fleet it can be seen that by the mid-1970s the Soviet bloc as a whole will be able to deploy 26–28 million deadweight tons of shipping. To a large extent the satellite fleets in this great Communist armada share the objectives of the USSR's Ministry of the Merchant Marine: to minimize their countries' dependence on Western shipping and then get out on the world's cross trade routes to earn foreign exchange. It is true that the animosities resulting from post-war subjugation are still alive and that new rivalries are bound to appear. But if the Kremlin has its way, they will be of little consolation to the capitalist shipowner.

The East European fleets

	million tons dwt.
Poland	1.7 (3.5–4.0 in 1975)
East Germany	1.1
Bulgaria	0.9 (2.5 in 1975)
Romania	0.5 (1.0 in 1973)
Total	4.2

Source: Various official statements

Fears that Soviet merchant shipping poses a threat, and not merely a challenge, to Western shipowners, are usually based on three facts. In the first place, the Russian fleet has been growing at the rate of about a million tons deadweight a year and will continue to expand at something like this rate throughout the 1970s. Secondly, it is state-owned, centrally directed, and to an increasing extent co-ordinates its activity with the other members of Comecon. And finally there have recently been examples – Australian wool, East African coffee, Malayan rubber and some of the South American and North Pacific trades – of determined rate bargaining by Communist lines to secure cargoes and/or eventual membership of a conference.

In trying to put these fears into perspective one must first tone down some of the lurid colours in which the picture is often painted, particularly by American commentators. To begin with it is sometimes forgotten that since the Norwegians, Japanese, Greeks and others have also been building fast throughout the 1960s, the Soviet fleet still represents only six per cent of the world's merchant tonnage.

Secondly, the Russians are not seriously competing with Western shipowners in the construction of large tankers, large bulk carriers or container ships. This is the result of various factors, including a large number of shallow ports, the need for operational flexibility, comparative commercial isolation and technical inexperience. The absence of large bulk carriers and tankers is particularly reassuring to freelance shipowners like the Norwegians, who specialize in these types.

Thirdly, the political nature of the Soviet fleet's central organization does not always work to Western competitors' disadvantage. A whole range of unpredictable demands may be made on its tonnage – arms shipments to the Middle East, aid cargoes to Africa, naval support – and in some cases such traffic may be established as a 'sea bridge', permanently absorbing capacity to support Cuba, Egypt or North Vietnam.

Fourthly, the Russians are cautious as well as suspicious, conservative as well as communist, and often show a remarkable concern to acquire commercial respectability. In spite of their attacks on the conferences for 'exploiting' the developing nations, they show signs of aspiring to membership wherever possible. In the most important instance in which they already have membership, they in fact settled for something approximating to their own wool trade, in spite of the loud bullying noises they made beforehand; and in the Malayan rubber trade there has so far been a similar discrepancy between words and action.

Finally, the Russians are natural bureaucrats. They are scrupulous about sticking to the terms of any formal contract they sign, and when they join a commercial or technical organization they follow the rules. (Not that this prevents them working the rules to their own advantage, any more than pedantic adherence to Communist Party procedure prevents them eliminating a Khrushchev or a Dubček; it will be fascinating to see them matched against the US Federal Maritime Commission.)

The trouble is, of course, that these same factors can be looked at from the opposite point of view. For example the arbitrary – in commercial terms – nature of the Soviet operation may well lead to trades being carved up at governmental level. Ships diverted on to the North Vietnamese supply routes may have nothing to lose by picking up a cheap cargo.

Equally, the USSR's 6 per cent of world tonnage looks much

more menacing when one realizes that for some purposes it is as if a single Western shipping group owned a fleet of this size: for example, when the Soviet negotiators confronted the Australian conferences, they were able to point out that Baltic Steamship's application was backed by 'unlimited funds'. Although the efficiency of a particular operation may be hampered by the need to maintain a flexible fleet, the Russians have the resources to build for any specialized requirement that justifies itself. And once they decide that a project is worthwhile – such as North Atlantic passenger operations to earn foreign currency – they will not easily be deterred by its being unprofitable in the conventional Western sense.

In general the Soviet Ministry of the Merchant Marine prides itself on taking the long view, on judging shipping by its contribution to the economic and political efficiency of the country as a whole. The immediate effect on an individual Western shipowner may be that he is confronted by a deliberate policy of subsidy. In the same way, the ostentatiously 'reciprocal' nature of a shipping agreement with one of the Soviet Union's trading partners is of little consolation to third nations if they are excluded.

In any case reciprocity should be accepted as a general principle, not merely as the response to somebody else's bargaining power. Is it ever likely to be worthwhile, for example, for foreign shipping agencies, banks or insurance companies to set up shop in Russian ports and cities, as Soviet organizations increasingly do in the West? And if it was, would they be allowed to do so?

In Britain the Russians are represented by the Anglo-Soviet Steamship Company, a member of the Baltic Exchange. A Belgian-Soviet shipbroking firm called Transworld Marine opened in Antwerp at the beginning of 1970. In Singapore, a Soviet shipping agency has been in operation for some time, and negotiations are currently under way to establish joint shareholding companies in Japan and Canada.

The point, of course, is that commercial relations with the Russians can never be fully reciprocal so long as Western firms are confronted with a set of customers who are really no more than the Soviet Government in different disguises. Imagine a British tramp owner going behind *Sovfrakht*'s back to sign up with *Exportliess* for the summer timber shipments out of Igarka; or a Greek cruise operator persuading the Russian miners' union to patronize his cut-rate holiday trips from Odessa. Yet the Russian liner *Aleksandr Pushkin* is now regularly cruising out of British ports during the winter, and her sister ship from the Black Sea, the *Shota Rustaveli*, has been able to step in and take charter work to Australia in free competition with British ships.

Returning to the basic question of whether the Russian merchant fleet represents a threat or a challenge, there is no doubt that the Russians are prepared to use threatening words – the merchant fleet is intended 'to contribute extensively to the economic competition between the Socialist and capitalist countries' – yet so far the words have usually been accompanied by restrained and reasonable action. Even where other shipowners complained that the Communist tactics were unfair, there have usually been shippers to welcome the new competition, if only as a lever with which to put pressure on the established lines.

But it is still too early to assume that the Soviet administration will never cultivate freight 'wars' purely for political ends. It has already used its membership of UNCTAD to exploit Asian and African suspicions of the European conferences, and the Europeans' resentment of American interference. All we know at the moment is that if serious disruption of Western shipping is an objective, the Russians intend to get themselves well dug in before they open hostilities. In the meantime, closer integration with the capitalist structure makes it increasingly difficult for them to lash out without getting hurt themselves.

Such integration should therefore be encouraged, provided of course that the terms continue to be reasonable. British shipowners should do less complaining about the Russians as newcomers, which merely puts their backs up, and indulge in more positive public propaganda on their own behalf. The inconsistencies in Soviet maritime policy – such as criticizing

147

American restrictions on aid cargoes while making similar arrangements themselves, or joining conferences while at the same time branding them for their capitalist 'exploitation' – should be persistently exposed, in public speeches as well as in the corridors of UNCTAD and the dining rooms of the Chamber of Shipping. Above all, the Russians should never be allowed to take for granted the commercial and personal freedom they enjoy in European, if not in American ports.

CHAPTER 9

Oceanography and Fish – and Submarines

One might have expected the Russians to at least hesitate when they came up against the full implications of becoming a world sea power: yet in fact they have shown a consistency and an attention to fundamentals which must send a chill down the spine of a Pentagon analyst. They have shown that for all its clumsiness, communist planning has its points when it comes to launching a national effort of this kind.

The unique feature of Soviet expansion is the way in which it ranges across the whole spectrum of sea power, from icebreaking tactics, through fishing, to commercial cargo operations and submarine missilry. And in the background is a massive programme of oceanography.

This increasingly important science is really an assembly of other scientific disciplines – mathematics, physics, chemistry, biology, geology, hydrography, meteorology and engineering – in so far as they can be applied to the study of the oceans and the seabed. The exploration of this watery world is less glamorous than travelling through space, but the oceans' immense potential as a source of food and minerals, apart from their military importance, may make it much the more useful of the two activities.

For many people, it was the International Geophysical Year of 1957/58 which made it clear that the Russians were on the move in oceanography. They mounted a bigger oceanographic programme than anyone else on that occasion and have been steadily forging ahead ever since. Having overhauled the British, French and Japanese, the scale of their effort is now comparable to that of the United States, and in some respects surpasses it. For example, the Soviet oceanographic research fleet had grown to the same size as the American fleet by 1964, and in tonnage terms is now about 50 per cent bigger.

For this sort of work vessels are often converted from other types. But ideally they should be purpose-built, to accommodate the elaborate winching systems needed to anchor in perhaps 4,000 fathoms of water, and to lower instruments or collect material from the seabed. The catamaran hull form, as used in at least one American oceanographic vessel, may prove to be just the job.

For naval research, where underwater acoustics is the most important element, an oceanographic ship should also be able to keep station almost silently when the water is too deep even for her to anchor. But the most exotic vessel in the US Navy's research fleet is the *Flip*, a 300 foot long craft which rides in the normal horizontal fashion until she starts work, when she upends herself leaving only the bows – if that is the right word – sticking out of the sea. It must be an eerie experience to serve on a ship so vividly reminiscent of those grotesque wartime pictures of torpedoed freighters just about to slide under the waves.

An example of current Soviet design is the 7,000 ton *Akademik Vernadsky*, a hydrographic research ship which made her first voyage in 1969. She has a crew of 95 in addition to 66 scientists manning 28 laboratories. A radio receiver on board collects data relayed from buoys dangling various measuring instruments under water. The information is then processed in a computer. The ship's winches can lower instruments weighing up to three tons to depths of more than 11,000 metres and her anchor cable is nine miles long. The Russians now operate something like two hundred research vessels and, provided the interdepartmental priority can be established, they can call on the help of a state-owned merchant marine and fishing fleet.

There are well over 2,000 qualified oceanographers in the Soviet Union, perhaps twice as many as in the United States. Taking the marine sciences as a whole, an American congressional delegation to the USSR estimated that even in 1966 there were 8,000–9,000 Russians working full time in this field, compared with 3,000 in the United States.[1] These figures have been questioned, but assuming some disparity existed then it can hardly have diminished, since the Russians are reported to be training five times as many students in marine subjects as the Americans.

If one turns from statistics to an expert personal assessment, Rear Admiral Waters, writing in the 1969 edition of the *US Naval Review*, sums it up in this way: 'Comparing efforts and achievements in oceanography, the United States and the Soviet Union are about equal.' The Admiral believed his country was ahead in the naval applications of oceanography and would stay ahead, but even here he saw no cause for complacency on the Americans' part.

The most chauvinistic of American observers would hardly deny Russian supremacy in the field of polar research, for which the Soviet Union has many obvious applications. It is equally natural, though nonetheless impressive as evidence of a systematic approach, that the Russians should mount a massive programme of applied research in support of their rapidly expanding fishing industry, though less attention seems to have been paid to basic research in marine biology, compared with the American programme. In the same way, the emphasis in Soviet ocean geology has been on work which might obviously yield practical results, such as offshore oil drilling in the Caspian and the Arctic, and the search for recoverable ores on the seabed. The congressional delegation referred to above noted this comparative neglect of pure research but found evidence – in the recently increased budget, and the greater freedom granted to the Institute for Oceanology in Moscow, for example – that the Russians saw the need to establish a wider base for their long term effort.

Other areas in which the American programme has been comparatively strong are ocean engineering – on which serious exploitation of the seabed must depend – instrumentation, laboratory facilities ashore, and that strange adjunct of modern

[1] *The Soviets and the Seas*, us House of Representatives Report No 1809, 1966.

science for which the Americans seem to have a unique enthusiasm, data handling.

The Russians may have large numbers of oceanographic surface ships, but only a few underwater research and recovery vehicles have so far been reported. Some of those that have appeared are similar in concept to American designs. For example the *Krab*, which has mechanical arms and television, and is controlled by cable from the surface, resembles the US Navy's CURV. The latter was built to recover torpedoes but achieved international fame – and stimulated further development – when it was used to find and attach a line to the missing nuclear bomb off Palomares, Spain, in 1966.

The Russians also operate a 25-foot deep-diving submarine *Sever II* whose performance (it can dive to 6,000 feet, has a maximum speed of six knots and carries a three-man crew) is comparable to the United States Alvin type, but seems to have been used mainly for fishery research. At least one former W class naval submarine has been converted for fishing work – an idea the Japanese also tried. The torpedo compartment has been rebuilt as a laboratory and she is fitted with portholes, searchlights and television. *Atlant I*, a towed, one-man craft which can descend to about 500 feet, is used specifically to study the operation of fishing gear and how fish react to it.

Russian experiments in living and working underwater for long periods – which in this context means up to two weeks – do not so far seem to have been as ambitious as the American 'man in the sea' programme (nor does Britain have a comparable programme, although her diving technology is of a high standard). The American 'Sealab' experiments began in 1964, tragically stimulated by the loss of the nuclear submarine *Thresher* in 8,000 feet of water off Massachusetts in April of the previous year. They involved teams of 'aquanauts' working in an artificial, pressurized atmosphere containing hardly any oxygen and frequently swimming out to work on the seabed.

One of the most fascinating subsidiary experiments was the use of a porpoise trained to respond to sound signals. It successfully delivered mail, tools and messages from the base ship at anchor on the surface to the underwater laboratory on the bottom, 200 feet down. It even carried a guideline out to an aquanaut who signalled that he was in trouble.[2] In similar experiments the French scientist Jacques Cousteau used young seals, rewarded at frequent intervals with juicy chunks of squid, to ferry samples between the seabed and his ship.

In the long run these pioneering efforts could open up a new dimension in oceanographic research, enabling man – accompanied perhaps by other mammals – to work and explore anywhere on the continental shelf, which generally slopes down to no more than about 100 fathoms. The associated techniques, such as 'saturation' diving, may well prove vital in exploiting the vast mineral resources of the oceans.

A whole range of military applications for underwater technology is also emerging. The Americans have for a long time had an array of submarine detection devices on the seabed off their eastern coastline. Their submarines may be using underwater navigational 'beacons' and it has even been suggested that nuclear submarines might have bases on the seabed.

The alarming prospect of a race between the great powers to deploy nuclear weapons on the ocean floor prompted the Geneva Disarmament Committee to try to stop this sinister form of warfare – which a few years ago might have been a subject for science fiction – before it could get started. By October 1969, the Committee had reached the stage of considering a draft treaty jointly submitted by the United States and the Soviet Union, to ban 'nuclear and other weapons of mass destruction' from the seabed.

The Soviet equivalent of the man in the sea programme seems to have centred on the Chernomor series of underwater laboratories. In 1968 *Chernomor I* spent five days 45 feet down on the bed of the Black Sea, with a five-man crew. In 1969 *Chernomor II* spent more than two weeks 80 feet down off the Caucasian town of Gelendjik. This is still a shallow dive compared with the 200 feet of *Sealab I* and *II*, but the programme director,

---

[2] For details of this and other aspects of the Sealab programme, see the article by Captain George F. Bond in the 1969 *US Naval Review*.

Professor Monin, said at the time that depths of 25–30 metres were only a transitional stage. Within the next two years they would increase to 100–150 metres.

Perhaps the most interesting feature of *Chernomor II* is that it has abandoned the 'umbilical cord' which supplies gas, water and power to the American vehicles; it is considered to be the prototype of a self-contained underwater house that could be 'mass produced'. Apart from the hull, all the parts and systems are said to be standard production items. The crew can apparently surface or submerge at will and although they would normally be connected to ship or shore by a communications cable, this can be abandoned and replaced by a radio buoy floating on the surface. In short, it seems the Russians intend to lose no time in putting the new technology to work, even at this early stage in their research programme.

The 1970 Chernomor programme was scheduled to continue biological and geological research, but at greater depths. Announcing this at a press conference, Professor Monin mentioned the possibility of cultivating a submarine 'garden', organizing dolphins to drive shoals of fish (a typical attempt to cap the American dolphins experiments) and placing two smaller laboratories near Chernomor to form an underwater 'village'.

If Soviet oceanography has weaknesses, the Russians are probably well aware of them. This is one of the fields in which they welcome exchanges with foreign scientists, and their active participation in international oceanographic organizations keeps them abreast of Western development. They have tried to buy research submarines developed by commercial concerns in the United States. New laboratories have been built and where they previously relied extensively on foreign instrumentation a wide range of Soviet designed equipment is now appearing. One of their most ingenious devices, developed by the Arctic and Antarctic Institute in Leningrad, is an automatic recorder which can be left moored beneath the ice all winter. In fact it is left under water for a whole year, measuring temperature and the direction and strength of the current. An acoustic signal then calls it to the surface, where it lies bleeping until its mother ship finds it.

In general, the speed and deliberate application of Soviet oceanographic development leave little doubt that any obvious gaps will sooner or later be filled. And the funds will apparently be there. Professor Matveitchuk, speaking at the international oceanology conference held in Brighton in 1969, forecast 'an expenditure one and a half times that of the present by the early 1970s.'[3] A big increase in expenditure is also planned by the United States. The next decade could see the race to dominate the underwater world of the oceans developing something of the national competitive spirit engendered by the space race of the 1960s. If the Americans have any sense, it will.

How much the rapid expansion of Soviet oceanography owes to its centralized direction is a fascinating question, but an extremely difficult one for an outsider to answer. At top level, the Council of Ministers has evidently been convinced that it should be given priority at a time when the Soviet Navy, merchant marine and fishing industry have successfully pressed claims for support. But at working level the research programme is divided between dozens of institutes responsible to different ministries, just as research in the United States is scattered among Federal, state, university and commercial laboratories. I would speculate that what the Russians gain in the formal establishment of national priorities is balanced by, among other things, the discipline of commercial involvement in the American programme.

A few years ago a Russian scientist commented that 'the administration of us oceanography reminds me of a contemporary abstract painting rendered by an ape'.[4] But since then a cabinet level council on marine resources and engineering development has been set up, and a commission drawing its members from government, industry and the universities has been working on plans to integrate the national effort and, in effect, to preserve American leadership in marine science and resource development.

In the Soviet Union much of the research is organized by

[3] *Guardian*, February 19, 1969.
[4] Quoted by us congressional delegation to Poland and ussr, August 1966.

institutes specifically attached to the ministries of geology, fisheries, merchant marine, education and so on. The work is co-ordinated and the results disseminated to other interested departments by a broadly based National Council for the Utilization of the Resources of the Sea. This comes under the powerful Committee for Science and Technology, which has budgetary responsibility for all large-scale research and development programmes. Basic research is co-ordinated by the Inter-agency Oceanographic Committee, under the Academy of Sciences.

Where does all this effort get the Russians?

It has already earned the respect of the international scientific community. This has in turn enabled the Soviet Union to offer welcome assistance in this field to countries like Cuba, Egypt, Greece, India and Indonesia. In 1966 the Second International Oceanographic Congress was held in the USSR.

As a financial investment it should eventually show a return in the recovery of minerals other than coal and oil from the seabed – the Russians seem to be setting the pace in dredging manganese from the bottom of the Pacific, for example[5] – and in the extraction of chemicals from the oceans themselves. The sea is not merely full of salt. It also contains millions of tons of magnesium, potassium and bromine, all of which are already being extracted. At present no more than 0.1 per cent of the world's mineral supply comes from the sea, but since the demand is expected to treble by the year 2000, there is plenty of room for the proportion to grow.

Russian work on tidal power stations looks highly relevant in the light of forecasts that the world will use three times as much energy during the next twenty years as it has in the whole of the previous 100 years. Most critical of all, the demand for food could apparently double by the end of the century, making it imperative that we catch more fish from the sea while at the same time preserving the stock.

The Soviet Union has got this message too. Much of its oceanographic work is directly geared to the needs of the

[5] Center for Strategic and International Studies report, *Soviet Sea Power.*

trawlermen. Fish already provides 20 per cent of the nation's food protein; and since the 1950s it has invested more than four thousand million dollars in the systematic expansion of an industry which it hopes will one day cease merely to hunt fish and begin instead to 'farm' them.

A Worldwide Fishing Industry

As an example of communist planning redirecting national resources and energies in the drastic manner often theoretically attributed to it, one could do worse than examine the recent history of the Soviet fishing industry.

The fact that the Soviet Navy is supported by government research establishments and is subjected to elaborate operational analysis does not distinguish it from the Royal Navy, while centralized control of the USSR's merchant marine has yet to realize its full potential. But the national campaign to expand the Russian fishing effort has already made a spectacular impact.

The resources of oceanographic research have been harnessed to the operation of co-ordinated fleets exploiting modern methods on a large scale. Preceded by their reconnaissance vessels, Soviet fishermen have ventured steadily further from their home waters, exploring traditional grounds more thoroughly than their competitors and then searching out fresh ones. In the process they have developed old ideas, such as the mother ship and the transfer of catches at sea, on a scale that makes them new. The same is to some extent true of the way in which they took up two recent British innovations, the factory trawler and the freezer trawler.

The net result has been to increase the Soviet catch from 2.6 million tons in 1958 to 6.1 million tons in 1968, setting the USSR in third place in the world league table of fishing nations, behind Peru and Japan. The planned catch in 1970 is 7.8 million tons (8.7 millions if you include whales and other marine mammals, as the Russians always do in their statistics).

This contrasts with the static record of the British industry and an American catch that has actually declined. But these comparisons alone would give an exaggerated impression of the Soviet achievement because in terms of production the American and British industries happen to be outstanding for their stagnation. In fact the Russians have done little more than keep pace with the rate of growth of the world catch, and if one compares the Soviet record with Peru's astonishing performance in the late 1950s and early 1960s it seems to show a steady, plodding progress (between 1958 and 1964 the Peruvian catch increased from 1.0 million tons to 9.1 millions).

Any comparison of the total Soviet catch must be treated with caution because with about two million miles of river, a quarter of a million lakes and two land-locked seas, the Russians naturally have important inland fisheries. Immediately after the Second World War they accounted for about 40 per cent of the country's fish supply. This proportion has fallen to more like 10 per cent, largely because of the heavy investment in deep-water fishing, but also because of difficulties in maintaining the absolute size of the inland catch.

Thus, for example, caviar may become still more of a luxury unless the Russians can reverse the damagine effects of pollution on the sturgeon. The Siberian sturgeon is said to be in danger of extinction from the untreated effluents of the new oil and gas industries flowing north to its spawning grounds. In the Caspian the situation has been aggravated by a falling water level which restricts the breeding grounds. The Soviet authorities have countered the problem by hatching millions of sturgeon fry to restock the grounds, by building purification plants – at the pulp factory on Lake Baikal, for example – and by cracking down on those industries which cause the trouble. The manager of one chemical works is reported to have been jailed for killing hundreds of thousands of small sturgeon in the local river.[6]

In spite of these difficulties the catch of freshwater fish was expected to increase fourfold between 1968 and 1970. But the basic point remains that it is the deep-sea fisheries that have been largely responsible for the Soviet Union's rising production.

[6] Report of US Congressional delegation to Poland and USSR, August 1966.

The Russian share

Year	Fish Catch – million metric tons live weight USSR	World	Soviet catch as % of World
1938	1.5	21.0	7.2
1948	1.5	19.6	7.6
1957	2.5	31.5	8.0
1958	2.6	33.2	7.9
1959	2.8	36.7	7.5
1960	3.1	40.0	7.6
1961	3.3	43.4	7.5
1962	3.6	47.0	7.7
1963	4.0	48.3	8.2
1964	4.5	52.7	8.5
1965	5.1	53.5	9.5
1966	5.4	57.3	9.3
1967	5.8	60.5	9.6
1968	6.1	64.0	9.5

Source: FAO *Yearbook of Fishery Statistics*

Catches compared

	Fish Catch – million metric tons live weight United Kingdom	United States	Soviet Union
1938	1.2	2.3	1.5
1948	1.2	2.5	1.5
1953	1.1	2.7	2.0
1958	1.0	2.7	2.6
1963	1.0	2.8	4.0
1968	1.0	2.4	6.1

Source: FAO *Yearbook of Fishery Statistics*

A Soviet fisheries journal[7] indicated in 1964 that domestic demand was 5.5–6.0 million tons, a level which production reached in 1967. But in 1968 it was admitted that in spite of the rapidly increased supply of frozen fish, neither the quantity nor the quality were satisfactory, and in 1969 the Russians were

[7] *Rybnoye Khozyaistvo*: 1964 No I, cited by Dr T. Armstrong, *Polar Record*, May 1966.

still talking about a substantial planned increase in overall fish consumption per head. Whether this level of production should be considered 'economic' is debatable to a certain point, beyond which the argument founders through lack of information.

The average British trawlerman would dismiss Russian competition as subsidized and possibly unfair. He has to reject perfectly good red soldier fish because they are not acceptable to the English housewife's conservative palate, let alone being able to count on 'planned' increases in consumption. He has to borrow capital on the open market to build an efficient new vessel instead of having investment funds allocated to him.

But what makes an operation truly uneconomic is not a different set of priorities or a different pattern of demand; it is an inefficient method of satisfying them. If the Soviet Government chooses to put a monetary value on the military or political byproducts of its fishing industry – such as a supply of experienced seamen for the navy – this becomes an element in its economics, even if one makes allowance for it in some external comparisons.

Using its own accounting system, the Ministry of Fisheries profit performance in 1967 was reported to be inferior to that of about twenty other Soviet ministries, and its half-yearly figures were 20 million roubles below the 'profit quota'.[8] But throughout the 1960s the main standard by which the Russians have judged their fishing industry must have been whether it could alleviate the national shortage of food protein more efficiently than an agricultural alternative. The indications are that catching more fish has been quicker, less unpredictable and probably cheaper in direct financial terms – even allowing for the heavy investment in ships – than rearing more cattle. In similar circumstances there would be plenty of scope for a Western commercial operator to fix high prices and pay high wages.

In fact the Soviet Union's catch has reached the point at which it is worthwhile exporting some fish. The table shows the balance of this trade and how it compares with the British and American position. While the Soviet Union's balance has

[8] *Fisheries Year Book*, 1968–69.

improved that of the United Kingdom has deteriorated, and Americans are now importing two out of every five fish they eat.

The trade in fishery commodities – *thousand metric tons*

Year	Soviet Union Catch	Imports	Exports	United States Catch	Imports	Exports	United Kingdom Catch	Imports	Exports
1958	2,620	140	30	2,700	590	70	1,000	470	50
1963	3,980	100	170	2,780	910	150	960	650	60
1967	5,780	60	320	2,380	1,230	80	1,030	900	80
1968	6,080	40	320	2,440	1,550	70	1,040	970	80

Source: FAO *Yearbook of Fishery Statistics*

In particular, Soviet vessels have landed frozen fish and fish meal in Nigeria, Ghana, and a number of other West African countries where much of it no doubt counts as part of the USSR's aid programme. Ghana and Senegal have been helped to develop their own industries; as has Egypt, where the Russians have built new fishing harbours on the Mediterranean and the Red Sea. Important fishery development aid has also gone to the communist regimes in North Vietnam and Cuba. In return for technical assistance in the construction of Havana's fish docks, Soviet fishing vessels are also serviced there. Some facilities are available in Senegal. Aid is politically valuable in so far as it creates goodwill (not that the recent arrest of two Soviet trawlers in Ghanaian waters seems to indicate too much of that), makes the recipients dependent on Russian technical advisers and may eventually lead to a profitable commercial relationship. Whatever the terms on which the first tuna ships and trawlers were supplied to Senegal, it may one day provide a welcome market for the Soviet shipbuilding industry. The following Soviet quotation from the president of a Kuwaiti fishing company – which to me shows signs of enthusiastic editing, or perhaps just Arab courtesy – indicates the sort of climate the Russians would like to develop:

We are trying to be consistent in buying Soviet-made vessels because they meet all present day shipbuilding standards. Despite short delivery terms, the seiners and trawlers we bought last year proved highly

F

seaworthy, reliable and economical. They are especially good in the conditions of the Persian Gulf. Moreover, we have a high opinion of *Sudoimport*. They are very attentive and reliable trade partners. The ships are always delivered on schedule and are of very good quality. This is why we stopped buying ships in the United States and other countries. We are planning to sign more contracts for Soviet seiners and trawlers.

An example of the way in which the Soviet Union is able to turn its oceanographic expertise to good political account is provided by the Mediterranean expedition of the fishery research *Akademik Knipovich* in 1968. This was organized under the auspices of the United Nations Food and Agricultural Organization (FAO). Scientists from Tunisia, Cyprus, Turkey, Algeria and other developing countries were invited to take part under Soviet guidance. The expedition discovered useful stocks of horse mackerel, sardine and prawns off the Tunisian and Algerian coast, and the Russians commented afterwards that cooperation with Mediterranean countries was now expected to grow rapidly in this field. Algeria invited Soviet experts to come back in 1969 to plan the development of local fisheries, and the Egyptians signed up for training in the operation of large fishing vessels.

The Arabs are not the only ones to be impressed by the Soviet industry's scientific support. The striking feature of its expansion in the Atlantic and Pacific has been the systematic way in which new areas are first explored by oceanographic ships, followed by fishing reconnaissance vessels which take sample catches, and finally, if the results are satisfactory, by the fishing fleet itself. Ashore, the research organization centres on the All-Union Research Institute of Sea Fisheries and Oceanography, under the Ministry of Fisheries, supported by regional institutes of which the Far Eastern is the most important. The freshwater fisheries have their own institute. In all, the Congressional Committee on Merchant Marine and Fisheries estimated in 1966 that a total of 135 laboratories employing about 2,000 scientists were active in this field.

In addition to hunting down shoals of fish, and discovering

how their movements are related to temperature changes, ocean currents and so on, Russian scientists have experimented with artificial methods of increasing the stock. These include breeding farms and attempts to transplant fish and crustacea from one sea to another; for example, pink salmon and king crabs have been taken from the Pacific and let loose in the Barents Sea.

As for new methods of actually catching fish, the Russians are particularly keen on electrical techniques, for example, lowering a powerful electric lamp over the side to attract the fish, which can either be netted in the normal way or simply pumped aboard. This kind of lure – which is by no means confined to the Soviet fleet – is said by the Russians to have been used to catch one-third of a million tons of fish in northern waters during 1967. They have also been trying to interest European fishermen in their equipment for putting fish temporarily to sleep by passing a powerful electric current under water. [9]

A form of research which particularly interested the congressional committee's delegation to the USSR was the development of fish protein concentrate, because of its political importance as a potential food supply for extremely poor countries. They considered that though the Russians could not yet match American expertise in turning whole fish into a sanitized, deodorized, tasteless, dehydrated product – which was then prohibited for human consumption by the US Food and Drug Administration on 'aesthetic' grounds – they were working on the problem. The delegation urged the United States to do 'all in its power' to get into large-scale production of fish concentrate before the Soviet Union, to ensure both a new market for the American fisherman and a new means by which the US could exert diplomatic leverage.

The characteristic elements in the Soviet fleet are the factory mother ship surrounded by her attendant catchers, the factory trawler and the freezer trawler. Although the Russians are firm believers in fleet fishing, these last two can and do sometimes work on their own. The main distinction between them is that

[9] *Fisheries Year Book,* 1968–69.

the factory ship fillets its catch and generally processes it into a final form, while the freezer simply guts the fish and freezes them whole. Additional equipment and crew make both these types bigger than the conventional deep-sea trawler, which simply buries its catch in crushed ice. The low, graceful sheerline of the traditional vessel, derived from the sailing trawler – and still the characteristic silhouette of the British fleet – has given way to a shape much closer to a small freighter. Instead of lifting the trawl net over the side, it is hauled up a stern ramp just as the whales are hauled aboard the Antarctic whaling factories. The modern trawler is far less beautiful than her ancestors, yet at the same time she provides some improvement in the incredibly tough working conditions deep-sea trawlermen are used to, compensating for the longer voyages these big vessels have to make to pay their way. Instead of slewing broadside to the waves, dipping her rail as the crew struggle to get the gear aboard, the stern fisher steams head to wind, shooting and hauling her trawl from the comparative shelter of the stern ramp.

The idea of mother ships is not new. The North Sea herring drifters had them, and the Grand Banks schooner surrounded by her cluster of little open dories played this role. But the Russians have taken the concept a big stage further in replacing the dories by deep-sea trawlers. They pass their catch to the mother ship for processing and storage, and she acts as fleet headquarters and supplies the catchers with fuel, stores and hospital facilities.

When her holds are full she may rendezvous with a refrigerated fish carrier rather than interrupt the fishing by returning to port herself. But in any case the fleet system involves transferring fish from one vessel to another at sea. Russian fishermen have well developed techniques for doing this – in contrast to the Soviet Navy's relative lack of experience in supporting warships afloat.

In the North Sea forty years ago, English crews would load open boats with boxes of fish and row them across from one vessel to another. Nowadays the Russians either winch the fish across in nets or pump them through a floating pipeline; while in fine weather the trawler may simply come alongside, with a big floating fender between her and the mother ship.

The development of mother ships, which enabled their trawler fleets to fish more distant grounds, was one of the ways in which the Russians responded to declining catches from the Barents Sea in the late 1950s. That British trawlermen, faced with the same problem, chose instead to build more freezer trawlers is symptomatic of a fundamental difference of approach.

Many British trawler skippers not only choose to fish alone, but defend their isolation even against other skippers in their own company – with whom they may one day be competing for a job. When three Hull trawlers went down within a few weeks in the arctic winter of 1968, it was pointed out that a vessel might be missing for several days without causing concern ashore because skippers are so reluctant to break radio silence. And the last thing they would do is lead the vessels of a rival firm to a good shoal by openly talking about it on the radio. Obviously one skipper may choose to help another because he happens to be a personal friend, and the owners ashore expect to be kept informed so they can make the best of their fleet. But in the latter case they pass messages in code, and one firm in Hull actually has a 'scrambler' on its radio receiver as if it were dealing with military secrets – its use is mentioned in Jeremy Tunstall's study of the Hull trawlermen, *The Fishermen*.

The Russian fisherman's wages, like those of his opposite number in the West, are related to how many fish his vessel catches. But the extent of his actual competition is severely limited by the fleet system, which is widely favoured in the Soviet industry, particularly for distant water fishing. The fleet is organized rather like a naval formation, with a commodore directing operations from the mother ship's bridge. He deploys some of his trawlers as reconnaissance ships; these lead the catchers to a promising area and leave them to fish it while they move on in search of further shoals. If there are any fish there, the chances are that somebody in the fleet is going to haul them in.

The individual skipper is in a curious position. He has the benefit of the information circulated by the mother ship, but relatively little discretion as to where he shoots his gear. He knows that his performance, good or bad, is constantly being compared with that of his colleagues in order to foster the spirit of 'socialist competition', yet he is expected to share any success with the rest of the fleet. It is true he has less incentive than his British opposite number to keep quiet about a heavy haul, because he will not be returning to land his catch on an open market, where the price fluctuates according to how much his rivals are landing. But even so it is difficult to swallow entirely the official line that Russian trawlers always inform their competitors when they find a good shoal.

The example of a factory mother ship chosen by the Russians for their Leningrad fishing exhibition in 1968 was the 15,000 ton deadweight *Ieronim Uborevich*. She is one of about fifteen similar vessels, each of which is really a floating cannery, working with a fleet of catchers; in this particular case in the Pacific, where she turns out high quality canned herring, saury and tuna, boiled and frozen shrimps, fishmeal and oil. In all, her crew of 520 can process 250 tons of fish a day. Most of the factory workers are women, who are divided into three watches. The catch is lifted on to the upper deck, sorted and fed down the appropriate conveyor to the production lines. Some of it may be temporarily frozen and stored for processing later when the fishing is slack. (Detailed reports from the Leningrad exhibition by Peter Hjul and Commander M. B. F. Ranken were published in the October and November issues of *Fishing News International*.)

But the mother ship concept in its purest form has been revived in the mighty *Vostok*, of 43,000 tons displacement; she carries her own flotilla of fourteen catchers on deck, just as the dories were stacked on the deck of a Grand Banks schooner. Her twin screw turbine installation enables her to steam to the grounds at 18 to 19 knots – compared with the *Ieronim Uborevich*'s 13 knots – and then unload the catchers from special gantries to port and starboard. The small satellite craft are made of glass fibre, each fitted with 350 horsepower engines driving twin scews, and have a capacity of about sixty tons. The *Vostok* herself can handle over 300 tons of fish a day – canning it, freezing it into blocks or turning it into fishmeal and oil.

The class of which *Vostok* is the first is designed to operate anywhere in the Atlantic, Pacific or Indian Oceans. She can stay at sea for up to four months compared with, say, two and a half months for the normal Soviet mother ship; and as the fuel tanks are emptied they can be used to store the processed catch. She is self-contained even to the point of operating her own reconnaissance helicopter. The crew of 600 factory workers and seamen are provided with a swimming pool, a 200-seat cinema and concert hall, shops, lounges, and according to one Soviet report, a hospital with no less than fifty beds. There is a normal ship's canteen but kitchens are also available for those who wish to cook their own food.

The development of what one must nowadays call the conventional factory trawler depended on research into quick freezing methods, the construction of a successful filleting machine, and means of turning the remains of the fish into meal. The first vessel to combine all these elements was the *Fairtry*, built in Britain in 1953. The idea was quickly taken up by the Russians, and has since been applied on a massive scale. Their basic type, of which there are more than a hundred, is the Mayakovsky class of 3,800 tons gross. It is designed to work in cold or temperate waters, catching fish from the seabed and near the surface, to be frozen, canned or turned into fishmeal and oil. With a crew of a hundred, it can handle sixty tons a day.

The factory trawler is a self-contained unit, catching its own fish. It is, however, less flexible than the basic freezer trawler because to be efficient it needs to find homogeneous shoals of a variety its filleting machines can handle. The freezer suits the British industry, which fishes the north-west Atlantic and is supported ashore by a highly developed system of processing and distribution. It also fits into the long range pattern of Soviet operations: for example in African waters, where there is a wide variety of fish. The Russian Tropik class, of 2,500 tons gross, is specially designed to operate in tropical Atlantic waters, and its slightly larger derivative, the Atlantik, is intended to range even further into the South Atlantic. Together the two classes amount to nearly 200 vessels.

In addition to the *Vostok*, the Russians have been experimenting with a variety of new hull forms and propulsion units. The Sever class, for example, are diesel electric, with the engine room forward. The *Progress*, launched in 1968, is powered by a gas turbine with a free-piston gas generator, claimed to weigh only two-thirds as much as a comparable diesel unit while burning the cheapest fuel.

Of more fundamental interest is the catamaran trawler *Experiment*, which spent five months on trials in the Atlantic during the summer of 1969, testing her twin-hulled structure and supplying fish to various mother ships. She really consists of two normal side fishing hulls joined together by a broad bridge deck and with twin ramps astern, and the idea is that she should carry a small crew for a vessel of her 1,000-ton displacement and fish continuously by shooting one trawl as the other comes aboard. She is also equipped to use seine nets near the surface, and would have freezing and processing equipment if she went into series production.

It sounds an ingenious concept provided the catamaran's inherent structural weakness – the tendency for the two hulls to flex independently and slowly break apart – can be suppressed in the winter sea conditions which fishing vessels have to take in their stride. The prototype is claimed to have steamed at full power into a Force 8 gale and kept her decks comfortably dry. Her skipper in 1969 estimated that she caught 75–80 per cent more than a single hulled vessel of the same tonnage; a more recent report put the figure at about 50 per cent. At any rate a second catamaran is being built before it is decided whether to introduce this type into the working fleet. The Russians may have come up with an important innovation.

Their naval architects are already thinking beyond the *Experiment* to the possibility of building a catamaran-hulled mother ship. A large self-propelled scale model of such a vessel has already been tried out successfully, according to a report in the *Economic Gazette*. The full-sized vessel would have a displacement of 23,000 tons. She would have refrigerated capacity for 5,000 tons of fish and could handle several catchers alongside at the same time.

Apart from the larger units, it is difficult to assemble detailed information on the make-up of the Soviet fleet. For example the total of '20,000 self-propelled vessels' referred to by the Deputy Minister of Fisheries in 1968 is almost meaningless by itself, though it is obviously a large number and the increase of 1,500 vessels during the 1966–70 five-year plan probably relates to it. The Soviet journal *Morskoi Flot* quoted a total of 2,600 fishing vessels of more than 100 gross tons on the Soviet register in January 1968.

By now there are probably about 4,000 sea-going craft, accounting for 80–90 per cent of the Soviet Union's total catch. Included in this number are well over a hundred factory mother ships, something like 350 factory trawlers and freezers, supported by about fifty refrigerated fish carriers.

Many of the designs are common to the fleets of East Germany and Poland, whose shipyards have supplied hundreds of vessels for the Soviet fleet. The Poles, for example, have supplied B64 and B69 factory mother ships of 10,000 tons deadweight, and a number of B62 herring mother ships, which were the first of their kind; while the important Tropik and Atlantik class freezer trawlers came from East Germany. It is also true that both Poland and East Germany have expanded their fleets alongside the Russians, and that there is some cooperation between them. They exchange technical information, their fishery research vessels run joint programmes and the Russians might, for example, provide a fish carrier for an East German fleet that was short of one. But the fishing operations themselves are not co-ordinated in the way that the Comecon cargo fleets operate joint freight services, each country providing a share of the capacity.

The inland fisheries of the Soviet Union are still organized extensively through the equivalent of collective farms. But the sea fisheries – in which the major expansion since the 1950s has taken place – are dominated by a pyramid of State organizations headed by the Ministry of Fisheries. The Ministry is divided into departments dealing with marine fisheries, inland fisheries, and the work of conservation and reproduction. The marine department is in turn divided into administrations controlling the Northern Fleet (based at Murmansk), the Western Fleet (Riga), the Far East Fleet (Vladivostok), the Black Sea Fleet (Sevastopol) and the Caspian Fleet (Astrakhan). The expansion programme has been supported by thirty training establishments turning out more than 5,000 specialists of one kind or another each year. But the Minister of Fisheries, Mr Ishkov, warned in 1968 that the industry would be in trouble unless it could attract more men who 'actually wanted to fish' instead of being fishery scientists or engineers.[10]

Russian fishermen are well paid. They earn much more, apparently, than merchant seamen. But then they expect, like British trawlermen, to work as long as the fish are there; and, in the case of the northern fleets, to carry on working through an arctic winter at sea. In addition to the production bonuses, their pay is adjusted by a coefficient which reflects the grim conditions on some of the grounds – the maximum is for fishing offshore in the Arctic Ocean or the Bering Sea.

With Soviet fishing fleets now ranging all over the world, it is easy to forget that until the end of the Second World War they never ventured beyond their own coastal waters. When they did begin to move it was the vessels from Murmansk and the Baltic which took the initiative; tentatively at first, and then with more urgency after 1957, when the Barents Sea catch sharply declined.

Herring boats went to Spitsbergen and Iceland in 1949, and by the early 1950s Russians were trawling in the Norwegian Sea and exploring the north-west corner of the Barents Sea. The first reconnaissance voyage to Newfoundland was made in 1954, and by the early 1960s the Russian boats were moving

[10] *Fisheries Year Book*, 1968–69.

down the eastern seaboard of the United States, reaching the Gulf of Mexico in 1962. Another two years and Soviet fleets were established on all the major grounds in the North Atlantic. Meanwhile, in their systematic way, reconnaissance ships had been feeling their way down the west coast of Africa since 1957; and by 1962, when they started large-scale fishing there, the first research ships had already visited the continental shelf of South America. This led to active fishing off South America in 1966 – prompting Argentina to declare a 200-mile fishery limit – and early in 1967 no less than a hundred Soviet vessels were reported off the shores of Patagonia, Tierra del Fuego and Antarctica.

The Atlantic naturally is the Soviet Union's most important fishing area. But a lot of effort in terms of research and equipment has gone into expanding the Far East fleet. Based on Vladivostok, it is already the largest of the five regional administrations, accounting for one-third of the total catch, mostly taken in the Pacific. It is receiving large numbers of new freezer trawlers and has set itself the task of attaining a 'leading position' in world tuna fishing.

In the Pacific, serious expansion did not begin until the late 1950s, the first move being into the Bering Sea rather than the ocean proper. From then on the pattern of southward movement seen in the Atlantic was repeated. In the early 1960s Russian vessels were regularly seen in the Gulf of Alaska and appeared off California in 1967. By the following year they were working off Hawaii, and reconnaissance vessels had reported dense concentrations of fish off the coasts of Australia, New Zealand and Antarctica, where the impact of their arrival has since been felt by the local industries.

Recent comments in the Soviet Press indicate that the Indian Ocean, where Russian vessels first appeared in 1964, is scheduled for the same systematic treatment.

The most important question arising from this story of steady, scientifically managed expansion is whether the Russians know when to stop – in the interests of conservation. As one might expect, it is a difficult one to answer.

There are several encouraging indications: the Russians practise conservation of their own inland fisheries; since the mid-1950s they have adhered to international conventions offering some measure of control over fishing in the North Atlantic, the Barents Sea and the North Pacific (in the last case it was largely a defensive agreement to prevent the Japanese depleting stocks of the salmon which breed in Russian rivers); and Soviet scientists repeatedly warn that world fish stocks may be exhausted unless some rational control is exercised to maximize the permanent supply.

But set against this is the irresponsible way in which Soviet whaling expeditions in the Antarctic seem to have ignored international efforts to halt the alarming decline of stocks which threatens to make some species extinct. It can be argued that the Russian approach is dictated by the desire to see some return from a comparatively new fleet of whale factory ships, built between 1959 and 1963; but to do so merely indicates that where conservation is concerned the Russians, like many others, are tempted to operate a dual standard. Everyone agrees with some conservation in principle: but in practice there is a great deal of difference between the men whose job it is to study the problem and those employed simply to catch fish – with payment by results.

The Ocean Sciences in Warfare

Another direct application of oceanographic research is in the operation of submarines, and in anti-submarine warfare (ASW). The Soviet Union's massive effort in the marine sciences is all the more appropriate when one considers that she operates the largest fleet of submarines in the world, and that one of her principal unsolved strategic problems is defence against American Polaris missile submarines.

Wandering blind in the ocean, a submarine's first need is obviously to know exactly where she is and the form of the seabed beneath her keel, so that she does not get stranded or run into an underwater cliff. The long range patrols now operated by the Soviet Navy, and the greater depths to which modern nuclear powered submarines can dive, therefore create a requirement for a wider range of accurate charts. This is particularly so in the case of the Russian missile-firing submarines which have recently appeared on patrol off the shores of the United States. The missile boat's commander might want to lie silently on the seabed in the shadow of a ridge. In any case a ballistic missile is no more accurate than the margin of error in the calculated position from which it is fired; a detailed survey of the seabed in the patrol area might provide the navigator with a useful cross check on his dead reckoning, however sophisticated that might be in these days of inertial navigation. (The inertial system depends on a device, incorporating gyros, which records any movement from a given starting point.)

But since the submarine has to remain undetected, its commander also wants to know as much as possible about the nature of the water round it, especially the temperature gradients, since this will determine the efficiency of detection devices in surface warships, in helicopters, 'hunter-killer' submarines and on the seabed. The principal ASW weapon is sound. It is used either in active sonar – that is sending out a rhythmic pinging sound and waiting for an echo to return – or passive sonar, which simply means listening with a hydrophone.

Sound travels remarkably well through water, as any yachtsman who has lain in his bunk listening to the ominous thump of an approaching freighter's propeller will confirm. A submarine might well be able to hear a fast-moving ship more than a hundred miles away, and experiments have shown that under the right circumstances, sound can be received as much as 10,000 miles from its source. The trouble is that for the anti-submarine frigate the circumstances are hardly ever quite right. It is one thing to know there is an enemy submarine in the vicinity and another to pin down its range and bearing with active sonar sufficiently accurately to deliver a weapon. At high speed, particularly pitching into a heavy sea, the frigate has difficulty in hearing above the noise of its own passage through the water. A submarine makes less noise, but even so the range of its active sonar is only a fraction of the distance at which it can hear ships approaching on its hydrophones.

The velocity of sound passing through water is a function of its density. Velocity therefore varies with changes in temperature, salinity and depth (pressure). The practical effect of this is that the conical beam of sound waves sent out by the sonar dome bends, often leaving a 'shadow' area in which a submarine cannot be detected because there is no way of directing sound at it. In some places, near the mouth of a big river, for example, or alongside melting pack ice, salinity changes may be critical, but the most important factor is temperature. In the open ocean there will normally be a surface layer that has been mixed up to an even temperature, and below that a thermocline or rapidly decreasing temperature, followed by a deep layer of nearly uniform temperature. This may mean that a surface ship's horizontal sonar beam is bent sharply downwards no more than half a mile away.

It could be that deep cold water has welled up and trapped the warmer surface water below it, in which case the sound will curve up to the surface, reflect downwards and curve up again. The ship may lower a sonar transducer on the end of a cable to search beneath a known layer. It may deliberately bounce its sonar off the bottom to extend its range or it might just find a sound 'channel' in which the beam wanders along between two opposing temperature gradients. But in any case it is important both for ASW and the submarine's defence to know what temperature layers are likely to exist in a given bit of sea at different times of the year, and if possible to check them on the spot.

Surface warships – and Russian oceanographic vessels – therefore take every opportunity to dip a bathythermograph over the side, to record temperature at various depths and eventually compile a 'sonar atlas'. Modern instruments can be used at 15–20 knots.

A warship escorting a convoy of merchant ships in the North Atlantic would also want to stay clear of the 'deep scattering layer', believed to consist of plankton – minute marine organisms

– and perhaps shoals of fish. A submarine could lurk there in the knowledge that sonar signals would rapidly be diffused and lost. Hence the recent mission of the American submersible *Ben Franklin*, drifting 600 feet down in the Gulf Stream, recording temperature, salinity and sound velocity. Its main purpose was to study the deep scattering layer as it rises from 150–250 fathoms at night and then sinks away from the sun each day, and to establish what it consists of and how sonar can be used to penetrate it. Equally, a submarine lying in wait, listening for the approach of an enemy merchant ship, would not want to find herself surrounded by chattering fish or shoals of snapping shrimp, which at their noisiest can drown most other sounds.

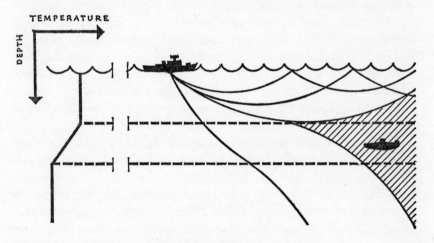

Sonar and the effect of temperature layers

Figure 4

A study of the noises made by these marine animals may not be operationally so important as a knowledge of temperature layers; but it is fascinating in its own right. The sounds range from the long moan of a whale to the crackle of a shrimp bed. The snapping shrimp produces its characteristic noise by opening and shutting its outsize left claw, which is as big as its entire body, and the noise produced by a shoal of them has been compared to frying fat or burning undergrowth. Whales, porpoises and dolphins force air through nasal sacks, while some fishes have air sacs which vibrate as they move through the water: others rub their fins together or grind their teeth. The squeteague croaks; the toadfish growls or grunts; the longhorn sculpin emits a low drumming like the hum of a generator; another species whoops like a ship's siren, while the rhythmic beat of a whale's tail may resemble the noise of a propeller.

It seems that whales and fishes, like submarines, use sound both to communicate and to locate other animals. For the most part there is no clash between the living and the mechanical worlds, but a shoal of fish 'chattering like a Women's Institute meeting' can be a nuisance. One submarine commander described to me how he became so irritated by the way they kept interrupting his underwater telephone conversation that he suddenly shouted into the instrument 'Why don't you fish just —— off'. For a moment there was absolute silence. Then even more excited chatter, slowly fading as they hurried away.

Fortunately, shrimp and fish noise is concentrated in coastal waters, mainly in warm and temperate latitudes.

Evidence of the practical usefulness of oceanographic data such as I have described can be seen in the US Navy's ASWEPS (Anti-Submarine Warfare Environmental Prediction Services). Information on water temperature, sound velocity, surface wave conditions and weather is collected from operational areas of the Atlantic, Pacific and Mediterranean, and broadcast daily to every ASW commander. The Soviet Navy has a similar system – in fact its forecasts can be received on western equipment – as does the Royal Navy, although it is less comprehensive than its American equivalent.

The Russians are comparative newcomers to many areas of ASW, both technically and geographically. They must still have a lot of leeway to make up before they can match the Americans. As for the Royal Navy, its anti-submarine forces are obviously limited in scale, but in technical quality they probably lead the world. In the circumstances, the wide-ranging activities of the Russian oceanographic fleet can be expected to receive the full backing of the Soviet naval hierarchy, and not merely for the purpose of submarine operations and ASW. Ocean research vessels make ideal platforms for electronic monitoring equipment, and can also test the long range communications required by Soviet squadrons venturing for the first time into the Indian Ocean and the South Atlantic.

Judging by the use Russian merchant ships now make of computer controlled weather routing, the Soviet Navy also operates an equivalent to the US Navy's Optimum Track Ship Routing System. This uses forecasts of weather, wave conditions and currents to provide each ship with a course across, say, the North Atlantic which gives the minimum voyage time even though the distance run may be increased. Some curious things turn up from this kind of study. For example, a warship which is nominally faster than another may consistently make slower time on passage because her length conflicts with the average wave length in that part of the ocean. Ideally, naval vessels should have dimensions which, like the air-conditioning, are related to that part of the world in which they will normally operate.

In Britain a great deal of theoretical work on the relation between wave forecasts and optimum ship design has been done by the National Physical Laboratory, and the Meteorological Office has been experimenting with a commercial weather routing service. The basic idea is to save time and fuel; and one shipowner who previously had to pay £7,000 to £8,000 a year to repair hull bottom damage caused by pounding when his ships were in ballast found he could avoid this cost by having them routed round bad weather.

Russian freighters are claimed to have saved an average of ten hours on each North Atlantic crossing during the winter, and about six hours in the summer, by following courses mapped out for them by shore-based computers. These figures, quoted by Dr Ziyadin Abuzyarov of the Soviet Hydrometeorological Centre,[11] were based on 358 winter crossings and 234 in summer. The computer comes into play in deciding just how far it pays to

[11] *Guardian*, February 28, 1969.

divert from the great circle track to avoid bad weather, given the type of vessel and her loading.

According to British experts, the savings claimed by the Russians are surprisingly high. But then the US Navy, most of whose ships use the OTSRS, claims to save an average of eighteen hours on an average Atlantic crossing and calculates that millions of dollars have already been saved on transport operations.

CHAPTER 10

The Evolution of Naval Strategy

Among the factors which have shaped the development of the Soviet Navy, four stand out. Its growth was stunted by the desperate economic condition of the USSR in the immediate post-revolutionary period, and has to some extent been distorted by later budgetry decisions. It has suffered from drastic political interference, ranging from Stalin's pre-war purges to Khrushchev's obsession with submarines. It took a long time to live down its subordinate Second World War role as a 'faithful helper of the Red Army'. And having achieved independent status within the Russian military establishment it has been faced with the continuing effort to keep abreast of an escalating 'enemy' technology, in the form of longer range carrier borne aircraft and the Polaris submarine.

The Navy in the Aftermath of Revolution

The Bolsheviks owed a great deal to the sailors of the Kronshtat naval base. The psychological and symbolic value of the cruiser *Aurora*'s presence in the heart of Leningrad in 1917, and her final bombardment of the Winter Palace, have been honoured ever since. But the abortive Kronshtat mutiny of 1921 showed that many sailors were still not satisfied. This prompted vigorous steps from the Communist regime to ensure that in future the correct Marxist-Leninist approach to naval affairs would prevail. It also helped to subordinate the Navy to the Red Army within the central defence administration.

In theoretical terms, the 1920s were marked by contention

between the 'old 'and 'young' schools of naval thought; between
the traditional concept of a fleet led by battleships and cruisers,
and the view that in future wars the important elements would be
submarines, destroyers and fast patrol boats. But there was never
much doubt about the outcome. The old school was suspect as
representing the views of former Czarist officers and the young
school's theories happened to be a rationalization of the fact
that there was no money to build a fleet of big, ocean-going
warships anyway.

The strategy of 'active defence' which actually emerged during
the late 1920s was a realistic expression of the Soviet Union's
capabilities at a time when she was struggling with the immense
post-revolutionary problems of social upheaval and industrial
reconstruction. The Navy's ambitions were limited to coastal
engagements using light surface forces, submarines and aircraft.
The few large vessels available were to be used as mobile shore
batteries.

Stalin and the Ocean-going Fleet

By the mid-1930s the Soviet regime not only had more resources
for naval construction; it also became uneasily aware that potential enemies such as Germany, Japan, and Italy seemed to regard
big navies as essential to their political ambitions. In particular,
the Russian's inability to intervene successfully in the Spanish
civil war seems to have impressed them with the value of long
range surface forces in something of the same way that the
Cuban crisis was to do later. Stalin emerged as an old school
man after all. He was going to have a navy 'equal to that of any
foreign power'. And like the German Navy, it was to include
battleships and carriers.[1]

By the outbreak of war more than 200 naval vessels were
being built in Russian shipyards, including 10 cruisers, 45

[1] For a full discussion of Stalin's policy and his attempts to get American
help in the construction of battleships, see *Soviet Naval Strategy* by R. W.
Herrick.

destroyers and 90 submarines.[2] But the battleships were never completed and the carriers not even laid down.

The Second World War and its Effects

The war came as a massive blow to the Soviet Navy's returning self-confidence. In the Baltic its vessels were quickly trapped in the Gulf of Finland, where they were largely reduced to providing artillery support. Sailors were placed under army command, as they were on other fronts, and went ashore to help in the defence of Leningrad. The Germans, having a vital air superiority, dive-bombed the escape route which light warships might have taken through the Baltic-White Sea Canal.

In the Black Sea naval units fared only a little better, although they showed a valuable flair for improvisation and undertook a number of limited offensive missions, including amphibious operations. Like their Baltic comrades, they indulged the Russian passion for minelaying. But whereas minefields played an obviously useful role in defending the sea approaches to Leningrad, Sokolovsky's *Military Strategy* argues that the mines laid in the Black Sea in 1941 did more harm than good: 'In view of the absence of major enemy naval forces in this theatre, there was no need for this. The minefields greatly hampered later operations by the Black Sea Fleet, causing us more damage than the Germans.'

The Northern Fleet retained some freedom of manœuvre, but it could hardly claim to have played a decisive role in the war. The Soviet war records show that it protected an impressive total of 1,600 convoys involving 4,400 ships, yet there never seemed to be many Russian warships or aircraft around in 1942 when Allied convoys – including some Soviet merchant ships – were running the German blockade to bring supplies to Murmansk and Arkhangelsk. Winston Churchill appealed to Stalin for more help, and the Russian leader promised that his 'naval

[2] *Soviet Sea Power:* Georgetown Center for Strategic and International Studies, 1969.

and air forces would do their utmost' east of the North Cape of Norway. But their utmost seems to have been little enough. When S. W. Roskill came to write the official British record[3] he judged that 'they never relieved the Home Fleet of any appreciable share of the responsibility for defending any arctic convoy.'

The Pacific Fleet may have had some deterrent value, but since the Russians only declared war on the Japanese right at the end of the Second World War there was no active enemy to fight. It simply moved in at the last moment to exploit the collapse of Japan.

The 'lessons' which influential Soviet strategists chose to draw from all this confirmed the Navy in a subordinate role as an auxiliary to the Red Army. Its primary mission was once again to be the 'active defence' of the coastline. Its most likely offensive role was in support of advancing ground forces. The Navy's Commander-in-Chief, Admiral Gorshkov, who devoted a large part of his career to extricating his service from this situation, gives a rueful description of it:

All this [wartime experience] unquestionably provided a solid foundation for the acceptance of joint operations with the ground forces, in defence and offence, as the main task of our fleet after the war. At the same time the belief that this concept was basic to the post-war period, ignoring changes in the international power structure, strengthened the dominant defensive tendencies in views about the strategic use of the fleet; and these being extended into the post-war years, confined the fleet to the coastal zone even more than before, controlled by the troops. Thus the Navy's role as a mere helper of the land forces was consolidated.[4]

At first sight, it might seem that the ocean-going fleet which Stalin once again started to build around 1950 would have been the answer to Gorshkov's subsequent criticism. It was to be led by two dozen Sverdlov class cruisers (according to Admiral Kuznetsov, Stalin had 'a curious passion for heavy cruisers'), and a large fleet of medium-sized W class submarines; there were even renewed plans for aircraft carriers.

[3] *History of the Second World War; The War at Sea*, Vol. II, HMSO, 1956.
[4] *Morskoi Sbornik*, February 1967.

But although the Russian leader apparently valued the nominal scope of his naval forces as a symbol of great power status – 'every nation that becomes a world power must have a navy', he told one American diplomat – its deployment in his time was almost neurotically defensive. For example only a few dozen submarines were attached to the Northern Fleet, where they had direct access to the open Atlantic. When Khrushchev took over the number was sharply increased. In 1970 it was estimated that 150 submarines (out of a total 370 to 380), including two-thirds of the nuclear powered ones, were based up there.

As Gorshkov explains, the earlier idea was to draw the enemy's carrier task forces into the coastal minefields where they could be destroyed by squadrons of fast torpedo boats and the combined bombardment of ships, shore batteries and land based aircraft. This was fair enough if the enemy was considered to be intent on invading Soviet territory, or even perhaps on launching air attacks against inland targets, since the range of carrier-borne aircraft was extremely short in those days. But it hardly amounted to naval power in the broad sense in which that term is used in the West.

Khrushchev, Submarines and 'Flying Torpedoes'

Stalin's death in 1953 released the USSR from some of its defensive paranoia. She began to look outwards again for the first time since the war, and this could only be good for the Navy. But once Khrushchev was firmly established, it appeared that in some ways his ideas on naval matters were even more cranky than his predecessor's.

In a commendable search for ways of reducing the crippling burden of the defence budget he convinced himself that 'enormously expensive' cruisers were redundant, let alone aircraft carriers. In the missile era which was about to dawn there would be hardly any naval missions that could not be accomplished by the submarine. He was about to make the same mistake, though on a grander scale, as Britain's defence minister Duncan Sandys, who forecast that the missile would rapidly make manned aircraft redundant.

During Khrushchev's visit to the United States in 1959, he gave a typically exuberant account of his policy. Cruising round San Francisco harbour aboard the US Coast Guard cutter *Gresham*, he decided to enlighten Captain Clark: 'I'll tell you a secret. We were starting to build a big fleet of ships, including many cruisers. But today they are outmoded. Cruisers have a very short range. They are enormously expensive. We are scrapping 90–95 per cent of them, including some that were just on the verge of being commissioned. From now on we will rely mainly on submarines.' The great merit of submarines, he added, was that their range had been increased by the installation of 'flying torpedoes'. 'I won't tell you how many submarines we have lest you think I am bragging – but we have enough to assign some of them to catch herring in the North Sea.'[5]

It was Khrushchev who replaced Admiral Kuznetsov by the present Commander-in-Chief of the Soviet Navy in 1955. The qualities in Gorshkov which probably appealed to him were his enthusiasm for missile technology and his comparative youth, combined with a record of political reliability. Reliable or not, the Admiral somehow outmanœuvred his leader on the issue of scrapping the cruisers – apparently by abandoning the uncompleted ships but stalling over the rest. According to *Jane's Fighting Ships*, fourteen Sverdlov class cruisers were completed by December 1960, fifteen months after Khrushchev's visit to the United States. Twenty keels had apparently been laid, but only three hulls were actually scrapped after being launched.

By 1962, Gorshkov was able to refer to surface vessels – admittedly in the context of their missile armament – as being just as important as the submarine fleet, which by then had grown to an astonishing total of about 500 boats: 'The basis of our Navy are the atomic submarines, equipped with powerful rockets and homing torpedoes with nuclear charges ... On a level with submarines in the armament of our fleet are the surface vessels, equipped with rockets and the latest technical aids.

[5] *New York Times*, September 22, 1959.

Naval missile carrying aircraft are also perfecting their efficiency.'[6]

It is perhaps difficult for a Western naval man – even after listening to Khrushchev – to appreciate the achievement represented by the words 'on a level with'. At the time Gorshkov was appointed, the Navy was about to go under (almost literally) for the third time. Pushing it down was an army-dominated military establishment, free since Stalin's death to do some stategic thinking of its own, but strongly recommended to express the answers in terms of nuclear missiles. In 'The Development of Soviet Naval Art'[7] the Admiral describes how extraordinary some of these answers were:

There appeared among us, unfortunately, highly influential 'authorities' who considered that with the arrival of atomic weapons, the Navy had completely lost its importance within the armed forces. In their opinion all the basic tasks in a future war could be carried out without any participation by the fleet, even when it was necessary to conduct military operations on the open sea and on the expanse of the oceans. It was often argued that to destroy striking forces of surface ships, and even submarines, a few missiles in launching sites on land would be sufficient.

In contrast to the views held during the early post-war years about the importance of joint operations with the land forces as one of the fleet's basic missions, the idea of joint coastal operations was completely rejected. It was considered that for land forces equipped with nuclear weapons, support from the sea was unnecessary; with their own resources they could cross water barriers and if necessary take on the enemy's fleet attempting to strike at them from the sea.

It was considered that even amphibious landings had completely lost their importance and that in the era of the nuclear missile, their purpose could more easily be accomplished by air assault or by ground forces using their own amphibious armoured vehicles.

Obviously, the spread of such opinions, coming on top of the defensive tendencies which still existed, not only interfered with the correct determination of the fleet's further development; it prevented our military-theoretical thought from moving forward.

Quite how the new Commander-in-Chief managed to prevent

[6] *Pravda*, July 29, 1962.
[7] *Morskoi Sbornik*, February 1967.

the Navy sinking under this weight of authoritative indifference he does not explain. It no doubt helped that he was a good party man and could not be accused of lacking enthusiasm for missiles as such. The Soviet leadership may also have been impressed by the freedom of manœuvre sea power gave to British and American forces operating in the eastern Mediterranean; at Suez in 1956 and in the Lebanon two years later. It was in this period that the Russians began to use military and economic aid to establish themselves in the Arab countries, but they were not in a position to create a significant presence at sea.

However it was achieved, Gorshkov claims in retrospect that the development of an ocean-going navy was accepted in principle at that time, even if Khrushchev himself remained far from convinced about the need for all those expensive cruisers:

In the mid-1950s the central committee of our party laid down the path of development for the Navy, taking the revolution in military affairs into account. The course was set for the construction of an ocean fleet capable of strategic missions of an offensive nature. The foremost position in this was taken by submarines and naval aircraft, equipped with nuclear missiles. So began a new era in the development of the Navy and of naval art.

By taking advantage of technological advances, he continues, it was possible within a short time to create a new form of armed force: 'an ocean fleet in which submarines, aircraft, surface vessels and other types of weapon are harmoniously distributed.' The basis of a 'well balanced fleet' had been laid down – 'one which in its formation and equipment has the ability to carry out missions both in a nuclear missile war and a conventional war, and also to safeguard the state's interests on the sea in time of peace'.

Before tackling some of the specific issues raised by Gorshkov – can one really have a 'well balanced fleet' without aircraft carriers, for example? – it is useful to examine how far he and his fellow admirals were able to get the implications of an ocean-going navy across to other military leaders by the end of the Khrushchev period. Judging by its treatment in *Military Strategy*, first published in 1962, not all that far.

It was written by a committee of soldiers under the chairman-ship of Marshal Sokolovsky. Although it accepts the by then official line on the Navy's independent role, it sometimes shows only a muddled grasp of the physical facts of naval warfare – as, for example, when discussing the 'vulnerability' of the Polaris submarine.

The book is nevertheless of immense importance in showing us what a conservative view of official Soviet naval strategy amounted to at about the time of the Cuban crisis. The following summary is taken from the 1963 edition, which was slightly revised to take account of naval criticism levelled at the first edition. The passages quoted were not changed in the 1968 edition, so the main elements of this strategy can be assumed to have held good at least until then.

The section on naval operations begins by explaining that in any future world conflict the Navy will have more scope and responsibility than in the 'Great Patriotic War', but 'will hardly be decisive for the outcome of the war':

The main aim of fleet operations in naval theatres is to defeat the enemy's navy and disrupt his maritime communications. In addition, it may be necessary to deliver nuclear missile attacks on coastal targets, carry out joint operations with the ground forces, provide transport and protect one's own sea communications ... Nuclear submarines and naval aircraft armed with missiles will make decisive naval opera-tions possible against a powerful maritime enemy.

The authors proceeded to examine each of the major missions in turn, beginning with the destruction of the NATO carrier task forces, which in those days carried much more responsibility for nuclear deterrence:

From the outset, one of our Navy's most important tasks will be to destroy the enemy carrier strike forces. The enemy will attempt to deploy these formations in the most important theatres near Socialist countries so as to deliver surprise nuclear strikes on major coastal targets (naval bases, airfields and missile sites) and possibly on targets much further inland. For example, in the NATO exercise 'Autumn – 60' a carrier strike force deployed in the Norwegian Sea simulated the delivery of 200 nuclear strikes on targets on our coast and deep within our territory . . . In the centre [of such formations] will be the attack carriers, which represent the main, and extremely vulnerable, target for nuclear missile and torpedo attacks. The carriers are protected by anti-submarine surface ships and anti-submarine aircraft. Radar pickets will be deployed on the perimeter of the area. But these forces can no longer be relied upon to protect the attack carriers from missile strikes launched by submarines and naval aircraft.

The presence in our fleet of submarines and aircraft equipped with missiles allows them to engage the carrier without entering the task force's anti-submarine and air defence zone. It is essential to attempt to destroy the attack carriers before they launch their aircraft; we must destroy the protective forces, the auxiliaries and the carrier bases. It should be remembered that these formations are extremely vulnerable on passage, during refuelling operations, and during the launch and recovery of their aircraft . . . The attack carrier is an extremely vulnerable target for nuclear strike.

An effective means of combating attack carriers and other surface forces is the nuclear powered missile submarine . . . New methods of submarine operations have come to replace the former methods of torpedo attack from short distances – missile strikes from great distances and from submerged positions. Previously it was necessary to concentrate several submarines for a mass torpedo attack to destroy a surface ship. Now, any surface ship can be destroyed with a single missile or torpedo with a nuclear warhead.

Attack carrier formations can be successfully engaged by naval aircraft and those of the Long Range Air Force. Armed with 'air-to-ship' missiles with nuclear warheads, these aircraft can strike without coming within the dense zone of fire of the carrier formation's anti-aircraft defences.

Soviet strategists were also beginning to grapple – hopefully – with the problem of countering the Polaris deterrent:

Combat with enemy submarines, particularly nuclear powered missile submarines, is also an important task for the fleet. In the aggressive plans of the Anglo-American bloc, great significance is attached to the use of submarines armed with Polaris missiles for nuclear attacks deep into the territory of the socialist countries. By the outbreak of war, such submarines can be deployed so as to launch rockets 800 kilo-metres from the coast, mainly in the Arctic Ocean and in the northern seas, in the North Atlantic and in the western Pacific . . . Submarines have become the main striking force at sea, not only in our Navy but also in the fleets of the Anglo-American bloc.

Nuclear submarines with Polaris missiles can be destroyed in their bases by the Strategic Rocket Forces and the Long Range Air Force and while on passage and in their patrol areas by hunter killer submarines, the Long Range Air Force and other anti-submarine forces. Combat with missile submarines has moved a long way from the coast, on to the open seas and oceans. The former coastal anti-submarine defences will no longer be effective against them. There is need for a reliable system of reconnaissance to ensure the timely detection of enemy submarines, particularly those carrying missiles, the exact determination of the co-ordinates of their positions, and the guidance on to them of active weapons ... Under such conditions (of co-ordinated operations) we can count on blocking the enemy missile strikes with the help of submarines and on safeguarding our naval forces and communications from submarine attack.

In a European war which is assumed to involve the United States, the Russians envisaged large-scale operations against shipping:

One of the Navy's main tasks in a future war will be to sever the enemy's ocean and sea transport routes and to disrupt his communications. We should remember that up to threequarters of the possible enemy's resources of men and material are on the other side of the ocean. According to the calculation of certain military theoreticians 80 to 100 large transports would arrive daily at European ports in the event of war and 1,500 to 2,000 ships, excluding escorts, would be at sea at any one time.

Operations against enemy lines of communication should be developed on a large scale from the very beginning of the war. This task might be carried out by strikes of the Strategic Rocket Forces, the Long Range Air Force and nuclear-powered missile submarines against naval bases and ports, against channels and narrow inlets, shipbuilding and ship repair yards; by destroying convoys and transports at sea using submarines and aircraft. The mobile use of nuclear submarines, ensuring the maximum concentration of effort against enemy communications within a limited time will be of great significance in this context. Diesel-electric submarines, which will obviously still be used in operations against enemy communications, can be deployed as mobile screens, in systematic operations or in free search.

Finally, there was still thought to be an important place for joint operations:

Although support of the land forces will not be one of the Navy's main tasks, considerable effort must be expended in this direction. In conjunction with the land forces, the fleet can foil enemy landings either at the point of assault or during the sea crossing. The fleet will in turn have the task of carrying out landings on the enemy's coast, and safeguarding the crossing of straits and large water obstacles by the land forces. The Navy will engage the enemy fleet, particularly its carrier and missile units so as to protect these same formations of troops from seaward attack.

The first point of interest in this analysis is the order in which the missions are placed. It implies that the NATO carrier strike forces were regarded as a more serious threat than the Polaris. However, one must remember that the book's original text was probably prepared only about a year after the deployment of the first operational Polaris submarine, the USS *George Washington*, in November 1960. By 1964, as Herrick points out in his *Soviet Naval Strategy*, the anti-Polaris mission was given top priority by a *Red Star* article of which Marshal Sokolovsky was the joint author.

The long discussion of the aircraft carrier's vulnerability to missile strikes from beyong the range of its defensive screen is a reminder of the most striking single feature of Soviet naval strategy – that it claims to find no place for the fixed-wing aircraft carrier. And this negative fact is closely related to a positive one. The Soviet fleet is alone among the world's major navies in placing great emphasis on the surface-to-surface cruise missile. The American and British navies have developed surface-to-air missiles which have a surface-to-surface capability, but so far no weapon which is optimized in this second role.

In the Russian Navy, the surface-to-surface missile serves two purposes. It gives formations of either surface ships or submarines an inflexible and limited equivalent of the long range striking power provided in other large navies by carrier-borne aircraft (the Royal Navy has been evaluating surface-to-surface systems in anticipation of its carriers being scrapped). In defence, it extends the reach of the screen the Russians would throw up against the advance of enemy strike or amphibious assault forces.

Its great merit by comparison with ship-borne air power in the strike role is that it can be fitted in more or less any shape or size of warship. Even the us Navy can only afford a small number of carriers, and they are far too important to risk without a screen of escorts. So although the surface-to-surface missile is in many ways inflexible – for example, once launched, it cannot be recalled – in this other sense it is highly flexible.

The Russian naval cruise missiles are credited with a range of up to about 300 miles. But to hit a target at that distance they would require mid-course guidance from an aircraft, making the system both much more difficult to set up and much more vulnerable. In any case the ship launching a missile would require some sort of long range reconnaissance to be aware of the target's existence and approximate location in the first place, whether provided by an aircraft or another ship.

Under some circumstances, however, the cruise missile is obviously an extremely formidable weapon: if it were, for example, to be launched at fairly close range from a Soviet E-class submarine, which would provide a poor radar echo as she wallowed in the wave clutter. Later generations of missile, travelling faster and probably skimming the surface more closely, will be even more difficult to stop.

As we have seen, the Russians claim that a combination of this weapon, the air-to-surface missile, the submerged launched ballistic type and the torpedo – all nuclear-armed if required – is an effective answer to the aircraft carrier. One can hardly doubt it, although if the carrier has launched her aircraft they still have to be dealt with, and it is not an issue one can discuss without making assumptions about the carrier task force's alertness, the success of Russian aircraft, surface ships and sub-marines in tailing it, and so on. But in the context of Khrushchev's budgetry restraint it was a hypothetical question anyway.

It is difficult to imagine the Soviet Navy turning down a fleet of aircraft carriers if it could get them, vulnerable to nuclear missiles or not. But Admiral Gorshkov had enough trouble getting the 'enormously expensive' cruiser construction programme reinstated without suggesting that the Central Committee might like to fund a completely new technology, involving a large type of ship never before built in Soviet shipyards, new types of aircraft and the formation of a specialized corps of sea-going aviators.[8]

When Gorshkov discusses the problem of aircraft carriers, therefore, his view may be as much a rationalization of the financial facts of life as a technical assessment:

An analysis of the military potential of the fleet's various forms of power in the dawn of the nuclear missile era led us to the conclusion that the carriers were irreversibly in decline. Although they were powerful then, and could for some time to come pose a serious threat to our country's security, there was nevertheless clearly no point in looking for a way to use them as main striking forces in naval warfare.

The fleets of the imperialist countries, with the help of carriers, have been able to carry out major missions in local wars against the peoples of the underdeveloped countries who do not possess modern means of waging war. It is also true that in the West, major tasks have still been assigned to carriers in a nuclear missile war.

Even now some people, yielding to the hypnosis – if I may say so – of this contemporary naval experience, continue to campaign for the construction of carriers. But this leaves out of account the important fact that the military ability of carriers, even with nuclear energy, does not stand comparison with the striking potential of submarine-air forces.[9]

The weak point in Gorshkov's argument is that it appears to take account of the carrier's usefulness in conventional and otherwise seriously limited wars without – by American standards at least – giving these roles anything like their due importance. Vietnam is an example. While the carrier task force survives, it can com-

[8] For a discussion of the Soviet Navy's budgetary tactics see 'Sea Power and Soviet Foreign Policy' by Lieutenant-Commander Cox, usn, *US Naval Institute Proceedings*, June 1969.
[9] *Morskoi Sbornik*, February 1967.

mand a sea area in a comprehensive, flexible way that is not remotely possible using only submarines and aircraft based on land at long range. It is an expensive system which offers great power provided one is prepared sometimes to face great risks. It has to be assessed for its cost effectiveness on a given scale over a certain range of circumstances. If the Admiral really thought the subject was adequately covered by his remarks in *Morskoi Sbornik*, they provided evidence of the defensive nature of Soviet naval strategy and the extent to which it was still focused on general nuclear war.

Back in 'the dawn of the nuclear missile era' his argument may have been both adequate *and* hypothetical. But in the Mediterranean since 1967 the Russians have evidently found a requirement for a visible, permanent, reasonably well-balanced naval force provided with its own air reconnaissance and the possibility of some air cover – from North African airfields. Their squadron has recently included a helicopter carrier whose primary role appears to be ASW but which could be used for amphibious operations together with the landing ships also deployed in the Mediterranean.

A fixed-wing aircraft carrier would fit neatly into this picture. Move the same squadron through the Suez Canal into areas where no land-based air support is available and the absence of a carrier could be a serious limitation. Even in European waters – where the Soviet Union does not have NATO's great chain of coastal air bases – the case for the carrier has been strengthened since Khrushchev's time by the increasing reluctance on both sides of the Iron Curtain to envisage a future war in terms of a devastating nuclear exchange. In limited conventional warfare – NATO's 'flexible response' instead of 'massive retaliation' – the carrier is more likely to survive. This factor must at least be weighed against its vulnerability to the greatly increased speed and endurance of the nuclear submarine.

So if Gorshkov and his colleagues really believe that 'the role of the Soviet Navy is to challenge capitalist naval supremacy in all the seas and oceans of the world', one might expect the carrier to become a live issue once more in Russian military thinking. By now the debate would be subject to a great deal of political inertia, and of course actual construction might continue to be ruled out financially. But a solution to this second problem may be at hand in the form of the vertical take-off aircraft.

The Royal Navy has been designing a 'through deck cruiser' (a political euphemism worthy of the Kremlin) which could operate either helicopters or a naval development of the Hawker Siddeley Harrier vertical take-off fixed-wing aircraft. It may succeed in producing a cheap 'mini carrier', in which case the Russians could do the same. They already have a Yakovlev-designed research aircraft which uses the vectored thrust engine principle of the Harrier. The Russian prototype was built back in 1964, so although at the time of writing there is no operational version, it could appear at any time. Such an aircraft could fly from the helicopter carrier *Moskva* – or indeed from any warship with a large helicopter pad – although she is by no means an ideal platform for it.[10] In the meantime the US Marines have already bought a first batch of Harriers for operation in support of amphibious operations.

When defending their coasts against NATO's carrier strike forces, the Russians face the naval air problem in another form. The increasing range of Western carrier-borne aircraft has made it possible for a carrier to stand progressively further offshore while threatening inland targets, and has at the same time increased the defensive reach of the carrier's interceptors.

The Soviet Navy has therefore come to depend on co-ordinating its ships' operations with those of long range aircraft, large numbers of which were transferred from the Long Range Air Force at the end of the 1960s. These provide essential reconnaissance services, plus the powerful additional striking power of their stand-off air-to-surface missiles.

Cruise missiles sited ashore have also in effect been put aboard ships and sent to sea. It has become increasingly important for surface warships to carry their own anti-aircraft defences: the fact that the Kresta class ships – which were laid down from 1964

[10] See Chapter 15.

onwards – have a larger proportion of surface-to-air missiles than the earlier Kynda class, started in 1960, may possibly reflect this factor, as well as a general intention to range further afield. Submarines designed to operate in the Baltic or the Black Sea have given way to longer range types.

The way in which this combined defensive screen might be expected to work was demonstrated in July 1968 by the Warsaw Pact navies' Exercise Sever (North). *Izvestia*'s correspondent, evidently well briefed on the Soviet Navy's ability to 'resolve independent, major operational strategic tasks', sent his first despatch on July 13:

Many tens of warships of various classes and types – atomic and diesel powered submarines, cruisers, missile ships, destroyers and trawlers – left their bases for the ocean. In the air were squadrons of bombers to take part in joint operations by the four fleets – Baltic, Northern, East German and Polish.

Taking part were two big naval groups, the 'Westerners' and the 'Easterners'. The Westerners had an aggressive intention to prepare to land ground forces from the sea. Theirs was a very big and powerful group of ships. The aggressive schemes of the Westerners were opposed by the Easterners. They, in an attempt to wrest the initiative from the Westerners, left their bases and took up positions for battle.

The 'battle' was spread over the next ten days. Eastern aircraft appear to have made contact with the Western task force about half-way up the Norwegian Sea, heading north. It was then confronted by a double screen of submarines, the first provided by the Polish Navy and the second by the Russians. At least one ballistic missile attack from a submerged submarine is reported to have been simulated. Finally, two amphibious landings were carried out, one apparently near Murmansk and the other in the Baltic.

The landings not only served to test the defences, which included coastal missile batteries; they also exercised the Warsaw Pact's marines. The Soviet 'naval infantry' was reactivated in the mid-1960s, and now numbers about 12,000 men. This is of course only a small force compared with the 300,000 men of the

US Marine Corps, which has major detachments afloat at all times, but its activities are rightly being closely watched by the West.

Gorshkov has, after all, spent a lot of effort playing down the importance of 'joint operations with the land forces' in the past. It is therefore reasonable to speculate that the new interest in 'naval infantry' is prompted by the 'ocean fleet's' intention to develop a long range amphibious intervention capability, similar to that possessed by the American and British navies, as much as by the continuing requirement to operate along the flanks of NATO, in the Baltic Approaches and the entrance to the Black Sea.

Since the Arab-Israeli war in 1967, Russian tank-landing ships have appeared in the Mediterranean. The helicopter carrier *Moskva* is reported to have taken part in amphibious exercises while she was working up the Black Sea.[11] If amphibious forces were later deployed on the other side of the Suez Canal it would be an important confirmation of the offensive posture many observers believe the Soviet Navy has already taken up. If they were actively used to intervene in some local conflict in the Middle East it would of course be an historic turning point in the Soviet Union's naval strategy.

The submarine plays an important part in three of the four major missions assigned to the Soviet Navy in Marshal Sokolovsky's book, and with its new ability to bombard coastal targets as well as providing a protective screen, it could conceivably be involved in the fourth. The Russians have an enormous number of submarines – more than twice as many as in the American and British navies put together – which in itself accounts for the continuing emphasis on anti-submarine warfare in NATO. In his statement on the 1969 budget, former US Secretary of Defence Robert McNamara described them as 'the main threat to our ability to win a war at sea'.

In Britain, those with memories of how nearly the German U–boats succeeded in starving us in the Second World War tend to regard the size of the Soviet force with particular uneasiness. But the numerical total of 370–380 Russian submarines

[11] *Soviet Sea Power*, Center for Strategic and International Studies, 1969.

should not be taken as a measure of the threat they constitute to Western Europe's supply lines. Something like 150 of these boats are in the Pacific and Black Sea fleets: and of the rest, about 150 are based in the Arctic and 70 in the Baltic. In war, some of them would remain in the Baltic or perhaps be trapped there; others would be assigned to defensive tasks or strategic missions against inland targets. The maximum available for long range anti-shipping operations would surely be less than 200.

At the height of the battle of the Atlantic the Germans had 430 U-boats of which 230 were operational. To make a comparison between the threats posed by German submarines then and Russian ones now, one would have to allow for the much greater effectiveness of nuclear submarines, the long passage from Murmansk for Russian diesel submarines, the effect of afloat support and so on. Robert McNamara summed up in fairly optimistic terms:

As I have stated in past years, our war at sea strategy is based essentially on the rapid emplacement of ASW forces, comprised of submarines and land and sea based ASW aircraft between the enemy submarines and their potential targets. Recent studies have reaffirmed the potential effectiveness of this concept and the probability that in an all-out war at sea we would be able to destroy a very large proportion of the Soviet submarine force in a matter of a few months while losing only a relatively small part of the free world merchant fleet.[12]

If that small part happened to be tankers bringing the oil on which Britain's industry is heavily dependent, she would be in difficult straits; she is, however, more self-sufficient in food production than she was during the Second World War.

In the United States the comparative reassurance of the Pentagon's assessment was attacked by Admiral Rickover as being dangerously complacent. The admiral is often referred to as the 'father' of the American nuclear submarine; a man of evident authority but inevitably suspected of overselling his own product. His arguments may be reduced to three main points

[12] Statement on 1969 US defence budget before Senate Armed Services Committee.

(quotations are from the Congressional hearings before the Joint Committee on Atomic Energy, April 1969):

1. The numerical superiority of the Russian submarine fleet was tolerable in the past because the US Navy had a larger number of the much more effective nuclear submarines, many of them equipped with Subroc anti-submarine ballistic missiles. But the Russians have recently expanded and modernized their nuclear submarine construction yards: 'already one Soviet shipyard has produced seven Polaris type submarines; a rate of twelve a year'. Other classes of nuclear submarine are also being built so that 'by the end of next year (1970) the Soviets will have more nuclear submarines than we do'.

2. Although the standard of Soviet submarine design has lagged behind the American – the main criteria are maximum submerged speed, the speed at which the boat can run 'silently', the depth to which it can dive and the range of its weapons – the Russians are putting a great deal of effort into this area and could overtake the United States: 'When you create an organization that can produce several new design submarines in one year, you have developed a tremendous national asset. One can only imagine what this [Russian] group is capable of producing in the next few years. We on the other hand turn out only one new design in ten years.'

3. The United States should therefore reactivate its own submarine development and construction programme. Whereas in the early 1960s eight or nine Polaris and nuclear attack submarines were being turned out each year, 'as presently planned we will be turning out about five new nuclear attack submarines a year from now on.' Existing plans will bring the American inventory of nuclear submarines to 106–109 by the middle of 1974, by which time the Soviet Navy could have 165 nuclear submarines.

In considering these arguments it is important to distinguish between the Russians' construction of long range ballistic missile submarines, which exist in the Alice in Wonderland world of nuclear deterrence, and the new C and V attack classes, which could play an important role in limited, conventional war as well as trying to neutralize the American seaborne deterrent. The US Navy has stopped building Polaris nuclear missile submarines, of which it has 41.

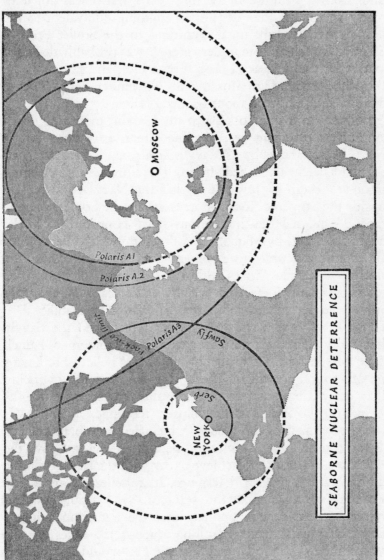

Figure 5 Polaris and its Soviet equivalents showing the areas of the ocean from which they can reach Moscow and New York respectively.

The Russians started modifying submarines to launch ballistic missiles from the surface in the mid-1950s, but it was not until the early 1960s that they developed anything equivalent to the Polaris system. In July 1962, according to the Soviet Press, a missile was launched from underwater. It was probably designed primarily for the nuclear H-class submarines, and similar to the Serb rocket paraded in Moscow in November 1964. This is credited with a range of about 600–700 miles.

From then on it was possible to think about mounting a sea-borne nuclear deterrent by patrolling American waters. But as late as 1966 statements by US Navy officials implied that no such patrols had been established. It may therefore be that Admiral Kasatonov's claim in July 1967 – that the Navy at last ranked alongside the Strategic Rocket Forces within the Soviet supreme command – marked the first serious naval contribution to the strategic deterrent. By May of the following year the Pentagon's head of research and development told Congress that 'the Soviets now operate patrols within missile range of the United States shores, and increasing activity indicates a significantly improved Soviet missile-submarine operational capability'.[13]

It was in 1967 that the Russians first displayed the Sawfly rocket on which their second generation submerged launch ballistic missile system is probably based. It is believed to have a range of about 2,000 miles. The Y class submarines now being built to carry it have sixteen missiles tubes, the same number as the American Polaris boats they closely resemble.

The deployment of the Y class, which became operational in 1968 and can be built at a rate of one a month, at last gave the Soviet Navy the chance to achieve parity with the US Navy in the realm of strategic nuclear deterrence. Its missiles can reach any part of the United States. By the spring of 1970 a deputy assistant secretary of defence said publicly that the Pentagon believed Y class submarines were patrolling 1,200–1,500 miles off the eastern seaboard of the United States.[14] He 'would not be surprised' if the Russians had one on regular station in the Atlantic.

[13] *Soviet Sea Power*, the Center for Strategic and International Studies.
[14] *Guardian*, April 25, 1970.

It was on September 28, 1964, that the uss *Daniel Webster* took the Polaris A–3 missile on operational patrol for the first time, 'leaving no land target inaccessible'. The A–3 has a range of 2,900 miles. It marks the end of a four-year progression from the original 1,400 mile range of the A–1, and the 1,700 miles of the A–2. The speed of this improvement must have infuriated Soviet anti-submarine experts. It means that American boats can back right off into the open ocean – notice how far offshore the Russian Y class boats are said to be – yet still remain within range of many targets inside the ussr. The optimistic statements about destroying them which appear in all three editions of *Military Strategy* are no more than examples of textbook technology: 'In fact even these weapons are vulnerable. An effective counter to nuclear powered missile submarines is provided by hunter-killer submarines with homing missiles and torpedoes, and also by surface vessels.'

Polaris is no doubt one of the major reasons for the increased emphasis the Russians have recently placed on anti-submarine warfare (ASW). In part this is based on their massive hydrographic programme, the other reasons for which we have discussed earlier. It no doubt includes the development of longer range sonar, better homing torpedoes, airborne magnetic anomaly detection equipment and experiments in the tactical use of reconnaissance satellites. Two visible signs of all this activity are the helicopter carrier *Moskva*, which spends a good deal of time trailing her variable depth sonar round the Mediterranean, and the intelligence 'trawlers' which lie rolling and pitching off Polaris bases such as the Holy Loch in Scotland. It may be that, beneath the waves, Soviet nuclear submarines attempt to trail the missile boats as they set off on patrol; and sonar arrays may have been laid on the bed of the Barents Sea.

NATO sources seem to be agreed that the Russians are catching up in this form of warfare. But Royal Navy experts – who reckon that their ASW technology is unmatched by even the Americans – indicate that the Soviet Navy still has some way to go. It is true that a technical breakthrough which would make the Polaris detection problem tractable could happen at any time:

but for the moment, and probably for years to come, it stands out as one mission the Red Fleet cannot accomplish – and a good reason why the Russians should be building their own equivalent of Polaris.

CHAPTER II

The Red Fleet in Blue Waters

In general, the range of Soviet naval activity has been increased in parallel with the rapid expansion of the Russian merchant fleet. The appearance of the Soviet Union's freighters on the great deep sea trade routes is matched by the increasing frequency with which her warships emerge from the Baltic and the Black Sea to cruise the warm waters of the Mediterranean, the Indian Ocean and even the Caribbean. Economic aid to the politically sensitive 'third world' is complemented by a supply of naval equipment. Merchant and naval fleets are together carrying the Red Flag into southern corners of the oceans where it has never been seen before.

Some of the direct ways in which Russian merchant vessels can assist their naval colleagues have already been discussed: a tanker sent out to refuel a submarine, a trawler collecting hydrographic data, a scientific research vessel monitoring NATO communications. But a merchant navy also creates a naval reserve of men who know what it means to go to sea, with experience of foreign ports and foreign people; it builds the maritime traditions and awareness that a nation like Britain takes for granted. The Royal Navy may feel that it gets a raw deal from the Treasury and from politicians, but at least they understand phrases like 'showing the flag' and can still joke about 'sending in a gunboat'. In the Soviet Union at the time of Khrushchev, there was even talk of dispensing with a conventional navy altogether, until the Cuban confrontation demonstrated the value of long range surface forces. And although the effectiveness of gunboat diplomacy in its more subtle twentieth-century forms is increasingly appreciated in Moscow, it seems to have been discovered almost by accident, primarily as a result of Soviet involvement in the Arab-Israeli conflict.

Once a country possesses a large merchant navy, its protection tends to become one of the stock arguments for maintaining or increasing the naval defence budget: 'The necessity of strenthening the naval might of the USSR is also stipulated by the rapid development of our cargo and commercial fleet, and the broadening of the state interests of our country on the seas and oceans'.[1]

This same argument has been used often enough by the Royal Navy. In the past, it was also assumed that the fortunes of commercial shipping were to some extent a function of naval power: 'Trade follows the Flag'. But there is a clear difference between this sort of indirect relationship and that which exists in the USSR. There, investment in both the merchant and naval fleets appears in the central budget, and areas where their functions and interests overlap – in foreign aid programmes or oceanographic research – can be closely co-ordinated. Admiral Moorer, formerly the US Navy's Chief of Operations, summed it up in this way:

The elements (of Soviet sea power) are so thoroughly integrated as to present a single structure. For all intents and purposes they are all a part of the Soviet Navy and can so operate to the levels of greatest efficiency for the state. We do need to consider that to make comparisons in terms of ships and capabilities, theirs to ours, may not be the point at all. The point could well be that the Soviets are further along than we are in understanding what technology is bringing to the oceans. They may be on the way to achieving the flexible presence of power I mentioned earlier – and they may get there first.[2]

Admiral Moorer was exaggerating in order to make his point. But then he views the Soviet maritime expansion from a country the government of which has direct control over only one of the three main elements of sea power. Congressional committees may issue dire warnings, but the American fishing industry's

[1] Soviet Navy Day editorial cited by Lieutenant-Commander Cox USN, *US Naval Institute Proceedings*, June 1969.

[2] From a speech to the Defence Orientation Conference Association, September 1968.

response to the Communist challenge was to allow its own catch to fall. The US Government obviously puts a high strategic value on its merchant marine – witness the six and a half million ton reserve fleet and the readiness to pay for 'defence features' but it has to be kept alive commercially by an elaborate system of subsidies, and by turning a blind eye to wholesale operation under other flags.

By comparison, the Russian communists appear to have combined all three elements into a smoothly co-ordinated national effort. Yet the Khrushchev regime was surprisingly slow to realize how a visible naval 'presence' might further its political, and even economic, aims throughout the world.

To an Englishman, life in the navy traditionally involves long blue water voyages, tropical awnings and 'runs ashore' in exotic foreign ports. But for the Soviet Navy the 13,000-mile voyage of the cruiser *Dzerzhinsky* in 1961 was an event, to be meticulously planned beforehand and talked about proudly for a long time afterwards. Apart from a few long-distance cruises by submarines, Russian warships were largely confined to their designated fleet areas, forming a close protective screen round their own coastline.

When the freighters carrying Khrushchev's missiles neared Cuba in 1962, their only naval protection consisted of a few submarines – invisible but not, apparently, undetected. This was presumably deliberate – rather than evidence that no surface ships were available – since the original purpose of the exercise was to install the missiles without the Americans' knowledge and then confront them with a *fait accompli*. But the all-or-nothing nature of Khrushchev's manœuvre was seen by Western naval strategists as demonstrating the narrow range of options open to him. The presence of a balanced naval force may have been irrelevant to the original plan, but had it been the United States or even Britain that was supporting Cuba, they would evidently have possessed the means to provide one and therefore been less dependent on secrecy. Khrushchev's freighters found themselves completely isolated once it became clear what they were up to. It was that much easier to call his bluff.

NATO admirals have never ceased to remind the Russians of this fact. Whatever Khrushchev thought at the time, this hopelessly uneven confrontation with the well-balanced might of the US Navy probably provided his naval commander-in-chief with just the political ammunition he needed to reassert the importance of long range surface forces.[3] It seems to be more than a coincidence that the 'visibility' of Soviet naval power has steadily increased since that year.

The chronology runs something like this:

1961 – Soviet warships carry out modest exercises in the Norwegian Sea instead of merely shuttling between the Northern and Baltic fleet areas.

1962 – ships from the Black Sea venture out into the Atlantic in order to join the Northern Fleet in the arctic.

1963 – what is to become a regular pattern of exercises in the North East corner of the Atlantic is established; one group of ships circumnavigates the British Isles.

1964 – a small squadron spends part of the year in the Mediterranean; ships visit Cuba.

1965 – the Mediterranean exercise is repeated, with more ships for a longer period.

1966 – for the first time Soviet vessels conduct basic work-up exercises out in the Iceland–Faroes gap.

1967 – the Mediterranean squadron becomes permanent and, after the June War, Soviet warships steam into Alexandria; research vessels begin to survey the Indian Ocean.

1968 – a Soviet naval squadron appears in the Indian Ocean.

1969 – the Soviet Mediterranean squadron is at times numerically superior to the US Sixth Fleet.

1970 – the world wide exercise 'Okean', celebrating the hundredth anniversary of Lenin's birth, puts massive emphasis on the oceanic nature of Soviet naval power.

Okean (Ocean) involved nearly a hundred ships in the North Atlantic, fifty in the Mediterranean, about two dozen in the Pacific between Japan and the Philippines, and fifteen in the Indian Ocean off the coast of Africa. Hundreds of aircraft took part,

[3] See Chapter 10.

including Tu 20s which flew non-stop from the northern Soviet Union to Cuba. The helicopter carrier *Leningrad* emerged – for the first time – from the Mediterranean to join anti-submarine forces off Iceland. An amphibious group headed north from the Baltic, and a landing took place near the North Cape. Surface warships, submarines, naval bombers and reconnaissance aircraft exercised against one another in various combinations.

The only thing which marred the dramatic effect was the loss of a nuclear submarine in deep Atlantic water right at the beginning. No doubt, as the original announcement said, Okean was designed to 'test and further improve the Navy's combat skill and operational preparedness', but the impact it was intended to have – and did have – on the West, was summed up by its name.

One of the striking things about this new oceanic presence is that it does not depend on having naval bases scattered throughout the world. Like other big modern navies, the Soviet fleet is truly independent of the land when it wants to be.

Britain's great Imperial navy operated along a chain of bases from Spithead to Singapore. A few, like Gibraltar, are still in her possession. But they are no longer essential. A squadron can be sent out from its home base in England and maintained – expensively – at sea by a technique known as 'afloat support'. In the same way the US Sixth Fleet in the Mediterranean consists almost entirely of ships rotated from the Atlantic. They remain on patrol, meeting whenever necessary with a naval auxiliary to take on supplies.

To do this the ships have no need to stop. Nowadays it is quite normal to see an oiler ploughing along at, say, 15 knots, while warships on either side refuel from the hoses rigged between them. The only limitation is that they must hold a steady course. Fuel can be transferred in half a gale, although the ships naturally reduce speed as the weather worsens. In calm conditions NATO squadrons have given spectacular demonstrations of five or six vessels linked together in line abreast, alternately warships and auxiliaries.

Since 1964, when according to Admiral Gorshkov 'the long

cruise became routine', the Soviet Navy too has rapidly developed its afloat support. Whereas the British and Americans did so because they were steadily losing overseas bases, the Russians had neither the opportunity nor, apparently, much desire to acquire them. For a while, until the ideological split with Albania, Russian submarines had a land base in the Mediterranean. Since 1967 the Soviet Navy has also been making extensive use of Egyptian and Syrian ports for repairs, fuelling, victualling and recreation. But this does not mean that Alexandria or Latakia has become a Soviet naval 'base' in the traditional Western sense, in spite of the way many commentators use that word.

Even if the Arab governments were prepared to grant formal, permanent base rights the USSR would gain nothing by demanding them. The Israelis may argue that from their point of view the distinction is academic, but the history of the former British presence in Egypt and Aden suggests that it may at some time be vital. The Soviet Union's objective must surely be to see the Arabs dependent on its support without in turn becoming dependent on them or wounding local political pride. Anything which helps to make the military commitments less than automatic is going to be welcome, and a modern navy's ability to do without fixed land bases if necessary is one of them.

But if avoiding shore base commitments is a general rule with the Russians, might they not consider it worth breaking in Cuba, which is much further from home than Alexandria – and a lot nearer Washington?

In the summer of 1970 a Soviet submarine tender berthed in the Cuban harbour of Cienfuegos – on the south coast about forty miles from the Bay of Pigs – and American U2 reconnaissance aircraft photographed construction work ashore 'of a type associated with submarine operations'.[4]

The way the affair developed provided a fascinating comparison with the Cuban crisis of 1962. Not that there were many visible signs of crisis this time; but the strength of the diplomatic undercurrents could be guessed at from the occasional eddies breaking the surface. At the end of September a US Government

[4] *Guardian*, September 26, 1970.

spokesman, evidently speaking with the authority of the President, warned that the establishment of a Soviet submarine base in the eastern Caribbean would be viewed with 'the utmost seriousness'. White House officials deliberately reminded the Press corps of the understanding reached between Khrushchev and Kennedy in 1962 – which amounted to an American promise not to invade if the Russian missiles were removed.

In Moscow, Pravda dismissed the new alarm as an unnecessary American propaganda campaign; but in mid–October 1970 the Kremlin issued a formal denial – except that by denying that the Soviet Union was establishing 'its military base' in Cuba, the Russians left open the possibility that they were building a naval base for the Cubans which Soviet warships could then use.[5]

The Pentagon evidently feared that a tender berthed in Cienfuegos would be used to service the Y class ballistic missile submarines (the Russian equivalent of the American Polaris boats) already lurking off the eastern seaboard of the United States. American officials had to admit, of course, that the facilities in Cienfuegos (reported to include barracks and shore cranes near the tender's berth) would be equivalent in that case to the US Navy's Polaris bases at Holy Loch, Scotland and Rota, in southern Spain. But they seem to have been no more impressed with this argument than their predecessors were in 1962 when reminded about American missiles in Turkey. The establishment of a Cuban base, they pointed out, would change the strategic balance just when that balance was under discussion in the Strategic Arms Limitation Talks (SALT).

However, the potential shift in the balance was far, far less than it had been eight years earlier. The Y class was not dependent on facilities in Cuba, though they might make life easier. Nor was the presence of Soviet warships in the Caribbean in itself a novelty by the summer of 1970. Admiral Gorshkov's long range naval forces had already quietly achieved for Brezhnev and Kosygin much of what Khrushchev's land missiles had dangerously failed to achieve in 1962.

[5] The Kremlin's statement was analysed by my colleague, Victor Zorza, in *The Guardian* of October 14, 1970.

At the time of writing, it remains to be seen what the Russians will eventually gain from this latest Cuban manœuvre. By mid-November the State Department claimed to have reached 'an understanding' with the Kremlin[6] but it is not clear whether construction work in Cienfuegos has been abandoned or whether the submarine tender will finally sail for home.

The Soviet Navy now operates a fleet of about 150 major auxiliaries, more or less equally divided between oilers, supply vessels and repair ships. The oilers can be supplemented by merchant marine tankers – like the *Karl Marx*, which accompanied the squadron paying a ceremonial visit to Cuba in 1969 – which are also used to supply the long range fishing fleets at sea.

Submarines were among the first Russian warships to take to the open ocean and they have cruised unsupported for periods of more than two months. But they now have available to them specialized classes of ocean-going depot ship, missile carriers and nuclear maintenance vessels, mostly built within the past five years. One nuclear submarine is known to have remained at sea for six months supported by a group of surface vessels, and a task force comprising several submarines patrolled the central Atlantic for a while, replenished and repaired by its own tenders.

However, in spite of such impressive demonstrations the normal Soviet practice of afloat support is still below Western standards. At sea, Russian warships generally use the older method of refuelling, from a hose trailing over the oiler's stern, as opposed to a multiple hose rig swung over the side. They are occasionally replenished under way, but most of the time they are content to lie alongside in some sheltered anchorage – a method which the American and British navies reckon makes their ships unnecessarily vulnerable.

A Russian naval chart of the Mediterranean, therefore, is sprinkled with anchorages not bases. The ones most frequently used have been near the island of Kithira, between Greece and Crete, in Salum Bay, west of Alexandria, in the Gulf of

[6] *Guardian*, November 18.

Hammamet on the Tunisian coast, and off the Spanish island of Alboran near Gibraltar.

To provide the one thing the Soviet Navy cannot take to sea with it – because it has no aircraft carriers – the Russians reached a discreet compromise with Egypt. By 1969 it was an open secret that a squadron of Tu 16 medium bombers based at a former RAF airfield near Cairo, and painted with Egyptian Air Force markings, was being flown by Russian pilots to maintain surveillance of NATO's naval forces. These aircraft sometimes landed in Algeria, at the other end of the Mediterranean, where a number of airstrips are reported to have been lengthened with Russian assistance. From this sort of arrangement, which has been repeated for different reasons with Egyptian MiG 21 interceptors, it is only a short step to regular Soviet Air Force squadrons being 'invited' in to meet some future 'imperialist threat'.

Between Algeria and Egypt is Libya, which became committed to the pan-Arab struggle against Israel after the 1969 coup, although maintaining many of her contacts with the West. As the American and British bases were being dismantled, the Soviet forces were no doubt angling for invitations from the new revolutionary regime. A few Russians moved in immediately as advisers to the Egyptian army instructors. But here, as in Algeria, the communists were met by a powerful diplomatic counter offensive from France, reflected in the sale of more than a hundred Mirage fighters to the Libyan Air Force and the French Navy's courtesy visit, in the spring of 1970, to the Algerian naval base at Mers-el-Kebir. This big base had, of course, formerly belonged to the French, but since their departure there had been repeated rumours that the Soviet Navy would be invited to replace them.

The French Government is probably concerned as much as anything to safeguard its oil supplies from North Africa, but worried NATO military commanders have naturally followed its effort with the greatest of interest. When Admiral Moorer, formerly US Navy chief of operations, gave his assessment of the naval balance in the Mediterranean to a House of Representatives

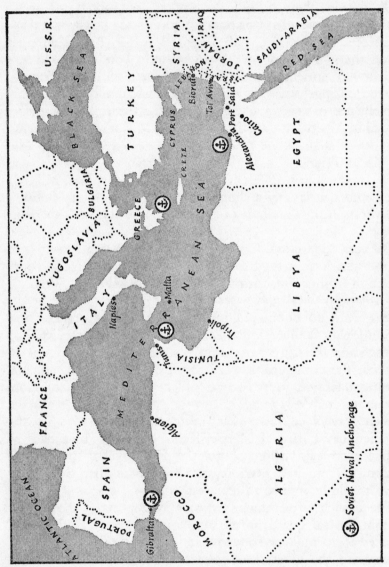

Figure 6 The Mediterranean showing Soviet naval anchorages.

appropriations sub-committee in February 1970, he said that the two serious threats to the Sixth Fleet were the Soviet submarines, and the possibility of Russian aircraft operating from a chain of airfields along the North African coast.

Even if the Mediterranean were not the scene of a bitter and unresolved conflict between Arabs and Jews, control of it would be of immense strategic importance. To the north it exposes the 'soft underbelly of NATO'; on its southern shore new wealth literally flows out of the ground. It has only three narrow entrances and the Soviet Navy's route from Sevastopol to the Atlantic lies through two of them. The third used to be the great maritime short cut which took Europe's manufactured goods to the Far East and brought back raw materials (on March 15, 1967, Lloyd's recorded 1,800 ocean-going merchant vessels in the Mediterranean and Black Sea, more than half of them flying one of the NATO flags and none of them more than 250 miles from land).

From the opening of the Suez Canal in 1869 until the Second World War, the dominant naval power in these waters was the Royal Navy, maintaining bases in Gibraltar, Malta and, later, in Port Said. With the creation of NATO the US Navy progressively assumed control until it came to be regarded for military purposes as virtually an American lake. Then came the Soviet challenge; tentative at first, but becoming more positive and more confident in the wake of the Arab-Israeli war of 1967. In December of that year the Soviet Army newspaper *Red Star* complained on its naval colleagues' behalf at the 'impudent' way US warships kept watch on the Soviet squadron but warned that 'the situation in the Mediterranean has changed, and will continue to change, not in favour of the aggressor'. By November of the following year, *Izvestia* was boldly demanding that the Americans call their ships home and leave the Soviet Navy to keep the peace.

NATO's formal response to the Soviet build-up was the forma-tion, in 1968, of Maritime Air Forces Mediterranean (Marairmed) to maintain continual surveillance of the Russian ships' activity, and a half-hearted decision to have an international squadron of frigates 'on call'. Marairmed is composed of an American squadron of Orions based in Italy, British Shackletons (to be replaced by Nimrod jets) in Gibraltar and Malta, and a mixed force of Italian aircraft in Sicily and Sardinia. Some of these aircraft would have been on patrol anyway, but the information they collected would not immediately have been exchanged and co-ordinated through NATO channels. It is hoped to include Greece and Turkey in the new command as soon as they have suitable equipment.

In that same year NATO was also quietly dusting off contingency plans to protect or support Yugoslavia if requested; this was, of course, the year in which the Red Army invaded Czechoslovakia. Such planning was reflected in the communique issued after the ministerial meeting in Brussels that November: 'Clearly any Soviet intervention directly or indirectly affecting the situation in Europe or other Mediterranean areas would create an international crisis with grave consequences.' If Yugoslavia were permanently overrun by Soviet forces the Italian Navy would find itself sharing the Adriatic with the Soviet Fleet. How far this lessened the Russians' reliance on the Turkish Straits would depend on circumstances. But important as the purely naval consequences might be, they would be swamped by much larger issues.

The Royal Navy's presence in the Mediterranean dwindled during the 1960s to a handful of minesweepers and frigates. In 1969 Britain offered to retain at least one major unit – carrier, commando ship or assault ship – for most of the time as evidence of its increased commitment to European defence, but even this modest promise has proved difficult to keep. Italy maintains a substantial navy (one of the two Allied naval commands in southern Europe is held by an Italian admiral) and the French Navy maintains close touch with NATO at some levels even though it has withdrawn from the integrated command structure. But the major Western force confronting the Russians in the Mediterranean is of course American.

The United States Sixth Fleet consists at present of about 40 vessels, 180 aircraft and 21,000 men operating as a self-contained unit independent of the shore. The combat ships are usually divided into two task forces, each led by an attack carrier, escorted by a cruiser and a squadron of destroyers. In addition there is an amphibious group of about half a dozen vessels with a reinforced battalion of Marines, a handful of submarines and a minesweeping squadron. The fleet 'train' comprises oilers, ammunition carriers, supply and repair ships.

Aircraft are the key; not only because they carry the American fleet's main punch, but also because the Soviet ships have to operate without air support except in so far as it can be provided from land bases in the Soviet Union or from borrowed Arab airfields. At any time of the day or night an attack carrier like the *USS Saratoga* has an early warning radar aircraft in the air, with a tanker and a mix of fighters, reconnaissance and strike aircraft. The ship pulses to the continuous cycle of launch and recovery. Even lying in one's bunk in the darkness one is aware of the same rhythmic pattern: the roar of jet afterburners quickly followed by the thump of a steam catapult; the scream of the arrester wire as another aircraft lands.

I mention *Saratoga* by name because a visit I made to her in 1969 illustrates another aspect of the Mediterranean confrontation – the curiosity which both sides have about the other. During my short time aboard only a few ships appeared above the carrier's horizon but two of them were Russian. One was an electronic 'spy' trawler that came plodding up from the westward and the other a freighter which came near to causing a really nasty collision.

The carrier was taking on fuel and stores from a naval supply ship steaming alongside, with hoses and a wire conveyor system rigged between them, when the freighter appeared ahead on an almost reciprocal course. Instead of turning to starboard, as one would expect in such circumstances, the Soviet vessel held on as if she were determined to plough straight between the two Americans. *Saratoga* cast off everything in a hurry. The auxiliary hauled in her gear and began to swing away. But at the last moment the oncoming freighter put her wheel hard over and swept by on the carrier's clear side, to starboard.

The chances are that whoever was manning the Russian's bridge was by then as concerned as we were at what might have happened – if, for example, the *Saratoga* had herself turned sharply to starboard she might literally have chopped the other vessel in two. But if the near collision was unintended, the Soviet freighter's decision to plot a course through the American exercise area may have been the result of deliberate curiosity. The intelligence trawler's obviously was.

The Russians presumably use trawler hulls for many of their intelligence ships because they are cheap and seaworthy, but in the Western press this has invested them with a peculiarly sinister quality, as if they went around pretending to be fishermen. In fact, of course, they are the equivalent of the *USS Pueblo*, captured by the North Koreans. Their jobs include listening to radio traffic, establishing the location of radar sites, and recording the electronic characteristics of NATO warships' equipment so that jamming devices can be designed.

The passive monitoring of the wallowing trawlers is supplemented by fast warships which can, and do, keep close station on NATO task forces, particularly during exercises. During Exercise Silver Tower, in 1968, for example, which involved more than a hundred NATO vessels, the Russians sent a mixed surveillance fleet equipped with its own oilers. It included three Kotlin class destroyers, two intelligence trawlers and about a dozen other vessels apparently diverted through the exercise area. In addition Tu 16, Tu 20 and Mya 4 aircraft (the last of these presumably from the Long Range Air Force) made daily, low level reconnaissance flights. Radio traffic was obviously being systematically monitored and manoeuvres recorded.

A NATO staff officer commented that 'the Russians' close interest was not unexpected and in fact it added a great deal to the realism of the exercise as far as our ships and pilots were concerned'. Indeed mutual surveillance of the other side's operations is such a routine affair these days one wonders how long it will be before NATO and the Warsaw Pact agree to simplify matters by holding their annual naval exercises together. Anyone watching the Royal Navy's commando ship *Bulwark*, during another exercise in 1968, escorted by no less than eight Soviet vessels including a Kresta class cruiser, might well have been puzzled as to which fleet was the interloper.

Although there must be many things Western commanders would rather the Russian sailors did not see or hear, the presence of strange warships weaving through a task force should not be a navigational hazard provided they follow the international collision avoidance rules. But obviously they can be a nuisance – for example to a carrier which wants to turn into wind to launch her aircraft. Inevitably, there are occasional complaints that curiosity has given way to deliberate harassment.

In May 1967 a Soviet destroyer actually scraped the length of the *USS Walker* during joint American and Japanese anti-submarine exercises in the Sea of Japan. Later that year in the Mediterranean, where the Russians had established a permanent squadron in the wake of the June War, the crew of the submarine tender *Mahomet Gadzhiyev* complained of being blinded by American aircraft flares and searchlights. Was this just a piece of air hooliganism? asked the subsequent article in *Red Star*.[7] In November 1970 two Russian sailors died when a Kotlin class destroyer was in collision with the British aircraft carrier *Ark Royal*, during night flying operations in the eastern Mediterranean. Both commanders complained of the other's bad seamanship, but the Royal Navy's account of the incident, putting the blame firmly on the shadowing destroyer, carried far more conviction.[8]

On several occasions recently, the numerical strength of the Soviet Navy's Mediterranean squadron has exceeded that of the US Sixth Fleet. But it varies a good deal, with the result that every few months there is a new 'Red build-up in the Med' which commentators can, if they feel inclined, attribute to 'renewed Middle East tension'. The most significant increase followed the Arab-Israeli war of June 1967. Since then the squadron's size has fluctuated according to a basic seasonal pattern, from 30–40 vessels during the winter months to 50–60 in the summer. Most

[7] *Guardian*, December 29, 1967.
[8] *Guardian*, November 11, 1970.

of these ships are drawn from the Soviet Black Sea fleet, with its headquarters at Sevastopol. But nowadays they are often joined by groups from the Baltic which may later proceed through the Bosphorus, and there is a certain amount of movement in the opposite direction. Gibraltar and Istanbul – particularly the latter, since submarines are required by the Montreux Convention to pass through the straits on the surface during daylight and would hardly remain undetected even if they could negotiate the shallows submerged – provide NATO with convenient checkpoints from which to monitor the ebb and flow. In a general war NATO should be able to close one or both of these entrances and make the sheer weight of its naval and air forces tell, whatever initial advantage the Russians might have gained. Its shore-based air support is still much better.

In April 1969 a record total of 65 Russian vessels assembled to monitor NATO's exercise Dawn Patrol. In August another peak of 63 ships was recorded during large-scale Soviet exercises led by the new 18,000 ton helicopter carrier *Moskva*. With her in the Mediterranean were 3 cruisers, 10 destroyers, 8 escorts, 8 landing ships, about 15 submarines and the usual assortment of tenders, supply ships and oilers.

The counting of hulls indicates the increasing size of the Russian presence, but it is a poor guide to the comparative strength of Soviet and American naval forces in this part of the world. For a start, the Russians would no doubt try to assemble an even larger number of ships if they really expected to go to war. But in any case differences in the type of warships facing each other could be more important than the nominal size of the two fleets, and there is also the question of whether the available weapons are actually used. The military balance would probably be quite different, for example, in a short nuclear exchange than it would be in a protracted conventional conflict that had escalated gradually from some local incident. These qualifications do not, however, upset the general statement that the Sixth Fleet's aircraft carrier groups – backed by other NATO navies and land-based air forces – are a far more powerful and flexible striking force than the carrier-less Soviet surface squadron, which has to rely on ship-to-ship missiles and limited land-based air support.

Whether NATO's superiority is as assured and overwhelming as the former British Defence Minister Denis Healey implied when he said that the Soviet warships would be sunk within minutes of the outbreak of general war, before they had time to fire their missiles, is another matter.[9] Mr Healey's main purpose was probably to divert public attention from the more immediately obvious problem of the purely military threat, towards the immense political importance of the Russian presence. But taking his words at face value the Soviet Navy's Commander-in-Chief, Admiral Gorshkov, can hardly be blamed for the sharpness of his rejoinder: 'Such unpardonable boasting does no credit to a British statesman. I think the British admirals would find it hard to fulfil their Minister's promise.'[10]

The Admiral confused the issue by pretending that Mr Healey was only talking about the Royal Navy. But the British Minister's picture of the Soviet squadron as a lot of sitting ducks appears to contain at least one important assumption – that the US Sixth Fleet could necessarily pre-empt a Russian attack. Are the carrier task forces invulnerable to a surprise multi-missile onslaught? No doubt the war game computers have an answer, but it may not be reassuring. And what of the large force of submarines the Russians maintain in the Mediterranean, equipped with torpedoes and cruise missiles? These are probably the most difficult waters in the world for sonar detection.

Commenting on the big Soviet build-up in the spring of 1969, the Allied Forces Commander in southern Europe, Admiral Rivero, USN, said that although he was comparatively confident about neutralizing the Russian surface fleet, 'the submarine threat is much more difficult to handle'. At that time there were probably about twenty Soviet submarines in the area, mostly of the diesel powered F-class, but some of them nuclear powered. A more usual number these days is about a dozen, accompanied by their own tenders and oilers. Most of them enter the Mediterranean through the Straits of Gibraltar.

[9] *Guardian*, February 12 and 20, 1969; *Sunday Times*, February 16, 1969.
[10] *The Times*, April 5, 1969.

In order to make the threat of their surface-to-surface missiles and torpedoes credible, the Russians must demonstrate that they can find the NATO forces whenever they wish and maintain close contact with them. One of the Soviet squadron's basic jobs, therefore, must be to practise maritime interception, for which the high speed of many Russian surface vessels makes them particularly well suited. Once having established contact, the time can profitably be spent observing the NATO ships' operational routines, looking for gaps in the radar and sonar screen and collecting 'electronic signatures'.

Meanwhile the anti-submarine vessels, led by the *Moskva* and the *Leningrad*, no doubt continue to work at the intractable technical problem of locating the nine Polaris ballistic missile submarines patrolling in deep water from American bases at Rota, in southern Spain, and the Holy Loch in Scotland.

But the Soviet Navy does not have to fight hypothetical world wars in order to see a return for its investment in a Mediterranean presence. In terms of political influence the profit is already a handsome one even if it derives – as Mr Healey reminded us – from an exaggerated idea of the Russian ships' military significance.

No country in the Middle East can doubt that NATO now takes the Soviet Navy's challenge seriously, whatever the reasons. For Arab countries which have temporarily at least placed themselves under Communist protection to further their struggle with Israel, this must be deeply reassuring. And every time a Western journalist writes another scare story about the sinister activities of the Red Fleet, or an American admiral defending his budget against the congressional axe adopts the same alarmist tone, they are further encouraged.

When a Soviet admiral declares that 'the Mediterranean is no longer an American lake' his words are nowadays only too obviously true. The Russians need not be capable of defeating the Sixth Fleet to inhibit its action; they merely need to place themselves in its line of fire. Far too much is at stake for the Americans to risk tangling directly with the communists unless their own interests are directly threatened. Hence the value to

Egypt of the large Russian warships which steamed into Alexandria after the war with Israel.

Nor is the effect necessarily confined to the Arabs. Clare
Hollingworth has pointed out[11] that if the Red Flag is waved
often enough it may make even the Turks wonder whether some
sort of political insurance policy might not be useful. They are
already uneasy about NATO's switch from a strategy of massive
retaliation to one of 'flexible response.' Now there seems to be a
widespread suspicion that if there were a Communist invasion of
Turkey, the Americans would be found watching it on their
television sets. Against this sort of background, the removal of
one of the US task forces from the Mediterranean as an economy
measure would present the American administration with a real
public relations problem.

The Russians' physical presence in Egypt also had a significant
effect in inhibiting Israeli retaliation against breaches of the 1967
ceasefire. Some observers believe that the Israelis would have hit
back directly at the missile patrol boat which sank their destroyer
Eilat, possibly from the shelter of Port Said, but for the Soviet
warships also berthed there. It is certainly true that Israeli jets
and artillery have taken care not to hit the former British naval
base in Port Said, now used by the Russians.

At first the area of immunity was extremely small. The edge of
the port was subjected to artillery bombardments and Israel Air
Force jets bombed targets immediately to the west – although
they seem to have taken care not to fly over the Soviet warships
in the process. It was accepted that some of the Russian military
advisers and technicians scattered throughout the country must
have been killed or injured in periodic raids intended to knock
holes in the southern perimeter of Cairo's air defences.

But when, in the spring of 1970, the Russians began to install
SA–3 low level missile defences around key targets in central
Egypt and brought in their own servicemen to man them, the
Israelis showed signs of hesitation. Shortly afterwards it was
announced from Tel Aviv that Russian pilots were flying MiG
interceptors on operational missions to provide air cover for the

[11] *Daily Telegraph*, April 9, 1969.

same central areas – as opposed to the canal zone – and that Israeli pilots would avoid combat with them unless it was absolutely essential. How long it can be avoided remains to be seen. It now depends on the missiles as well as the men.

A deliberately visible presence therefore has its uses; but the point about ships, as opposed to soldiers or aircraft, is that they can if necessary remain invisible from the land. In fact, varying degrees of visibility can be arranged at will.

If the requirement is to 'show the flag', then nothing can match a freshly painted warship sweeping up to the town quay, with a band playing and the crew lining the decks. Local dignitaries can be entertained on board (the Royal Navy's rum and gin drinking traditions, and the plentiful supply of vodka the Soviet Navy always offers its guests, give them a big advantage here over the 'dry' American ships) and the ship's company sent off to fraternize on whatever scale seems diplomatically appropriate. Ashore, the Russians seem to rely somewhat heavily on earnest cultural tours, while British and American sailors can be relied upon to boost the income of the local bars and clubs.

The important thing about a ship is that as soon as she feels that she has overstayed her welcome she can cast off and slide away over the horizon. There she can wait unseen, far less likely to become a focus for the resentment so often aroused by army camps and noisy military airfields. She offers protection without occupation; the possibility of intervention without commitment.

CHAPTER 12

Military Aid and Political Influence

The primary mechanism of communist imperialism in the Mediterranean area is military aid, supplemented by the economic aid discussed earlier. Yet in comparison with the Western powers, the Soviet Union is a newcomer to the international arms trade. In the first decade after the Second World War the USA and Britain scattered large quantities of military surplus equipment round the world, while the USSR concentrated on building the armed strength of her immediate circle of Communist satellites.

The year 1955, which saw the first Russian arms deal with Egypt, through Czechoslovakia (accompanied by an offer to help build the Aswan Dam), proved to be a turning point in Soviet foreign policy. Since then, although the transfers of Russian arms have still been on a smaller scale than those from the Americans,[1] they have made a spectacular political impact.

The total for all countries outside the Soviet bloc is probably something like £2,500 millions and more than half of the two dozeu or so recipients have been helped to build up their navies. Non-Warsaw Pact countries using Russian warships include Egypt, Syria, Algeria, India, Indonesia, North Vietnam and North Korea.

In the case of Indonesia, the Russians supplied what amounted to a complete navy of more than a hundred vessels, including a Sverdlov cruiser, a dozen W class submarines, seven Skory class destroyers, seven Riga class frigates and twelve Komar patrol boats equipped with Styx guided missiles. However, the support for these vessels was abruptly withdrawn when the Sukarno

[1] See Geoffrey Kemp's *Arms Traffic and Third World Conflicts*, International Conciliation, March 1970 for a full analysis.

regime was ousted, and it is believed that a substantial number of them soon ceased to be operational. The commander-in-chief apparently managed to obtain a few spares from Moscow virtually on a 'cash and carry' basis, but this was hardly a substitute for properly organized technical support. Quite apart from this, there is the problem of Indonesia's hot, humid climate, which is said to have ruined much of the electronic equipment in ships designed to operate in cool northern waters.

Here then is a moral tale for other nations, notably in the Arab world, that have become dependent on the Soviet Union for their major arms supplies; to which the Russians would no doubt reply by pointing to similar situations involving Western suppliers, such as General de Gaulle's refusal to deliver the Mirage aircraft bought by Israel and the partial embargo applied in the Middle East by the United States and Britain.

The object of Anglo-American policy is to maintain a military 'balance', the absolute level of which is largely determined by Soviet deliveries to the Arabs. Egypt alone is estimated to have received something like £1,000 million in Russian military aid. Substantial arms shipments have also gone to Syria, Iraq and Algeria.

The first Soviet arms for Egypt, valued at £80 million, were actually sold through Czechoslovakia. By the outbreak of the war with Israel in June, 1967, the Egyptians were operating hundreds of Russian aircraft, tanks and ships. Many of their officers had attended training courses in Moscow, and in Egypt they were assisted by Russian technicians and military advisers.

Then in six days the Israelis proceeded to destroy almost the entire Egyptian air force on the ground and capture much of the armour. After a horrified pause, the Soviet Union responded by replacing the tanks and fighters with more recent models, and on even easier terms, according to the Israelis. But this time there were not only more advisers; it was made clear from the start that their advice would be listened to. If there was going to be another war, the Soviet equipment had better be on the winning side.

In return for this 'fraternal' support the Arabs must accept the dependence created by the need for training, a continuing supply of spare parts, the extension of long term credit and whatever political strings are attached to the aid package. The Russians, for their part, have acquired an influence proportional to that dependence – although if the Arabs ever make peace with the Jews their influence may quickly evaporate – and a powerful lever with which to exert pressure on the United States and her allies. They are also building a military infrastructure. Stocks of spare parts for T 54/55 tanks, MiG 21 fighters and Komar missile patrol boats are now located all over the Middle East. Soviet aircraft are reported to have staging rights in Syria and Iraq – as well they might since military transports have been in and out so frequently with deliveries of arms. In Egypt, staging rights have already merged into something more ambitious.

It is obvious that any state which buys its arms abroad sacrifices its independence in some degree, some of the time. The important distinction among the developing nations which 'buy Russian' is the extent to which they are capable of maintaining and using the equipment when they get it. There is, for example, a vast difference between India, whose economy has a broad enough technological base to dispense with Soviet technicians once its own people have trained to operate a particular piece of gear, and Egypt, where the whole fabric of the armed forces is of necessity permeated by Soviet technicians, advisers, pilots and anti-aircraft gunners. (At the time of writing there are estimated to be about 10,000 of them.) Their main jobs have been establishing a sound training routine, making better preparations against surprise attack, attempting to alleviate the serious shortage of Egyptian pilots, rebuilding and manning the country's inner air defences and trying to put some heart back into the Egyptian armoured regiments.

The scale of arms deliveries means that Egypt's economy is mortgaged to pay for them for years to come, while cutting herself off from alternative sources of supply. That a country like India is able to buy from Britain, France and the United States as well as from the USSR helps to keep some freedom of manœuvre. But this approach has its own problems: the Royal

Navy, for example, is likely to be far less forthcoming with operational information now the Indian Navy is in close touch with the Russians. Soviet intrusion into this traditionally British arms market also inhibits commercial sales because of British Government security restrictions on advanced equipment and certain technical information. And from the Indian point of view the mixture of equipment has its drawbacks, quite apart from the diplomatic need to keep one country's weapons out of the other's hands.

However, these are minor difficulties compared with Egypt's humiliating and no doubt widely resented dependence on the Soviet Union. It is true that the Egyptians do possess some valuable bargaining counters; the convenience, if not the necessity, of naval port facilities, permission for Soviet pilots to fly reconnaissance missions from Egyptian territory and the tantalizing possibilities connected with a reopened Suez Canal. But there is now a significant range of policy options for which Egypt is virtually subject to a Soviet veto.

Most observers agree that the Russians have been restraining their clients' impulsive desire to hit back piecemeal at the Israelis in circumstances which invited retaliation, without doing that much to raise the Arabs' desperately low morale. One notable exception, which not only boosted the Egyptians' morale but also made a world-wide impact on military thinking and politics was the sinking of the Israeli destroyer *Eilat* by Russian-supplied Styx missiles in 1967. Even here, however, the Egyptians lost a lot of the prestige outside their own country, since Western commentators assumed that Soviet advisers set the operation up, even if an Egyptian sailor actually pressed the firing button.

Styx is a cruise missile which flies at just under the speed of sound a few hundred feet above the surface. In fact the word missile may be a bit misleading; with a twenty-foot fuselage and stubby delta wings spanning about nine feet, the thing is more like a small aircraft. It is boosted off its launching ramp by a solid fuelled rocket which it then jettisons, flying on with its main liquid fuelled motor. The course is fed into the missile's autopilot before the launch and it carries on without any further instructions until, perhaps, five miles from the target, when a small radar set in the nose switches on. This scans the surface until it picks up an echo, when the missile turns and glides down its own reflected radar beam on to the target. The Russians may also have fitted some Styx's with an infra-red homing head, which is attracted by the heat radiated by a warship. Fitted with radar, the missile's effective range against a target the size of a destroyer is probably about fifteen nautical miles.

In spite of its bulk, Styx is the smallest of the cruise missiles installed in Soviet warships. The Osa class fast patrol boat (*Osa* is the Russian word for wasp) carries four launching ramps and the smaller Komar (mosquito) has two. By supplying numbers of these inexpensive but deadly little craft to countries like Indonesia and Egypt, not to mention the members of the Warsaw Pact, the Russians have created an irritant – and under some circumstances a serious threat – to NATO navies in many parts of the world.

In addition to the Soviet Navy's own fleet of about 130 boats, the Institute of Strategic Studies lists ten other countries to which they have been supplied (noticeably excluding North Vietnam):

East Germany	12 Osa
Poland	12 Osa
Romania	5 Osa
Yugoslavia	10 Osa
Egypt	12 Osa, 7 Komar
Algeria	9 Osa/Komar
Syria	10 Komar
Indonesia	12 Komar
North Korea	4 Komar
Cuba	18 Komar

The missile patrol boat is particularly dangerous when the opposing naval forces are operating without air support, since aircraft are the obvious way of dealing with it. During the Malaysian confrontation with Indonesia, for example, one of the jobs assigned to the RAF Hunter squadrons was to keep an eye on the Komars lurking among the Indonesian islands. An alternative counter might seem to be a cruise missile of one's own, equalling or exceeding the Styx's range. But its usefulness would depend on having immediate political clearance to strike first on suspicion – bearing in mind that once launched, the missile cannot be recalled – and the means to identify a small target like a Komar on the limits of the radar horizon. In the attack on the *Eilat* it was noticeable that the Israeli destroyer never saw its enemy on a radar screen, probably because it lay in the 'shadow' of the land – or even in Port Said harbour itself.

So for British naval planners in particular, who had just been told that the defence budget would not stretch to replacing their four ageing aircraft carriers in the 1970s, the events of October 21, 1967, were bound to come as a cold shock.

At about 5.30 in the evening of that day the *Eilat*, an ex-British Z class escort which first saw service in 1944, was steaming through a quiet sea about fifteen miles off Port Said. She was alone, without air cover. But nobody worried much about that. Militarily, Egypt would take years to recover from the Israelis' brilliant six-day campaign in June. Their destroyer was merely carrying out a routine patrol that had been maintained since the ceasefire. Most of her crew were relaxing in the forecastle.

The first warning came from a lookout who sighted the trail of a missile coming in fast from the south. The watch on deck had time to attempt an evasive manœuvre and open up with their Bofors anti-aircraft guns. But when the missile was quite near, the crew noticed it change course and head straight for them – no doubt the point where its homing guidance head locked on. A few seconds later the eight-ton Styx struck the destroyer amidships; two minutes later it was followed by another in almost the same spot.

Between them they smashed boilers and engine room, started a fire, and left the elderly Israeli vessel wallowing in the gentle swell without either power or radio communications. Rather than drift inshore, her crew dropped anchor and spent the next couple of hours fighting the fire, treating the wounded and struggling to establish an emergency radio link with their base. But they were just too late. The message got through at last, but at 7.30 a third missile struck the stern. The *Eilat* slowly capsized and sank. The final missile exploded in the water among the survivors, causing a lot more casualties; 54 of the crew died, 45 were wounded.

This was not only the first time a warship had been sunk by a surface-to-surface missile launched from another vessel; it was also the first time an attacking ship – which its victim never saw – had sunk a much bigger one with anything but the weaker combatant's traditional weapon at sea, the torpedo.

In theory, Western gunnery officers knew well enough that the Styx could do a great deal of damage. Modern supersonic missiles will mangle a great chunk of superstructure even without an explosive warhead. But there were plenty of politicians and civil servants with an influence on naval procurement who had not realized quite what it could do; and even the experts had not seen a live demonstration of the Styx scoring four hits out of four at long range, and sinking a 2,500 ton vessel with only three of them.

As a piece of technological propaganda the sinking of the *Eilat* could hardly have been equalled. It provided an answer to the disillusioned Arabs who wondered just where all their shiny new Russian equipment was getting them. It gave them something to boast about, however pointless – the semi-official Cairo newspaper *Al-Ahram* used it a few days later to illustrate the clean manliness of the Egyptian forces approach to the war:

'The enemy goaded us, carrying it to extremes by the repeated encroachments of the destroyer *Eilat* upon our waters, whereupon we decided to act. The *Eilat* was a large destroyer equipped with cannons of all types. Two Egyptian missile boats went forth to meet it – armament against armament; a destroyer against two boats; cannon against cannon. And behold, the enemy destroyer sank to its grave sixty metres below the surface of the sea.'

But if the signal was meant for the Arabs, it was read much

further afield. A number of NATO navies dusted off shelved plans for their own surface-to-surface missiles and began to think more seriously about defending their ships against them. French naval officers anxiously counted the Styx launching ramps afloat in the Mediterranean. The Germans remembered that the Baltic, too, was full of Komars belonging to the Warsaw Pact navies. The Royal Navy, with its carriers on the way out, began an urgent evaluation of missile systems it might adapt or develop for its own ships, particularly the French Exocet; and as a cheap interim defensive measure, it rushed through a programme to equip its shipborne Wasp helicopters with the Nord Aviation AS 12 wire guided missile – which has just enough range to stay beyond the reach of a Komar's anti-aircraft guns.

The *Eilat* sinking was also one of the factors which prompted the Royal Navy's renewed interest in putting the Harrier vertical take-off aircraft to sea in a limited strike, fighter and reconnaissance role, operating from commando ships (converted fixed wing aircraft carriers, although in their present form they only carry helicopters) or a new class of 'through deck' cruiser. In short, the Soviet Union's decision to make small, missile carrying craft widely available to her friends has produced clear, even spectacular, results.

But in general, the multi-dimensional political problems in which the USSR is now involved through its military aid programme are a far cry from the crude, clear logic of the 1950s and early 1960s. In those days aid was a matter of helping the Arabs to throw off the yoke of Anglo-French colonialism, the Indonesians to settle with the Dutch and then confront British-dominated Malaysia; while the Cubans were to gnaw at the very roots of Western imperialism.

Since then things have become more complicated. In the Mediterranean, where the USSR challenges the United States, her role as the Arabs' friend brings dangers and responsibilities as well as opportunities. Prudence dictates that she should restrain any further Arab ultimatum at least until her protégés are capable of forcing major concessions from Israel – yet many Egyptians blame Russian restraint for their defeat in 1967. If the Arabs are some day really able to push Israel into the sea, the Soviet Union may be content that they should do so (although she herself has always acknowledged the Jewish state's right to exist) but not, on present evidence, if it involves her in the risk of a direct clash with the United States.

One can only hope that the risk continues to be visible, on both sides. In the meantime the USSR may become more interested in a stable Middle East – as a source of oil, for instance. There is also the possibility that the prospect of war on her Far Eastern border will at some point transform caution into genuine co-operation in other areas. In Iran, Pakistan and India, the Soviet Union's military and economic aid programme already overlaps with that of the United States as she attempts, apparently, to secure her southern flank in anticipation of further confrontation with China.

CHAPTER 13

East of Suez

The arrival of the Soviet Navy in the Indian Ocean means that for
the first time since Vasco de Gama, Western naval supremacy is faced
with a serious challenge.

The quotation comes from an Indian newspaper article written
after the visit of a handful of Russian warships led by an obsolescent cruiser. Its grandiose language reflects the quite disproportionate impact that a small, militarily insignificant Soviet
presence in the Indian Ocean has already made.

Russian activity in this area dates back to 1967, when vessels
associated with the Soviet space programme appeared and an
extensive hydrographic survey was begun. The first warships –
the ones referred to by the Indian journalist – arrived in the
spring of the following year from the Pacific Fleet. A small
force including a Sverdlov class cruiser and a Kashin guided
missile destroyer spent four months showing the flag in Madras,
Bombay, Karachi, Colombo, Basra and Unm Qasr (both in
Iraq), Bandar Abbass (Iran), Mogadishu (Somalia) and Aden
before returning to Vladivostok.

In the winter of that year a much more ambitious exercise was
planned, involving units of all four Soviet fleets. From Vladivostok, a group including a missile destroyer and several
auxiliaries came westwards through the Malacca Straits, linking
up with a squadron assembled from the European fleets, including two submarines, which made the long haul round the
Cape of Good Hope. By the middle of December there were
more than two dozen Russian ships gathered near the Seychelles,
including a number of space tracking and recovery vessels.

Since then the Soviet presence has been virtually continuous in some form or another. The Fortune Bank, in international waters off the Seychelles, is now more than a Russian anchorage. In 1969 the Soviet Union issued a notice to mariners stating that two red mooring buoys had been laid 35 miles east of Coetivy Island. They are painted with the inscription 'Property of the USSR' in English and Russian.

The buoys can of course be used by vessels servicing the space programme. But Western naval intelligence is more concerned with their potential in catering for a continuous rotation of submarine support ships – particularly now that other buoys have started to appear in the Arabian Sea, off Madagascar and Mauritius (with which the Russians signed a fisheries agreement in the summer of 1970).

Since parts of the Soviet Union are now within range of Polaris missiles launched from the northern Indian Ocean, any attempt to counter this potential threat must include those waters. But given that the USSR has a brand new navy and a growing number of political and economic contacts in southern Asia, one would expect her warships to put in an appearance there anyway. To some extent this is a case of the flag following trade. And once the warships are there they are bound, as in any other navy, to practise the arts of sea warfare: to check the coverage of potential enemy reconnaissance, study the environment for submarine operations, test communications, search out sheltered anchorages and improve replenishment techniques. By now they must feel reasonably at home in these blue waters. Two ships, for example, were away from their base in Vladivostok for the whole of the 1968/69 winter, from November to April.

Natural or not, the creation of a Soviet presence in the Indian Ocean has been watched internationally with the greatest interest and, in some cases, with alarm. There are many reasons for this, the most obvious being the sheer novelty of Russian naval activity so far from home. Another is that the closure of the Suez Canal increased the commercial and strategic importance of the shipping lanes leading south through the Mozambique Channel and round the Cape of Good Hope. A large proportion of Europe's vital oil supplies was diverted along this route.

In Britain, the Russian naval 'threat' to these supplies became something of a red herring in the passionate argument over whether arms should be sold to South Africa in defiance of the United Nations embargo. The military implications of the Russian presence were exaggerated by those who wanted Britain to supply anti-submarine ships and aircraft, if not a full range of arms. Others claimed that the Cape is one of the last places on the oil route between the Persian Gulf and Europe where Russian submarines would be likely to lie in wait for a Western tanker, because it is so far away from their bases. Yet in a curious way even this argument served to illustrate the disproportionate value the Russians were getting from a handful of warships when measured against their more immediate political objectives. The fact that the nature of their threat was sometimes misunderstood, as it had been in the Mediterranean, did not matter. The South African arms row simultaneously publicized the USSR's emergence as an oceanic power and stirred up renewed tension between the black and white countries of southern Africa.

Another reason for anxiety among Western commentators was Britain's announcement (partially revoked when the Government changed in June 1970) that she intended to pull out of Singapore and the Persian Gulf by the end of 1971, having already abandoned her base in Aden and with little sign from the Americans that they intended physically to fill the gap.

The fear was, of course, that it would in fact be filled by the Soviet Navy. But whether the gap would ever be significant has been the subject of continuing debate, not least between the political parties in the British Parliament. Indian politicians seem to have written the Royal Navy off in any case, even though some of them are at the same time concerned about the Soviet build up. Yet the Prime Minister of Singapore, one of the world's shrewdest statesmen, vigorously opposed the British withdrawal from his own country on military as well as economic and political grounds.

If there is a danger, it lies not in the immediate, quantifiable changes in the military balance produced by removing a few ships from Singapore, Bahrain or Aden, but in the consequential changes – in relations between Malaysia and Singapore, for example, or among the Gulf sheikhdoms – and the possibility of their being exploited from outside. With so many unknowns in the equation – the effect of American disengagement in Vietnam, China's intentions towards South-East Asia and her relationship with India and Pakistan, the result of the Arab-Israeli conflict – nobody can predict with any degree of confidence. But nor can anyone guarantee that the creation of even a partial, local vacuum will not lead to an explosion.

Individual governments will view the rapidly changing pattern of political forces around the Indian Ocean with alarm or satisfaction, according to their particular position. The only certainties are that a nation of limited military means like Britain cannot cover more than a small number of the possible contingencies even if she does stay 'east of Suez', and that a wealthy newcomer like the Soviet Union is sooner or later bound to find an opportunity to exploit her sea power.

Those who believe that Britain should somehow find the money to retain a military presence in the Indian Ocean throughout the 1970s should take consolation from the fact that many of the political changes and international realignments resulting from her intention to leave Singapore and the Gulf at the end of 1971 were put quietly and sensibly under way the moment the announcement was made. In consequence it is now far easier to find a modest role she can afford than it was in the 1960s.

In the meantime the Royal Navy will have to concede that the Russian sailors have won a major public relations victory. An Australian newspaper discussed the situation under the banner headline: INDIAN OCEAN – A RUSSIAN LAKE. The next question is whether the scattered Russian presence which has been responsible for all the excitement coalesces into a permanently patrolling fleet, served by a re-opened Suez Canal, and backed by a comprehensive support network. There have been periodic rumours, for example, that India was about to grant the USSR naval base rights. This seems unlikely, for the reasons already discussed in a Mediterranean context. But India has accepted large quantities of Soviet military aid, and a common fear of China could draw the two countries much closer together.

In May 1970 the Indian Parliament was warned by the Minister of State for Defence Production, Mr L. N. Mishra, that China too was trying to establish some sort of naval presence in the Indian Ocean.[1] It was reported that Chinese warships had been sighted by Indian naval patrols off the Andaman Islands in the Bay of Bengal. On the same day President Nyerere of Tanzania laid the foundation stone of a naval base being built with Chinese aid in Dar-es-Salaam harbour from which, it was reported locally, Chinese-built patrol boats would soon be operating.

If Mr Mishra was right about Chinese intentions, the appearance of even a single warship west of the Malacca Straits would be a portent of great significance. But for the moment it cannot be more than a portent. The Chinese Navy consists almost entirely of coastal defence forces, organized into a North Sea Fleet, an East Sea Fleet (which has about half the total forces) and a South Sea Fleet. It has hundreds of gunboats, fast patrol boats, ten of which are armed with missiles, and landing craft, but only a few dozen ocean-going ships – destroyers, escorts and submarines. At least some of the destroyers were built in Chinese yards, which have also been turning out submarines to the Russian W class design, plus one G class boat intended to fire ballistic missiles. So there is some basis from which to expand long range naval elements, but it is likely to be an extremely slow, painful business.

The Asian navy which is both capable of following the Russians into the Indian Ocean and probably interested in doing so is that of Japan. For all the inhibitions of her pacifist constitution, Japan is already considering the possibility of translating more of her enormous economic strength, as the world's third largest industrial nation, into military power. British plans to withdraw from the Far East prompted Japanese military commentators to remind their Government that 90 per cent of the country's oil supply comes by sea through the Malacca Straits, and that she

[1] *Guardian*, May 8, 1970.

is increasingly dependent on ore shipments from Australia. An article in the *Oriental Economist* in April 1968 suggested that the United States had already asked Japan to consider how she might help to replace the British presence.

It may be more than a coincidence, therefore, that in 1969 a Japanese naval squadron conducted a long training cruise into the Indian Ocean, visiting Singapore for the first time since the end of the Second World War. Japan already maintains a navy twice the size of those maintained by India or Australia in terms of manpower, with the emphasis on anti-submarine operations. The hardware includes two dozen destroyers, sixteen frigates, about three dozen escorts and eight submarines. The construction of helicopter carriers has been discussed, and with the resources of the world's largest shipbuilding industry, capable of producing a nuclear merchant ship, a rapid expansion should present no problem.

At present Japan's armed forces are limited by her constitution to purely defensive operations. Any change to a potentially offensive role would meet passionate political resistance. But against a background of deliberate American disengagement from South-East Asia, she is bound to keep her policy under continuous review. This must include the question of whether under some circumstances she should develop an independent nuclear deterrent against China and North Korea, even though the mere mention of the word nuclear is liable to send Japanese domestic politics into convulsions (a healthier reaction, perhaps, than the way in which such concepts as 'massive nuclear retaliation' are idly bandied about in NATO countries).

Less ambitious is the proposal that the constitution should be amended or reinterpreted to allow Japanese forces to take part in United Nations operations – again with an eye on North Korea. And hard as it may be for Allied ex-servicemen who fought in the Far East during the Second World War to accept the idea, it would be a perfectly logical next step, for Japan eventually to associate herself with the peacekeeping arrangements between Britain, Australia, New Zealand, Singapore and Malaysia. A naval contribution to this would be both the easiest to accept politically and the most suitable to Japan's own interests. During a tour of the Far East in 1970, Sir Alec Douglas Home apparently found the Australians discussing the possibility of joint arrangements with the Japanese, for patrolling their mutual trade troutes, as a major item of future defence policy.

The appearance of Soviet naval squadrons in the Persian Gulf, visiting Unm Qasr and Bandar Abbas, is almost bound to be viewed with suspicion by Britain, which gets so much of her oil from that area. Only a few years ago British troops landed in Kuwait to protect her – and Britain's oil interests – against Iraqi threats. Since then Baghdad has become, in the words of a British politician, 'like an advanced Russian base'.

The potential for troublemaking of the kind practised by Egypt before 1967 is probably there (my use of the word 'trouble-making' does not imply any sympathy with the absolute and in some ways barbarous power wielded by the local sheikhs). But would it serve the Soviet Union's purpose? Controlled communist subversion is one thing; extreme Arab nationalism – or communist subversion that happens to be directed from Peking – is another. The rebel movement in Muscat and Oman, for example, looks to China for its inspiration and for most of its arms. Where such influence exists, the Russians could decide to outbid the Maoist offers of support. But it was noticeable that when the scale of Arab guerrilla operations against Israel seemed to be threatening President Nasser's international leadership in 1969, statements critical of these operations began to appear in the Soviet Press. If the USSR's strategic ambition is to establish herself permanently as a major influence in the Middle East, then she requires a reasonable degree of internal stability among her client states; though a simmering external conflict with Israel is just the thing to maintain their dependence on her.

In the Gulf itself, it seems inconceivable that the sheikhdoms lining the southern shore can long survive the departure of the British without an upheaval of some kind. And the Russians may well try to exploit the situation to extend their political base from Iraq, where they are helping to work the Rumaila oilfield. But there is no reason to assume they will simply be interested in disrupting oil supplies to the West.

For one thing the Soviet Union has to reckon with her suspicious neighbour Iran, whose friendship she has been cultivating with various forms of aid, and whose navy has acquired some smart new warships – partly in anticipation of the Royal Navy's departure. One of the few things about which Middle East states in general seem to be wholly realistic is their dependence on selling oil. A Soviet presence which isolated them from their Western markets would not be welcome. But the Russians might acquire more influence as customers and suppliers of technical assistance – with naval forces just over the horizon to emphasize a threat or accept an invitation.

The Soviet Navy has been particularly active in the most western corner of the Indian Ocean, at the entrance to the Red Sea. Its ships turn up every year at Massawa for what amounts to an international flag-showing competition for the benefit of the Emperor of Ethiopia. The military aid supplied to the Yemen and Somalia includes help in developing the ports of Hodeida and Berbera – which enables Russian warships to berth there. The Republic of South Yemen, which includes the former British base at Aden, receives military and economic aid.

What these bargains lead to remains to be seen. The Russians have certainly not acquired bases in the traditional sense, and – for what it is worth – the Yemeni Prime Minister declared in 1969 that his country was aligned neither with the East nor the West. But while the Suez Canal remains closed any sort of supply or repair facility must be welcome in this part of the world, for by sea it is just about as far from Sevastopol as it is possible to get. And if the Russians ever wanted to blockade the Israeli port of Eilat they could do so just as effectively at the southern bottleneck of the Red Sea as the Egyptians did – for a while – by closing the Straits of Tiran.

With Western warships heading for home and those from the Far East still hull down on the horizon, the Soviet Navy's long term strategic aim must surely be to command the southern approaches to a re-opened Suez Canal, as the great British naval base at Aden used to do. Assuming that the Soviet leaders are more interested in seeing a return on their investment in the Arab cause than in an immediate settlement of the conflict with Israel, the ideal course of events from their point of view would seem to be as follows.[2]

She would continue support and training of the Egyptian forces, aimed particularly at eroding the vital Israeli air superiority in the Canal zone, which could lead to the establishment of a bridgehead on the eastern bank. The Israelis, taking heavier casualties and worried by the possibility of serious clashes with the Russians, would then agree to negotiate a withdrawal from Sinai. (At the time of writing an uneasy ceasefire, of which advantage has been taken by the Russians and Egyptians to strengthen greatly their missile defences on the west bank of the Canal, has led to the possibility of negotiation – and of renewed war.)

Russian salvage teams would promptly move in to get the Canal going on an emergency basis. With Western shipowners still worried by the possibility of another lightning Israeli attack, the Soviet Union would offer to act as guarantor and propose to Egypt that a new joint Authority be set up to run the waterway. Soviet warships would then guard the approaches and be frequently seen in the Canal itself on their way to join the much enlarged squadron permanently patrolling the Indian Ocean and the Persian Gulf from bases in the Black Sea.

But the irony of such wishful thinking on the Kremlin's behalf is that this glittering strategic prize – control of the world's greatest artificial waterway – is now known to be far less valuable to the West than most of us imagined. And while it remains out of reach it is the Russians, as much as anybody, who suffer.

[2] This is not meant to be in any sense a prediction of actual events, but merely a description of the way Soviet strategists would probably like to see them develop, that can later be compared with what really happened.

CHAPTER 14

Anticlimax

The Suez Maritime Canal shall always be free and open, in time of war as in time of peace, to every vessel of commerce or of war, without distinction of flag. Consequently, the High Contracting Parties agree not in any way to interfere with the free use of the Canal, in time of war as in time of peace. The Canal shall never be subjected to the exercise of the right of blockade. *Article 1 of the convention signed at Constantinople in 1888 by Great Britain, Germany, Austria-Hungary, Spain, France, Italy, the Netherlands, Russia and Turkey.*

Until June 5, 1967, the Suez Canal was the pivot of the world's maritime trade routes, handling more than 250 million net tons of shipping a year. Whether to remain 'East of Suez' was the great issue of defence policy in Britain. Six days later it was not which end of the canal you were at that mattered, but which side. It had become a ceasefire line across which Arabs and Israelis could snipe at one another; a superb anti-tank ditch that prevented the Egyptians from launching anything but a really determined offensive in Sinai, and cut off their retreat if they failed.

Immediately after the war, closure of the canal seemed to have given the Egyptians a powerful bargaining lever. It was argued that the Western powers, with ships trapped in the waterway itself and hundreds of others making expensive detours round the Cape of Good Hope, would soon force concessions from the Israelis in order to get it open again. But Israel had a different bargain in mind. Why should she allow the canal to be reopened without a guarantee that her own vessels could use it? Until then, not only had ships flying the Israeli flag been denied passage, in violation of the 1888 convention, but ships of other nations were searched for 'foodstuffs and other merchandise that might increase the military potential of Israel.'

At one point, in January 1968, it seemed that at least the fourteen ships anchored in the Great Bitter Lake might be released. Israel agreed they might go south through Suez, but when Egyptian salvage craft appeared in the northern section of the canal the Israelis opened fire, apparently fearing that they were being tricked into allowing the whole length of the canal to be cleared. On the anniversary of their imprisonment, the fourteen paraded slowly round the lake, forlornly sounding their sirens. At the time of writing they are still there – four British vessels, two Swedish, two West German, two Polish and one each from the USA, France, Bulgaria and Czechoslovakia (a really bad piece of luck considering how few ships she has).

Meanwhile, in Western shipping circles the initial alarm was subsiding. Some owners were already cashing in on the boom in tanker freight rates, as they had in 1956. And even where there was no direct compensation, companies began to realize that they could live without Suez after all. The P & O announcement that its eleven liners – the world's largest passenger fleet – were being scheduled round the Cape for the whole of 1968 and 1969 adopted a calm, even an optimistic tone:

The position will be reviewed on the canal's re-opening. Whether any voyages are then re-routed through it will depend on circumstances at the time, and passengers' preference. In order to maintain an efficient service it is vital that we plan well ahead and are not influenced by the uncertainty which surrounds the Suez Canal. By scheduling the ships to call at a number of attractive ports and by giving plenty of time for sightseeing we are making certain that our passengers have a really interesting and enjoyable voyage. We are sure that this new route will prove very popular.

By the summer of 1970 Port Line, one of the cargo shipping companies with a vessel trapped in the Great Bitter Lake, seemed inclined to abandon the Suez route even if it was reopened. 'I cannot see us going through the canal again', said Lord Mancroft, Deputy Chairman of the line's parent company:[1] 'the stranding of the *Port Invercargill* has been a bitter lesson.'

In Government departments, the frantic initial reaction gave way to sober calculation of just who was being hit by the closure and how. The canal had carried about 15 per cent of the world's trade, and threequarters of this was oil. Somebody had to bear the extra cost of going the long way round in time, shipping capacity and therefore in freight rates: a 30,000 ton tanker, for example, steaming at 16 knots now took thirty instead of seventeen days to reach London from Basra, in the Persian Gulf. But the total effect of the re-routing on a particular country depended on how near it was to one end of the canal, how much it depended on Middle East oil supplies – Italy, for example, was hard hit on both these counts – and whether it possessed a large merchant fleet which could recoup some of the extra cost.

One of the first indications was the range of freight surcharges promptly slapped on by shipping lines trading from north-west Europe to various points east of Suez: to Australia the surcharge was 5 per cent, to the Far East 10 per cent, to East Africa 15 per cent, to India and Pakistan $17\frac{1}{2}$ per cent, and to the Red Sea 50 per cent.

Most surprising to many people was the realization that the Soviet Union would herself pay a heavy price for the closure. In the last full year of operation her expanding merchant fleet sent through ten million net tons of shipping, putting it in seventh place among users of the canal.

If one considers American-controlled shipping, as opposed to that under the US flag – if, in other words, one includes a large percentage of Liberian and Panamanian tonnage – then the United States also emerges as one of the major users. She used to send some of her supplies to South Vietnam by that route. But geographically she was better placed than the USSR because her ships have to make less of a detour to reach the Indian Ocean or the China Sea.

[1] *Journal of Commerce*, June 4, 1970.

Transits of the Suez Canal in 1966

Flag	No. of Ships	Million net tons
Liberia	2,700	56.5
UK	3,600	45.6
Norway	2,300	43.8
France	1,100	16.5
Italy	1,200	15.2
Greece	1,500	12.6
USSR	1,500	10.2
Holland	900	9.1
Sweden	500	8.2
West Germany	800	7.9
Panama	700	7.8
Denmark	500	6.8
USA	800	6.7
Japan	500	5.9
India	400	3.2
Other flags	2,300	18.3
Total traffic	21,300	274.3

Source: Suez Canal report

Suez as a short cut

Route	New York – Bombay	Batum–Bombay
Distance via Suez	7,700	4,400
Distance via Cape	10,900	12,000
Miles saved	3,200	7,600

From the point of view of increased mileage, the Russian Black Sea ports could hardly be worse placed: they are, for example, at one end of the sea 'bridge' to India. An article on 'The Influence of the Closure of the Suez Canal on the Development of the Freighter Market' in the July 1969 issue of *Morskoi Flot* points out that the amount of foreign tonnage which had to be chartered to carry goods from the Black Sea to ports east of Suez rose from 475,000 tons in the first five months of 1967 to 835,000 tons (presumably in a comparable period after the

244

closure) because the voyages were so much longer. The rates paid were also high, and as a result it became uneconomic to move some commodities – for example the cement previously shipped out to Nakhodka. The article might have added that a lot more Soviet tonnage would be required to keep the same volume of war supplies moving along the route between Odessa and Haiphong, which had almost doubled in length.

As for Soviet warships and their auxiliaries, units of the Black Sea fleet might by now have been operating in far greater numbers east of Suez. But the sudden remoteness of the Indian Ocean may have encouraged the acquisition of port facilities and the development of afloat support techniques we should not otherwise have seen and which in the long run will increase the Russian Navy's effectiveness.

Perhaps the most direct reaction came from the Israelis, who in 1968 started laying a giant 42-inch pipeline from Eilat, on the Gulf of Aqaba, to Ashkelon on the Mediterranean. It pumped its first oil in February 1970 and once it is in full operation it will have an annual throughput of up to 60 million tons – compared with the 167 million tons of oil carried through the canal in its last full year.

The Russians themselves promised to open a spectacular arctic route between Europe and the Far East in 1967, saving thousands of miles on the Cape route. But as explained earlier, this plan was formed long before the Arab-Israeli war and it has even been suggested that its abandonment was influenced by a reluctance to take advantage of the Suez closure, rather than the other way round. What the Soviet shipping authorities did do was to press ahead with the development of a ship canal route from Western Europe to Iranian ports on the Caspian in competition with conventional services which now had to go right round Africa to reach the Persian Gulf.

The most widespread influence of the Suez closure was on Western tanker owners, among whom the tendency to build bigger and bigger ships was accelerated. In February 1970, Fairplay's *World Ships on Order* listed an astonishing total of 219 tankers each with a deadweight of more than 150,000 tons.

Their combined deadweight was 51 million compared with the 425 ships, totalling 11 million, with individual deadweights of less than 150,000 tons.

Tankers of more than 150,000 tons dwt. on order

Flag	No. of ships	M. tons dwt.	Average size
Liberia	66	14.7	223,000
UK	38	9.0	237,000
Norway	31	7.5	241,000
France	18	4.2	232,000
Japan	10	2.4	239,000
Denmark	6	1.6	272,000
Others	50	12.0	239,000
Total	219	51.4	235,000

Source: *Fairplay International*

I use the word 'accelerated' deliberately, because it is sometimes implied that today's 200,000 tonners were originally conceived as an answer to the Suez closure and that they will have no use for the canal when it is reopened. In fact Shell's trend-setting class of that size was planned back in 1964/65. The beam of these ships was limited to 155 feet so that they could pass one way through the canal in ballast and return loaded round the Cape. The alternative, rejected by Shell, was to build 70,000 tonners which by 1968 could have used the canal in both directions between Europe and the Persian Gulf.

The arithmetic of tanker design was complicated during the mid-1960s by the programme of improvements to the canal known as the Nasser Plan. By 1967, the original depth of 26 feet – dug a century ago by Ferdinand de Lesseps' great army of Arab labourers and mechanical dredgers – had been increased to permit the passage of ships drawing 38 feet: in other words, a laden tanker of about 55,000 tons. The plan involved increasing the depth to 48 feet by 1972 (deep enough for a laden tanker of about 110,000 tons) and about 60 feet by 1980 (i.e. 200,000 tons). But nobody could be quite sure how much canal dues might increase in the meantime.

With dues at the 1967 level, a 200,000 tonner going one way round the Cape could carry oil between the Persian Gulf and North-west Europe something like ten shillings a ton cheaper than the 70,000 tonner using the canal in both directions (other factors affecting Shell's calculation were the construction of new port facilities and a temporary scheme to unload part of the big ships' cargo at sea). Further size increases towards the 300,000 and 400,000 tonners now being built continue to reduce the direct cost per ton, but the descending curve eventually flattens out. The jump from a 20,000 tonner to an 80,000 tonner roughly halves the shipping cost while the much bigger step – in absolute tonnage terms – to 200,000 tons only reduces it by a third.

Shell therefore found it paid to fix their designs at this tonnage, so they could ballast through the canal, and many of the vessels now ordered by other companies will be able to do the same when it reopens. However, only a small increase in dues would send all these ships round the Cape eastbound as well as westbound. Faced with heavy dredging and salvage costs simply in order to restore the canal to its 1967 condition, the authority's decision on how to proceed with the Nasser Plan will require fine judgment.

Other factors also made Suez less vital to many countries than the last time it was blocked, when Britain and France went to war to regain control of it. The development of oilfields in Libya, Algeria and Nigeria, coming on top of the trend towards bigger tankers, helped to reduce the proportion of Britain's oil supplies coming through the canal from 60 per cent in 1956 to about 25 per cent by 1967.

Ships are getting faster as well as bigger. Modern cargo liners and container ships have service speeds of more than twenty knots, with the result that on a voyage from Europe to the Far East they take only a few days longer to go round the Cape. And the rapid growth of air transport is steadily replacing the passenger ship services that used to pass through the canal. Even the P & O line to India, which gave the English language the word 'posh' (Port Out, Starboard Home), has been abandoned. Commercial air cargo is still, of course, severely limited by cost.

But the armed services now have strategic transports like the American C5A, the Russian An-22 and the British Belfast, which can move even heavy vehicles around the world at high speed. Soviet arms for the Yemen, for example, can be airlifted across the Middle East without difficulty.

Back in 1967, the closure of the Suez Canal appeared to put the Egyptians and their Communist patrons in a powerful negotiating position. Three years later, it seems far more likely to be useful to the Israelis. In that time Egypt has lost a direct foreign exchange revenue of well over £200 million and her tourist industry has been crippled. Any Soviet plans to establish a controlling presence astride the isthmus are unfulfilled.

All this time the waterway has gradually been choked by the desert sand. When it reopens the canal authority will have to fight hard to regain the tanker traffic on which it used to depend – some of which is irretrievably lost. The canal will once again be a great trading route, but it will no longer divide two halves of the world in quite the way it used to. For Britain in particular, the phrase 'East of Suez' will have lost a lot of its meaning.

CHAPTER 15

The Hardware

'Now we have an ocean fleet, which can challenge the enemy in the open seas of the world.'[1]

The Soviet Navy is big, young and fast. Its specialities are the submarine, the surface-to-surface cruise missile mounted aboard a range of ships, from cruisers to patrol boats, and the mine. The inventory does not include fixed wing aircraft carriers.

By comparison with, say, the Royal Navy, with its weakness for sophisticated weaponry, some of the Soviet Navy's equipment looks rather 'agricultural', and its approach to tactics somewhat crude – as a NATO staff officer put it, the Russians appear to ask themselves such questions as 'Can we sink the NATO strike fleet at 0905 on August 17th?' But there is nothing unsophisticated about their application of gas turbine propulsion to light cruisers and destroyers. They also show great ingenuity and a flair for improvisation in the way they make use of their technical resources – in their enthusiasm for mines of all shapes and sizes, including nuclear ones, for example, or in their introduction of the cruise missile into the submarine fleet (first bolting it on to anything which could take it to sea, then modifying existing craft, and finally designing a new class from scratch).[2]

The Soviet Fleet in Perspective

The total tonnage of the Russian fleet puts it in second place among the world's navies. Its manpower, including the Naval Air Force, is about 460,000 compared with the US Navy's 760,000 and the Royal Navy's 90,000.

[1] Admiral Gorshkov, Commander-in-Chief of the Soviet Navy.

[2] Cmdr. M. K. MacGwire, 'the Background to Russian Naval Policy', *Brassey's Annual* 1968.

Active fleets

	USSR	USA	UK
Attack Carriers	0	15	3
Anti-submarine Carriers	0	7	0
Helicopter Carriers and Commando Ships	2	8	2
Amphibious Assault Ships	100	150	4
Nuclear-powered Ballistic Missile Submarines	18	41	3
Nuclear-powered Cruise Missile Submarines	25	0	0
Nuclear-powered Attack Submarines	17	40	3
Conventional Ballistic Missile Submarines	35	0	0
Conventional Cruise Missile Submarines	22	0	0
Conventional Attack Submarines	263	62	22
Surface-to-surface Missile Cruisers	8	0	0
Other Missile Cruisers	1	9	0
Conventional Cruisers	11	4	1
Large Missile Destroyers and Frigates	24	60	6
Ocean-going Escorts	176	200	56
Missile Patrol Boats	130	0	0

Source: Institute of Strategic Studies and *Jane's Fighting Ships*

Even in these days of nuclear propulsion and afloat support, the numerical strength of the Russian Navy looks less formidable when one breaks it down into four fleets, which can rely on one another only to a limited extent. Of course the US Navy, divided between the Atlantic and the Pacific, has a similar problem – as does any navy which operates throughout the world. But the effect is far more serious in the Russian case because the fleets' home areas, particularly in the Baltic and the Black Sea, can so easily be blockaded.

One of the main things that worries the American admirals trying to evoke more response from their Government to the Russian naval build-up is that so many US warships are really elderly. The average age of ships in the US Navy in 1969 was $17\frac{1}{2}$. Nearly 60 per cent of the combat units were 20 or over, whereas less than 1 per cent of Soviet warships was that old. What is more, the Russians have seven major shipbuilding yards, largely rebuilt since the war, capable of adding new tonnage to their fleet in a hurry. The capacity of their submarine yards, able to turn out twenty nuclear submarines a year and provided with covered berths for all-weather working, is particularly impressive.

The four fleets

	Northern	Baltic	Black Sea	Pacific
Nuclear Submarines	45	0	0	25
Conventional Submarines	105	75	40	80
Helicopter Carriers	0	0	2	0
Cruisers	5	6	7	7
Missile Destroyers	5	6	13	6
Conventional Destroyers	15	12	20	23
Missile Patrol Boats	20	40	20	50
Naval Aircraft	250	250	250	250

Note: These figures, intended merely to show the approximate distribution of the Soviet fleet in the spring of 1970, do not necessarily add up to the totals given in the table of comparative strengths; they are from a different, NATO source, using different criteria.

Russian surface warships show comparatively good seakeeping ability and they often have an advantage of a few knots over their NATO equivalents. The Kashin class gas turbine powered destroyers are reputed to be the fastest in the world. This extra speed may be obtained by good hull design, building in a lot of power, or simply resisting the temptation to overload an old hull with new equipment: whatever the reasons, its usefulness is undeniable – in tailing NATO task forces, for example.

Although the Russians have not yet applied nuclear power to a surface warship – which would give them the cruising ability now required by their long range operations – their Kresta class light cruisers, as well as the Kashin destroyers, use gas turbines. This is in contrast to the US Navy, which in the past has virtually ignored gas turbine propulsion. The Royal Navy has some ships with a combination of steam and gas turbines, and intends to make extensive use of pure gas turbine propulsion in future.

Another significant general characteristic of the Soviet Navy is that a large number of its ships, from cruisers to submarines, are equipped for minelaying. It also possesses a vast fleet of minesweepers.

Comparative age of the Russian and American fleets

Distribution by Age	Number of Ships	
	USA	USSR
0–4 years	108	431
5–9 years	96	486
10–14 years	130	589
15–19 years	39	67
More than 19 years	521	2

Source: Report to the House of Representatives Committee on Armed Services, March 1969.

Distribution by Type	USA		USSR	
	Number	Average Age	Number	Average Age
Cruisers	14	21	20	12
Conventional Submarines	69	21	300	10
Ballistic Missile Submarines	41	4	15	5
Nuclear Attack Submarines	36	4	20	5
Destroyers	171	22	50	15
Frigates	59	4	30	5
Amphibious Ships	156	19	40	5

Source: Report to the House Committee on Armed Services, March 1969.

The Main Classes of Warship

The 18,000 ton helicopter carrier *Moskva* ran trials in the Black Sea during the summer of 1967. A sister ship, the *Leningrad*, has since appeared, and others will probably follow. The *Moskva* carries twenty large anti-submarine helicopters: these can park with folded rotors in a central hangar and operate from the flight deck which covers the after half of the hull. They use 'dunking' sonar to supplement the ship's own variable depth equipment. She is fitted forward with anti-aircraft missiles and guns, anti-submarine mortars and torpedoes. Her speed is probably about thirty knots.

As soon as the *Moskva* appeared Western commentators began to link her with the experimental Yakovlev vertical take-off aircraft, two examples of which appeared at the Domodedovo air show in July 1967. This appeared to be a crude equivalent of the British Hawker Siddeley Harrier, using only two swivelling exhaust nozzles, a cumbersome hinged door to stop re-ingestion and a long puff pipe out front to give pitch control.

An operational version of this aircraft could of course fly from the *Moskva* and may one day do so. But the popular idea that the ship was intended from the start to evolve into a small fixed wing aircraft carrier seems unlikely. An aircraft like the Harrier gains a great deal of range or payload from using a short rolling take-off, and for that it needs a minimum run of about 400 feet – whereas the *Moskva*'s flight deck is less than 300 feet long.

This could be lengthened and angled in a derivative design, but it would seem more satisfactory to go for some kind of 'through deck' concept as the Royal Navy is doing. At any rate it seems to me highly probable that as soon as the Russians have a vertical take-off aircraft worth taking to sea – something the Harrier is only just becoming after years of engine development, and which the Americans have nowhere near achieved – they will build ships to carry it. If Admiral Gorshkov is still in command, I look forward to hearing him explain why the construction of these 'mini carriers' does not represent a change in Soviet naval strategy after the years of propaganda he has put in against the 'obsolete' conventional carriers of the imperialist navies.

The first of the remarkable Kresta class multi-purpose light cruisers was laid down in 1964 and completed in 1967. They are equipped with a mix of long range surface-to-surface missiles, anti-aircraft missiles and guns, anti-submarine rocket launchers and torpedoes. Two helicopters are carried in a hangar aft. Gas turbines give the 7,000 ton hull a speed of about thirty-six knots.

In a sense the Kresta design is a combination of the earlier

Kynda class light cruisers, which have more surface-to-surface missiles but less anti-aircraft armament, and the fast Kashin class destroyers, which are armed with advanced anti-submarine missiles and torpedoes, anti-aircraft missiles but no surface-to-surface missile launchers.

The 19,000 ton Sverdlov class cruisers, one of which caused a stir at the Royal Navy's Spithead review in 1953 – and which Khrushchev wanted to scrap – are some of the most powerful conventional warships afloat. The Russians still have a dozen of them, and gave one to the Indonesian Navy in the days when it was 'progressive'. They are armed with twelve 5.9 inch and twelve 3.9 inch guns, torpedoes and up to 250 mines. They are credited with a speed of 34 knots.

The USSR is believed to be building five types of submarine at the moment. These include the Y class long range ballistic missile boats, resembling the American Polaris design, and the bulbous-bowed nuclear powered C class. These are reported to have a displacement of 4,000–5,000 tons and may carry some new form of anti-submarine or anti-shipping missile – perhaps an equivalent of Subroc.

It is noticeable that the Russian programme also includes an apparently new class of diesel-powered attack submarines, whereas the United States has abandoned diesel construction. There are a number of possible reasons for this. The Russians may have produced an especially silent design which they want to mass produce cheaply for anti-shipping work. They may have future military aid programmes in mind. One also has to remember that they will eventually have to face the bloc obsolescence of their existing diesel types.

At least 170 of the ubiquitous W class medium-sized but apparently long range diesel submarines were built during the 1950s. Some of them were used for the gradual introduction of cruise missiles, either housed in tanks behind the fin, or faired into it. They are said to have a submerged speed of fifteen knots and to be capable of seventeen knots on the surface. The largest Russian diesel attack submarines are the F class, forty of which were built. They are a development of the Z class boats, with a submerged displacement of 2,300 tons.

The most important class of cruise-missile submarines are the twenty-five nuclear-powered E2 boats, each carrying eight Shaddock missiles and credited with a 22–25 knots speed. The early 'Sark' surface-launched ballistic missiles (apparently developed from the rocket paraded in Moscow in 1962) are mainly carried in the 25 diesel-powered G class boats. These missiles are believed to have a range of about 350 miles. The 'Serb' ballistic missile, with a probable range of about 700 miles, was introduced in the fifteen nuclear-powered HI class submarines which have a speed of 25–30 knots.

Among the specialized support vessels are three 9,000 ton Ugra class ships, probably used primarily for servicing nuclear submarines, half a dozen Don class 6,000 tonners for long range submarine afloat support and three Lama class missile supply ships. One of the curiosities of the Soviet fleet – but highly appropriate for all that – is a 3,000 ton icebreaking 'frigate'. She is armed with four-inch guns and mines, and *Jane's Fighting Ships* gives her a speed of 18 knots.

Two important classes of amphibious assault ships are the 4,000 ton Alligator, which first appeared in the mid 1960s, and the 1,000 ton Polnocny, more than two dozen of which have been built. The Alligator could carry perhaps five dozen tanks and the Polnocny up to ten.

The Russians have about 130 missile patrol boats in their own navy in addition to those they have distributed round the world. Perhaps eighty of these are of the 35-knot Osa (Wasp) class, and the rest are 40-knot Komars (Mosquitoes). They both carry the Styx cruise missile, which has a range of 15-20 miles; the Osa has four launchers, and the Komar two. As we have seen, the Styx is a formidable weapon, particularly in Mediterranean or Baltic conditions. But one should remember that the patrol boats are coastal craft of limited range, and their missiles are shock sensitive – the missiles which sank the *Eilat* may have been launched from the calm of Port Said harbour. It is thought that operation of a Komar's missiles might be limited to Force 3 waves, and those on the bigger Osa to about Force 4.

Last, but by no means least in the public interest they have aroused, are the intelligence 'trawlers'. Their gross tonnage varies from 300 to 700. *Jane's Fighting Ships* records nineteen appropriate names for them, such as *Barograf*, *Giroskop*, *Lotsman* and *Protraktor*.

The three main aircraft in the Soviet Naval Air Force are the extremely long range Tu 20 (Bear) turbo-prop, the subsonic Tu 16 (Badger) jet which has been operating from Egypt flown by Russian pilots, and the supersonic Tu 22 (Blinder). The Tu 20 has a loaded range of about 8,000 miles. It is intended primarily for strategic reconnaissance and electronic counter-measures, but it can carry a primitive (Kangaroo) missile, built like a small jet fighter. The Tu 16, with a 3,000 mile loaded range (4,000 miles maximum) has been equipped since about 1960 with a (Kipper) stand-off missile, which probably has a range of about 100 miles. The medium range Tu 22 carries a more advanced (Kitchen) missile, which it is believed could be launched from about 150 miles away, and no doubt has a radar homing device to steer it on to its ship target. Tu 22s are being phased in to replace some of the Tu 16s and now represent the Naval Air Force's main weapon against NATO's carrier strike forces.

CHAPTER 16

Soviet Naval Strategy Today

My immediate concern is the shift of Soviet grand strategy to an offensive posture on the high seas. Where earlier, the Soviet Union intended to deny the United States and our allies freedom to use the seas, she now intends to contest control. This is a fundamental shift, of grave impact for the future.[1]

If one were to ask a Russian naval officer whether the Soviet fleet is on the offensive there could be no doubt as to the ideologically correct reply. In the words of his Commander-in-Chief, its role is 'to challenge capitalist naval supremacy in all the seas and oceans of the world.'

Under Gorshkov's leadership for the past fifteen years, it has struggled to free itself from the dominance of the Red Army's allegedly 'defensive' mentality. Its first big opportunity came when it endorsed Khrushchev's enthusiasm for the nuclear missile without really accepting his corollary – that the short, devastating nuclear exchange would substantially reduce the need for conventional forces. By 1967 – after having demonstrated the previous year that its nuclear submarines could circumnavigate the world submerged[2] and with its long range ballistic missile available – it was able to assert the right to carry out 'strategic missions of an offensive nature'. And as far as nuclear deterrence is concerned, this seems to find acceptance in Defence Minister Malinovsky's statement, made just before he died, 'First priority is being given to the strategic rocket forces and the nuclear missile launching submarines – forces which are

[1] Admiral Turner F. Caldwell, USN, Director of Anti-submarine Warfare Programs, October 8, 1968.

[2] Malcolm Mackintosh, *Juggernaut*, London, 1967.

the principal means of deterring the aggressor and decisively defeating him in war.'[3]

But this much is still largely domestic politics. A navy which had merely succeeded in giving less training priority to 'joint operations with the ground forces' and contributing to its country's strategic nuclear deterrent could hardly be considered to have adopted an aggressive posture in the sense that this phrase is used in the West.

The test of Gorshkov's challenge and Caldwell's assessment must surely be how far the Soviet Navy has followed the Royal Navy and the US Navy in devoting a great deal of effort to exerting a positive influence at long range: demonstrating the ability to intervene in local wars, providing what we like to call 'peacekeeping' forces, protecting its government's property abroad, filling strategic areas of the ocean in peacetime with a visible presence and not merely an invisible deterrent, creating dependence, symbolizing commitment and offering friendship.

More to the point, therefore, are those statements by Gorshkov which relate his navy's ambitions to what others are already doing – 'Sooner or later, the United States will have to understand that it no longer has mastery of the seas' – and discuss the broader uses of naval power to protect 'state interests' such as a merchant fleet increasingly exposed in Western waters:

Soviet sailors ... well understand the meaning of naval power in strengthening the international prestige of our country and its military capacity, in the defence of its enveloping sea borders and the safeguarding of the state interests of the USSR in the seas and oceans ...

With the growth of the Soviet Union's economic strength, her interests on the seas and oceans are all the more widespread, and it follows that the Navy will be faced with new demands to protect them from the encroachment of the imperialists.[4]

Clearly, the expanded scope of the operations I have described in the Mediterranean, the Atlantic and the Indian Ocean shows that the Navy is already allowed to put down its textbook of

[3] *Current History*, October 1967.
[4] *Morskoi Sbornik*, February 1967.

nuclear warfare sometimes and take a wider view. To an extent, this was bound to happen as soon as the Soviet Union exchanged the eccentric dictates of Stalin or Khrushchev for the collective leadership of today. And this process is cumulative. Once it is agreed that a naval presence in, say, the Persian Gulf might at some stage further the political aims of the government, the naval staff start planning exercises and demanding the equipment to carry them out; and once the equipment is available both the sailors and the politicians think of new ways to use it. In Egypt, by a mixture of accident and design, the Soviet Navy is involved in a new form of 'joint operations' that includes economic aid, physical protection, technical infiltration and political control.

It is equally clear that the Russians are still operating with a naval instrument fashioned primarily for the deterrence of nuclear war and strategic defence against it. It still has no carriers. It concentrates instead on submarines – which are, of course, extremely powerful offensive weapons but are nevertheless inflexible, in spite of a widening range of armament – land-based aircraft and coastal forces; on long range missiles and mines.

Yet if the shift towards an offensive strategy most Western commentators claim to detect is fundamental, it must eventually be reflected in the physical shape of the Soviet Navy. If requirements are being made, some sort of ship will eventually emerge to meet them; subject of course to the financial resources being available – thus conventional fixed wing aircraft carriers would have to be given an extremely high priority before the cost of developing them from scratch was worthwhile.

What we have seen is the interaction of experience and theory. The concept of long range operations began as a theoretical denial of the idea that in general war the Soviet Navy should be confined to a subordinate coastal role. A number of things then combined to encourage Gorshkov to follow through the positive implications of his denial, and help convert others to his way of thinking: the immediate requirements of supporting a submarine nuclear deterrent, the reaction to the Cuban crisis and the Arab-Israeli war (the Suez crisis of 1956 probably made an impact at the time, but it seems to have been lost in Khrushchev's missile mania) and the rapidly widening scope of Russian commercial shipping and fisheries, which offer the West valuable hostages.

This experience has in turn tended to broaden the theoretical base of Soviet naval strategy to make more room for missions in limited war, and peacetime roles other than those of deterrence, vaguely defined as the protection of 'state interests'. It is not clear how widely the political leadership and the conservative military establishment understood the full implications of Gorshkov's preparation for 'broad offensive operations to strike against the imperialists' sea and land objectives in any part of the high seas.' But the feedback from deployment in the eastern Mediterranean and the Indian Ocean must eventually bring home both the implications and the immense potential.

As for the physical evidence of naval hardware, much of the Soviet construction effort is still going into the improvement of the seaborne nuclear deterrent and other submarine forces, the primary use of which could be in an all out war, either defensive or offensive. However, there are already signs of a broader, more flexible concept of naval power: the creation of afloat support for surface ships in addition to submarines, the re-activation of the naval infantry with new equipment, and the secondary amphibious role which appears to have been written into the requirement for the *Moskva*.

If I had to choose a single indicator for the future it would be the development of the *Moskva* concept: that is whether making life difficult for American submarines continues to be the primary mission of later units in this class; whether a specialist amphibious assault version appears and whether – as I would guess – it is eventually succeeded by a fixed wing vertical take-off aircraft carrier, with some kind of 'through deck'.

My answer to the question of how far the Soviet Union has changed her traditionally defensive naval strategy for an offensive one would be as follows. In the negative sense Admiral Gorshkov seems to have won his battle to free the Navy from the 'defensive' influence of the Red Army. There are limited signs that he is now reshaping his forces to suit a more offensive theoretical war strategy. As an instrument of 'cold war' diplomacy, to bolster Egyptian morale, to organize military aid for India or show the flag in Cuba, the Soviet Navy has been clearly on the offensive for years.

The age old dreams of our people have become reality. The pennants of the Soviet ships now flutter in the most remote corners of the seas and oceans. Our Navy is a real force and possesses the ability to resolve successfully the tasks of defending the state interests of the Soviet Union and of the whole socialist world.[5]

[5] *Red Star* April 16, 1970.

CHAPTER 17

Who Gets Hurt?

If one examines all the elements of Russian sea power in their own context, the one which shows the most aggressive policy – ironically – is the fishing industry. Deep-sea fishermen are likely to be among the toughest members of the community, whatever their nationality. But the almost military organization of the Russian trawlermen, with their mother ships surrounded by concentric rings of catchers, reconnaissance trawlers and fishery research vessels, indicates a unique determination to exploit the world's oceans systematically and comprehensively. By comparison the dogged individualism of the British trawler-man seems almost amateur.

The Soviet Union's navy may not have a carrier task force, but her fishing fleet has the *Vostok*; a self-contained floating factory with her own catchers, which she is ready to send off into any corner of the ocean where fish may be found. This is the sort of competition Western fleets will be up against as the explosive growth of world population makes the sea more and more valuable as a source of food protein.

For the time being the British trawler industry is a private affair – though state subsidized – dependent on the finicky taste of the British housewife. Its problems attract little public attention. The level of government support is hardly a burning political issue. But if food becomes as scarce in the world as some scientists predict, an aggressive national policy of fisheries development such as the Russians have, based on a strong programme of biological and operational research, may literally be vital – in the United States as well as in Britain.

One thing which can only be tackled at international level is the conservation of fish stocks in the North Atlantic. Judging by the disastrous experience of the whaling industry, it is imperative that Western scientists and governments take every possible opportunity to remind the Russians of the heavy responsibility they now share for seeing that the fish do not disappear as the whales have done.

In merchant shipping there can be no doubt about the aggressive nature of Russian commercial tactics. But, as with the Soviet Navy, the hardware reflects a transitional phase. Many of the ship types the Russians must deploy if they are to make a big impact on the cross trade freight market – the really fast cargo liner, the container ship, the supertanker and the giant bulk carrier – are only just beginning to appear.

One of the hopeful things about the 'container revolution' is that this type of integrated, door-to-door service is dependent on international cooperation. In such ways the expansion of Communist merchant fleets may bring political benefits, even if it does deprive the West of some markets. For the moment, therefore, I tend to regard the expansion hopefully as more of a challenge than a threat. But it will only remain hopeful if the Communists are persuaded to adopt economic standards which make sense internationally and to uphold, within limits, the principle of non-discrimination.

Of course in this context the elaborately protected American merchant marine is something of a skeleton in the Western family cupboard. But President Nixon's new support policy appears to be a move in the right direction, and if European shipowners ever feel irritated – for example when they have to compete with the subsidized speed of some of the US flag cargo liners – they must remember that Federal assistance programmes are part of the United States commitment to defend Europe in war. At the same time it might help diplomatically if the Americans were less coy about their large-scale shipping operations under flags of convenience.

The reason many British shipowners fear a Communist challenge is that they suspect it will not be a straight commercial fight. They are suspicious of the rouble's arbitrary exchange rate.

They simply do not trust Bakayev's declarations about competition and the freedom of the seas, although they will be delighted if he proves them wrong. In this situation one of the best ways of encouraging the Russians to practise what they preach would be a policy of maximum publicity for the issues involved, through political, diplomatic and press channels. Unfortunately British shipping – apart from a few exceptional individuals and the special case of the oil companies – is just about as ignorant of public relations as a major industry could be. This is one reason why in spite of hopeful signs that the impact of Russian competition can be absorbed – for example by the Europe-Australia conferences – I believe the underlying danger remains: that the Soviet fleet will one day justify its present capitalist means by achieving communist ends.

In contrast, it is because people like Admiral Rickover make such an effort to get their message across that the United States Government is unlikely to allow a dangerous gap in naval technology to develop. American naval supremacy is assured for the foreseeable future. However, the extent to which that supremacy guarantees European security, and Western influence in other parts of the world, may change a great deal. The United States is reconsidering the form, if not the extent, of its commitment to NATO, and is struggling to disengage from South-East Asia.

Against this uncertain background, it is important that Britain's long term naval planning should ensure the development of balanced, self reliant forces. Ideally this means continuing to operate aircraft carriers. But since new carriers have been ruled out by their comparative cost, we should press ahead with plans to put the Harrier vertical take-off aircraft on a 'through deck cruiser'. And in the meantime the Russian method of providing stand-off striking power with missiles should not be ignored (at the time of writing, Britain is negotiating to purchase the French Exocet missile).

East of Suez, the process of British withdrawal is obviously to a large extent irreversible. But membership of an international peacekeeping force in Singapore may provide a new way of using residual goodwill and experience. Both this concept and the alternative one of providing a 'general capability' to intervene require balanced, long range naval forces; and the arrival of the Soviet Navy simply reinforces this requirement.

The most impressive thing about Russia's maritime ambitions is not their specific impact but their scope; the fact that they embrace every aspect of sea power and are based on such a broad programme of research and education. They remind us of things of which a 'natural' sea power like Britain should be much more aware, such as the vast, scarcely touched potential of the oceans as a source of food and minerals.

The apparent co-ordination of the various elements – research, fishing, commercial, naval – is a major test of communist state planning. Their political direction is the test of whether the Russian communist system can match the Western capitalist one as an instrument of worldwide imperialism. Russia, the great land power, has curiously chosen to fight the ideological battle at sea.

Convention regarding the Regime of the Straits

MONTREUX, JULY 20, 1936
His Majesty the King of the Bulgarians, the President of the French Republic, His Majesty the King of Great Britain, Ireland and the British Dominions beyond the Seas, Emperor of India, His Majesty the King of the Hellenes, His Majesty the Emperor of Japan, His Majesty the King of Roumania, the President of the Turkish Republic, the Central Executive Committee of the Union of Soviet Socialist Republics, and His Majesty the King of Yugoslavia;

Desiring to regulate transit and navigation in the Straits of the Dardanelles, the Sea of Marmora and the Bosphorus, comprised under the general term 'Straits', in such manner as to safeguard within the framework of Turkish security and of the security, in the Black Sea, of the riparian states, the principle enshrined in article 23 of the Treaty of Peace signed at Lausanne on 24th July, 1923:

Have resolved to replace by the present Convention the Convention signed at Lausanne on the 24th July, 1923 and have . . . agreed on the following provisions:–

Article 1
The High Contracting Parties recognize and affirm the principle of freedom of transit and navigation by sea in the Straits.

Article 2
In time of peace, merchant vessels shall enjoy complete freedom of transit and navigation in the Straits, by day and by night, under any flag and with any kind of cargo.

Article 4
In time of war, Turkey not being belligerent, merchant vessels under any flag or with any kind of cargo, shall enjoy freedom of transit and navigation in the Straits.

Article 5

In time of war, Turkey being belligerent, merchant vessels not belonging to a country at war with Turkey shall enjoy freedom of transit and navigation in the Straits on condition that they do not in any way assist the enemy.

Article 10

In time of peace, light surface vessels, minor war vessels and auxiliary vessels . . . whatever their flag, shall enjoy freedom of transit through the Straits . . . provided that such transit is begun during daylight. Vessels of war other than those which fall into the categories specified in the preceding paragraph shall only enjoy a right of transit under the special conditions provided by articles 11 and 12.

Article 11

Black Sea powers may send through the Straits capital ships of a tonnage greater than that laid down in the first paragraph of article 14, on condition that these vessels pass through the Straits singly, escorted by not more than two destroyers.

Article 12

Black Sea powers shall have the right to send through the Straits, for the purpose of rejoining their base, submarines constructed or purchased outside the Black Sea . . . submarines belonging to the said powers shall also be entitled to pass through the Straits to be repaired in the dockyards outside . . . in either case the said submarines must travel by day and on the surface and must pass through the Straits singly.

Article 14

The maximum aggregate tonnage of all foreign naval forces which may be in course of transit through the Straits shall not exceed 15,000 tons except in the cases provided for in article 11 and in annexe III.

Article 17

Nothing in the provisions of the preceding articles shall prevent a naval force of any tonnage or composition paying a courtesy visit of limited duration to a port in the Straits at the invitation of the Turkish Government.

Article 18

(1) The aggregate tonnage which non-Black Sea powers may have in that sea in time of peace shall be limited as follows:

(a) Except as provided in paragraph (b) the aggregate tonnage of the said powers shall not exceed 30,000 tons

(b) If at any time the tonnage of the strongest fleet in the Black Sea shall exceed by at least 10,000 tons the tonnage of the strongest fleet in the sea at the date of the signature of the present convention, the aggregate tonnage of 30,000 tons mentioned in paragraph (a) shall be increased by the same amount up to a maximum of 45,000 tons.

(2) Vessels of war belonging to non-Black Sea powers shall not remain in the Black Sea more than twenty one days, whatever be the object of their presence there.

Article 19

In time of war, Turkey not being belligerent, warships shall enjoy complete freedom of transit and navigation through the Straits under the same conditions as those laid down in articles 10 to 18

Article 20

In time of war, Turkey being belligerent, the provisions of articles 10 to 18 shall not be applicable; the passage of warships shall be left entirely to the discretion of the Turkish Government.

Article 21

Should Turkey consider herself to be threatened with imminent danger of war she shall have the right to apply the provisions of article 20.

Article 28

The present convention shall remain in force for twenty years from the date of its entry into force. The principle of freedom of transit and navigation affirmed in article 1 shall however continue without limit of time. If, two years prior to the expiry of the said twenty years no High Contracting Party shall have given notice of denunciation to the French Government the present convention shall continue in force until two years after such notice shall have been given. . . . In the event of the present convention being denounced in accordance with the provisions of the present article, the High Contracting Parties agree to be represented at a conference for the purpose of concluding a new convention.

Article 29

At the expiry of each period of five years ... the High Contracting Parties shall be entitled to initiate a proposal for amending one or more of the provisions. To be valid, any request for revision formulated by one of the High Contracting Parties must be supported, in the case of modifications to articles 14 or 18, by one other High Contracting Party, and in the case of any other article, by two other High Contracting Parties. Should it be found impossible to reach agreement through the diplomatic channel the High Contracting Parties agree to be represented at a conference (which) may only take decisions by a unanimous vote except as regards articles 14 and 18, for which a majority of two thirds shall suffice.

Annexe II – Categories

(1) Capital ships are surface vessels of war belonging to one of the following sub-categories:

(a) surface vessels of war, other than aircraft carriers, auxiliary vessels or capital ships of sub-category (b), the standard displacement of which exceeds 10,000 tons or which carry a gun with a calibre exceeding 8 ins (203 mm);

(b) surface vessels of war, other than aircraft carriers, the standard displacement of which does not exceed 8,000 tons and which carry a gun with a calibre exceeding 8 ins.

(2) Aircraft carriers are surface vessels of war, whatever their displacement, designed or adapted primarily for the purpose of carrying and operating aircraft at sea.

(3) Light surface vessels are surface vessels of war other than aircraft carriers, minor warships or auxiliary vessels, the standard displacement of which exceeds 100 tons and does not exceed 10,000 tons and which do not carry a gun with a calibre exceeding 8 ins (203 mm).

Fleets of Nato and Warsaw Pact Compared

NATO	Ballistic Missile Submarines	Other Submarines	Attack Carriers	Other Carriers	Cruisers	Destroyers, Frigates and Ocean-going Escorts
Canada	0	4	0	1	0	22
Denmark	0	4	0	0	0	2
France	1	19	2	2	2	44
Germany (West)	0	11	0	0	0	18
Greece	0	2	0	0	0	12
Holland	0	6	0	0	2	19
Italy	0	10	0	0	4	22
Norway	0	15	0	0	0	5
Portugal	0	4	0	0	0	13
Turkey	0	10	0	0	0	10
UK	3	25	3	2	1	62
USA	41	102	15	15	13	260
Warsaw Pact						
Bulgaria	0	2	0	0	0	2
Germany (East)	0	0	0	0	0	4
Poland	0	5	0	0	0	3
USSR	53	327	0	2	18	200

Source: Institute of Strategic Studies and *Jane's Fighting Ships*.

Select Bibliography

Voyenaya Strategia (Military Strategy), edited Marshal V. D. Sokolovsky, Soviet Ministry of Defence, Moscow 1962; second edition 1963; third edition 1968.

Razvitie Morskovo Flota SSSR (Development of the Soviet Merchant Fleet), Ministry of the Merchant Marine, Moscow 1967.

SSSR na Mirovykh Putiakh (Soviet Ships on World Sea Routes), V. Bakayev, Soviet Ministry of the Merchant Marine, Moscow 1969.

The Soviet Merchant Marine Today and Tomorrow, Soviet External Trade Press, 1967.

Soviet Naval Strategy, Cmdr. R. W. Herrick, USN, US Naval Institute, 1968.

Soviet Sea Power, Center for Strategic and International Studies, Washington 1969.

'Oceanography and Underwater Sound for Naval Application', reprinted by Ministry of Defence in 1968 from *US Naval Oceanographic Office's Special Publication No. 84*.

Stalin and his Generals, edited Seweryn Bialer, Souvenir Press, London 1970.

Russia at War, Alexander Werth, Barrie and Rockcliff, London 1964.

Communist Ships and Shipping, John D. Harbron, Adlard Coles, London 1962.

The Northern Sea Route: Soviet Exploitation of the North East Passage, Dr Terence Armstrong, Cambridge University Press, 1952.

To the North, Jeannette Mirsky, The Viking Press, New York 1934.

The Suez Canal in Peace and War, Hugh J. Schonfield, Valentine, Mitchell, London 1969.

Khrushchev, Edward Crankshaw, Collins, London 1966.

The Russian Revolution, Alan Moorehead, Collins with Hamish Hamilton, London 1960.

Soviet Merchant Ships, anonymous, Kenneth Mason Publications, Havant 1969.

'The War at Sea', Vol. II, S. W. Roskill, *History of the Second World War*, HMSO, London 1956.

Jane's Fighting Ships, edited R. V. B. Blackman, Sampson Low, Marston, London.

The Military Balance, Institute of Strategic Studies, London 1969.

Fisheries Year Book and Directory 1968/69, British-Continental Trade Press, London.

'World Ships on Order', *Fairplay International Shipping Journal*, London.

Jane's Surface Skimmer Systems, Sampson Low, Marston, London.

The Soviet Drive for Maritime Power, report to Committee on Commerce, US Senate 1967.

The Changing Strategic Naval Balance, USSR vs. USA, report to Committee on Armed Services, House of Representatives, December 1968.

Status of Naval Ships, report to Committee on Armed Services, House of Representatives, March 1969.

The Soviets and the Seas, US House of Representatives Report No. 1809, 1966.

The Soviet Merchant Marine, US Department of Commerce/Maritime Administration 1967.

Report of the Rochdale Committee of Inquiry into Shipping, Cmnd. 4337, HMSO, May 1970.

Hearings before US Congressional Committee on Atomic Energy, April 1969.

Morskoi Sbornik, Feb. 1967, Admiral Gorshkov on 'The Development of Soviet Naval Art'.

Brassey's Annual 1968, Cmdr. M. K. MccGwire, RN (Retd.) on 'The Background to Russian Naval Policy'.

US Naval Institute Proceedings, June 1969, Lt. Cmdr. Cox, USN on *Sea Power and Soviet Foreign Policy*.

US Naval Review, 1969, Rear Admiral O. D. Waters, USN on *The Ocean Sciences and the Navy*.

US Naval Institute Proceedings, June 1967, Capt. O. P. Araldsen, RNN on *The Soviet Union and the Arctic*.

US Naval Review, 1969, Captain G. F. Bond, USN on *Man's Future Beneath the Sea*.

US Naval Institute Proceedings, July 1967, V. P. Petrov on *Soviet Canals*.

Soldat und Technik, June 1969, Siegfried Breyer on 'Soviet Warship Construction'.

Inter Nord, March 1968, T. E. Armstrong on 'The Northern Sea Route in 1966'.

US Naval Review, 1969, Cmdr. K. B. Schumacher, US Coast Guard on *The New Icebreakers*.

Shipping World and Shipbuilder, January 1968, Cmdr. Edgar P. Young, RN (Retd.) on 'Open Gateways of the USSR'.

Shipping World and Shipbuilder, July 1968, Cmdr. Edgar P. Young, RN (Retd.) on 'The Soviet Merchant Fleet'.

Polar Record, May 1966, Terence Armstrong on 'Soviet Sea Fisheries since the Second World War'.

Fishing News International, October and November 1968, Peter Hjul and Cmdr. M. B. F. Ranken, RN (Retd.) on 'Inrybprom – 68'.

International Conciliation, March 1970, Geoffrey Kemp on 'Arms Traffic and Third World Conflicts'.

Adelphi Papers 59 and 60, Institute of Strategic Studies, London, Robert E. Hunter on 'The Soviet Dilemma in the Middle East'.

Index